IN A CULT OF THEIR OWN

Amborish Roychoudhury is an advertising professional by day and movie maniac by night. He's been trying his hand at writing about movies, and blogs at amborish.com. This is his first book.

AMBORISH ROYCHOUDHURY

RUPA

Published by
Rupa Publications India Pvt. Ltd 2018
7/16, Ansari Road, Daryaganj
New Delhi 110002

Sales centres:
Allahabad Bengaluru Chennai
Hyderabad Jaipur Kathmandu
Kolkata Mumbai

Copyright © Amborish Roychoudhury 2018

The views and opinions expressed in this book are the author's own and the facts are as reported by him which have been verified to the extent possible, and the publishers are not in any way liable for the same.

All rights reserved.

No part of this publication may be reproduced, transmitted, or stored in a retrieval system, in any form or by any means, electronic, mechanical, photocopying, recording or otherwise, without the prior permission of the publisher.

ISBN: 978-81-291-5135-3

First impression 2018

10 9 8 7 6 5 4 3 2 1

The moral right of the author has been asserted.

Printed by Thomson Press India Ltd., Faridabad

This book is sold subject to the condition that it shall not, by way of trade or otherwise, be lent, resold, hired out, or otherwise circulated, without the publisher's prior consent, in any form of binding or cover other than that in which it is published.

To Baba...

'Amalkanti roddur hote cheyechhilo'

Contents

Foreword		*ix*
Introduction		*xiii*
1.	*Kaagaz Ke Phool*	1
	Paper flowers wilt too	
2.	*Mera Naam Joker*	10
	He made Christ laugh	
3.	*Surakksha*	20
	Gunmaster G-9	
4.	*Chashme Buddoor*	32
	Avert the evil eye	
5.	*Silsila*	47
	When the reel and the real collide	
6.	*Jaane Bhi Do Yaaro*	58
	Hum honge kaamyaab	
7.	*Katha*	71
	Grandma's tales	
8.	*Chameli Ki Shaadi*	81
	Naari nark ka dwaar hai	

9.	*Andheri Raat Mein Diya Tere Haath Mein*	90
	It's not what you think it is	
10.	*Superman*	97
	Duryodhan in tights	
11.	*Shahenshah*	109
	One Calcutta morning	
12.	*Raakh*	122
	Sizzling ember	
13.	*Clerk*	139
	Cardiac arrest	
14.	*Agneepath*	147
	Of coconuts, dapper suits and a poem	
15.	*Andaz Apna Apna*	162
	Mad misadventures	
16.	*Jo Jeeta Wohi Sikandar*	182
	There and back again	
17.	*Gunda*	195
	Where leaders steal shrouds	
18.	*RGV Ki Aag*	205
	Sholay, demolished	
19.	*No Smoking*	216
	King, Kashyap and Kafka	
20.	*Deshdrohi*	225
	No identification with actual persons	
21.	*Joginder, The Magnificent*	233
22.	*The Ramsay Brothers*	242
	Veerana, Purana Mandir and	
	Do Gaz Zameen Ke Neeche	
23.	*The Also-rans*	251

Epilogue   259

Foreword

Despite a punishing work schedule, if you ever want to know how activist turned Delhi Chief Minister Arvind Kejriwal remains such a major movie-buff—Twitter folk often look forward to his weekly film reviews before anyone else's—you only have to step into Kejriwal's alma mater, the Indian Institute of Technology Kharagpur (IIT KGP). It's a 2,100 acre campus housing 22,000 students—a self-sufficient city, with no civilization bordering it for as long as you can walk outside its main gates.

I did spot a Domino's somewhere, driving down to a dimly lit dhaba, several kilometres ahead, that served drinks on charpoys, where boys primarily mixed with other boys. What's the high point of one's social life in such a monastery, surrounded by young celibates, given a severely unfair gender ratio? Movies, obviously—downloaded, pirated, shared, all day, all night. Which is probably why IIT KGP had invited me over to deliver a TEDx talk—on movies, of course.

On my way, fellows on social media had already alerted me about how the nation's oldest IIT was pretty much the 'gadh' or fortress for a film called *Gunda* (1998)—a stress buster discovered on the local area networks of the campus in the early 2000s—that everyone had watched several times over, having mugged up dialogues of the Kanti Shah gem, which is entirely in verse, while the totally nutso Mithun starrer is set in an alternate universe where rape is the national sport.

I began my talk with a censored clip from *Gunda*. With the audience on my side, I spoke briefly about why Bollywood makes bad movies. Why does it, really? Because we love watching 'bad' movies. Quote-unquote very much underlined, since there is no such thing as a bad movie—only what we make of it.

What does one make of the IITian's (and several male engineering students') love for *Gunda*? Well, maybe the fact that there are multiple reasons why we love a movie. They could be anything—the fact that we simply love the hero/heroine on screen, or the songs in the film, or where the film is shot (location), or what people wear in it (fashion). How incredibly bizarre is a movie (with a world view so separate from our own) could equally be worth a return ticket to escape from the mundane. Movies talk to us in different (and unexpected) ways. Critical acclaim, or reviewers' ratings, in that sense, is rather overrated: Which is to take away nothing from the value of scripts, or stories being told. Religions, mythologies, are essentially stories that a society repeatedly tells itself. Films are evidently no different. Do we thoroughly enjoy movies that are only different in their sameness? Yes, in the same way that we reread the Bible, Koran, or listen to the same pravachan (discourse) from the Ramayan, or watch the Ram Leela year after year.

In the context of films, I suspect, this is how cults get formed. Box-office figures merely report the number of people who watched a movie upon its release. What they don't reveal is how many of them actually loved the movie, when they left the theatre. Furthermore, they don't predict or register how the film will survive the passage of time, finding newer devotees along the way, who would watch the same film again, and again, building a minor religion of sorts, eventually.

Andaz Apna Apna (1994), or *Jaane Bhi Do Yaaro* (1983), made no money for their producers. Very few people got to see them in theatres. Decades down, there are enough followers of the two cults, who can recite both films backwards, almost verbatim. *Sholay* (1975) shattered box-office records. *RGV Ki Aag* (2007), director Ram Gopal Varma's version of *Sholay*, also starring Amitabh Bachchan, remains the biggest box-office flop ever. And yet, both *Sholay* and *Aag*, by the looks of it, appear to be cult films. In fact, if the number of people who talk about *Aag* had actually bothered to see it in theatres, it would have also been one of the greatest hits ever!

But discussing is really at the heart of what makes viewing movies so joyful in the first place. It helps grow halos over them. Some of the stuff in movies attains the glory of legends, and folklore, or at any rate family secrets shared among the close few. It could be Ashok Kumar marching to the tune of Indian National Army's anthem 'Kadam Kadam Badhaye Ja' while palpitating during a cardiac arrest in *Clerk* (1989). Or it could be ham-star Joginder dancing with lota before his potty in *Teen Ikkey* (1980).

This is what I don't get about people who walk out of theatres mid-way, because they don't quite like a movie. So what if your mind's switched off from the main plot; hey, there's so much else to observe, embellish, exaggerate, and chat about forever. Having said that, I believe a picture should be either great (cult-good), or totally trashy (cult-bad); it's the middle ones, essentially attempting to be the former, that are utterly boring. Nothing you watch still is a waste of time. You just never know. There are gems in a lot of gunk.

Sometime around 2010, a bunch of millennial binge-watchers from IIT KGP, whose heads had been spinning with sweet-smelling garbage such as *Gunda*, formed a YouTube channel called The Viral Fever (TVF) to spoof cult pictures they hated enough to love, or loved to hate. They basically did spoofs of spoofs. Within no time, TVF had stormed the Internet, capturing millions of viewers. As did the stand-up comedian Biswa Kalyan Rath, another IIT KGP alumnus (go figure), beginning his YouTube career with a show called the 'Pretentious Movie Reviews', that took strikingly philosophical potshots at pictures (*Gunda* included) that he'd make love to between engineering classes. Both Rath and TVF's contribution to pop-culture exceeds most IITians' to science and technology.

Movies are how we also collectively laugh at ourselves. Amborish Roychoudhary's *In A Cult Of Their Own* is a welcome addition to the running joke. Done with the foreword, I look forward to the book. As should you.

Mayank Shekhar
Broadcaster, author, film critic

Introduction

Films are a religion in India, there are no two ways about it. It's full of myths and legends, stars are worshipped as demi-gods, we chant film dialogues with unflinching devotion, and people defend their favourites with deep aggression and resolve. Also, our abiding obsession with hits and misses — if today it's the Crores Clubs, back in the day it was Jubilees. In fact, so intense was our preoccupation with films completing Silver and Golden and Diamond Jubilees, a celebrated sixties' hero derived a moniker out of the term.

There are some films, however, whose stories don't end with the box office. Though they are deemed not so successful and fizzle out of the theatres in a heartbeat, these films lead charmed lives — they figure out a way to survive. When it's time, a torrent is leaked online or an old bootlegged DVD or VHS lands up in the right hands. Still better, our old friend YouTube throws a surprise. Before you know it, people are blogging and tweeting about it, and it becomes an Internet phenomenon. The film forms a cult of its own. And then there's The Trash — 'bad' films that we have come to love, even adore. They are called by many names: So Bad It's Good,

Trashy Films, Subaltern Films.

This book celebrates these 'cult films' of Hindi cinema, films that didn't exactly set the box office on fire but attained cult status later.

For the purpose of this book, there are three criteria for a film to be termed a 'cult film'. First, the films that (a) flopped at release or weren't released at all, or (b) are insufferably trashy but entertaining nonetheless, or (c) were successful but not considered 'mainstream'. Secondly, these films gained a cult following over the years and are often discussed, analysed online and have become a pop culture phenomenon.

This attempt is unique in that it celebrates the underdogs, films that were pulled out of obscurity for some reason and had their time in the sun all over again. A tongue-in-cheek ode to the cult movies of Hindi filmdom, its objective is to entertain, amuse and hopefully, inform.

For most films, I have tried to speak to the artists associated with them. This book contains excerpts from interviews with the likes of Naseeruddin Shah (*Jaane Bhi Do Yaaro*), Aamir Khan (*Andaz Apna Apna, Raakh, Jo Jeeta Wohi Sikandar*), Rajkumar Santoshi (*Andaz Apna Apna*), Tinnu Anand (*Shahenshah*), Deepti Naval (*Chashme Buddoor, Katha*), Sai Paranjpye (*Chashme Buddoor, Katha*), Mansoor Khan (*Jo Jeeta Wohi Sikandar*), Aditya Bhattacharya (*Raakh*), Rakesh Bedi (*Chashme Buddoor*) and Pankaj Kapur (*Raakh, Chameli Ki Shaadi*), among others. These interviews were conducted between early February 2014 and late March 2015.

Wherever necessary, I have tried my best to provide translations to Hindi songs and dialogues in an (often inadequate) attempt to make this book more enjoyable to Hindi film buffs across the globe, who don't essentially speak the language. When it came to classics like *Gunda* and

Andaz Apna Apna, although it felt like it would be humanly impossible to even venture such an enterprise, I have hazarded it in some instances. Some of the dialogues, however, were left untouched.

Needless to say, any list of cult films cannot claim to be exhaustive. There are titles in the list whose cult status many won't agree with. But those are the kind of discussions the book hopes to spark. Enjoy!

⌒

While the author has been named on the cover of the book, he didn't do it alone. He had to fall back on a number of mentors and friends who tirelessly provided direction and feedback at every stage.

Someone whom I'm fortunate to call a mentor and a friend, the affable Diptakirti Chaudhuri, writer of priceless film books like *Kitnay Aadmi Thay, Bollybook* and *Written By Salim Javed*.

Ankit Saxena, you are a rock star. Thanks for being a perpetual sounding board and egging me on every bit of the way.

Reema Prasanna for getting me started on this path, making me feel like a bestselling author time and again, and extending an ever-helping hand.

Jitesh Pillai for the immeasurable guidance and support.

Oorvazi Irani and Adhiraj Bose for help in reaching out to Naseer.

Madhu D. Roy and Parijat Sen—you guys are lifesavers! Thanks for transcribing some of the interviews.

Mohan Siddharth for the encouragement and part of the transcription.

My wife, Moutushi Roychoudhury for putting up with

the thousands of sleepless nights with a movie-crazy maniac.

Ma and Baba—Indrani and Amalkanti Roychoudhury—for unwittingly laying the seeds of my filmophilia from an early age.

Ipsita Roychoudhury Shee for believing in me.

The good folks at Rupa Publications, especially Dharini Bhaskar, Amrita Mukerji, Tanima Saha, Rinita Banerjee and Elina Majumdar for thinking the ramblings of this film-crazy bloke can be put on print.

Finally, the hordes of film buffs from my college days back in Guwahati. You guys can give the greatest film experts in the country a run for their money. Mainak Dutta, Subhamoy Roy, Anik Dasgupta, Sanjit Das, Subhashis Purkayastha, Subhasish Bhattacharjee, Arindam Bhattacharya and SO many others...

Special thanks to Sajid Khan, the greatest Hindi film buff this planet has known, for (unknowingly) providing the impetus for this book, through his impeccable shows 'Kehne Mein Kya Harj Hai' and 'Ikke Pe Ikka'.

Kaagaz Ke Phool

Paper flowers wilt too

Release: 1959

Cast: Guru Dutt, Waheeda Rehman, Johnny Walker, Baby Naaz, Mahesh Kaul, Veena Sapru, Ruby Meyers, Mehmood, Mohan Choti, Tun Tun

Directed by: Guru Dutt

Plot Summary: An acclaimed film-maker (Guru Dutt) bumps into an unforgettable face and takes it upon himself to chisel her (Waheeda Rehman) into a star. Inevitably, the creator and his muse are drawn to each other. But he is stuck in a troubled marriage and has a daughter. His films start flopping and he is dubbed a failure in a heartbeat. As he sinks deeper and deeper into oblivion, he pays one last visit to the studio.

✧

There is something intensely romantic about the concept of self-destruction. Especially in postcolonial India, literature and cinema were crowded with heroes who wallowed in self-pity, sorrow and misery. If Raj Kapoor and Dilip Kumar's roles in the 1940s and fifties propagated the tragic hero, Devdas became an icon and a poster-boy of the youth. 'Loser' was not a bad word, but in a morbid way, it was something to aspire towards. Pain and pathos were synonymous. It's another matter that this wasn't exclusive to an era—self-destructive themes spilled over to independent cinema and literature of the West and took a different shape in the nineties, through works like Irvine Welsh's *Trainspotting*, Chuck Palahniuk's *Fight Club*, Fatih Akin's *Head-On*, Mike Figgis' *Leaving Las Vegas* and many others. But that is beyond our scope of discussion. This obsession with melancholy and sadness was a prime characteristic of Guru Dutt's cinema, and is probably best displayed in three films: *Pyaasa, Kaagaz Ke Phool* and *Sahib Bibi Aur Ghulam*. But it was probably most poignant in *Kaagaz Ke Phool*. In *Pyaasa*, the poet Vijay finds redemption and walks off into the moonlight with his muse, Gulabo. In *Sahib Bibi Aur Ghulam*, Bhootnath witnesses the enchanting Choti Bahu drink herself to oblivion but he himself moves on to a better life. In *Kaagaz Ke Phool* however, Guru Dutt offers his protagonist no such relief. The destruction is absolute. It is also his most indulgent work, and that has been the greatest piece of criticism held against the film. But as it happens, this unbridled indulgence also gives *Kaagaz Ke Phool* its artistry and magnificence. Worldwide, film fans and critics have long hailed the merits of personal narratives, films that retain the distinctive stamp of their makers. And *Kaagaz Ke Phool* is personal cinema at its unadulterated best.

The Irony of *Kaagaz Ke Phool*

Kaagaz Ke Phool is staggeringly ironic on so many levels. It tells of a master film-maker who immerses himself in his work and his muse, eventually falling from grace and subsequently dying an untimely death. In many ways, this mirrors Guru Dutt's own fate not only in the making of the film, but even after it. A dishevelled, haggard old man staggers into a film studio and looks around the abandoned set. Everyone has dispersed for lunch and there's nobody to stop him. The old man looks at each prop, camera and trolley with almost familial longing and affection. Once, he belonged here, quite literally calling the shots. Flashback to not so long ago, when this man was a celebrated film director—Suresh Sinha. A sea of faces surrounds the successful director, hankering for his autograph. Mohammad Rafi's refrain wafts in the background:

Waqt hai meherbaan, arzoo hai jawaan
Fikr kal ki karein, aisi fursat kahaan
Daur ye chalta rahe, rang uchhalta rahe
Roop machalta rahe, jaam badalta rahe ...
Pal bhar ki khushiyan hai saari
Badhne lagi beqaraari
Dekhi zamaane ki yaari
Bichhde sabhi baari baari...

Time is bountiful, passion ablaze,
To dwell upon tomorrow—where is such leisure?
Let this moment continue, the colours splash,
Let beauty dazzle, the wine spellbind...
It's all fleeting—all the happiness,
The restlessness intensifies,
Alas, I've seen friendships, loyalties—
They all parted, one by one by one...

Sinha's misdemeanour and Kaifi Azmi's flawless poetry tell you that something is amiss. Even among this deluge of adulation, Sinha knows that life will not be like this forever.

Fame is fleeting, and all this glitter and sheen will go away in the blink of an eye. His estranged wife and her family detest him, and won't allow him to visit his daughter at her boarding school. Nobody at work agrees with his methods, but everyone puts up with him as he can still pull the crowds to the theatre. It is as if they are all waiting for that one misstep, one lapse of judgement to pounce on him and rip him apart. One stormy evening he meets Shanti (Waheeda Rehman) as they take refuge under a tree. Some time later, Shanti pays a visit to his studio to return his coat and gets captured on the camera rather unwittingly. While going through the footage, her winsome, almost ethereal face catches Sinha's fancy and he wants her to play Paro in his next film, *Devdas*. It's another delicious irony that the film he is making is an adaptation of Sarat Chandra Chattopadhyay's *Devdas*, the epitome of self-loathing and misery. *Kaagaz Ke Phool* itself, like *Pyaasa* before it, draws on elements from *Devdas*. Suresh Sinha sees in Shanti the modesty and plainness that he had visualized for the character of Paro. (Incidentally, the journey from Parvati to Paro is singularly curious. In Chattopadhyay's original Bengali novel, Parvati was affectionately addressed as 'Paaru', while the first Hindi translation preferred to call her 'Patto'. In P.C. Barua's 1936 *Devdas*, Kundan Lal Saigal called his heroine 'Paaru' as in the original text. It is the sheer power of cinema that the version used by Bimal Roy in his seminal 1955 *Devdas*, 'Paro', got stuck and the character was forever known by that name.) Needless to say, Shanti is cast for the role and becomes an overnight sensation. While working with his muse and preparing her for the role, the two are inevitably drawn towards each other. Love and longing have never been so pristine yet so delicate. Kaifi Azmi works his magic again, ably complemented by Sachin Dev Burman's music:

Beqaraar dil, iss tarah miley
Jiss tarah kabhi hum juda na thhey
Tum bhi kho gaye, hum bhi kho gaye
Ek raah par chal ke do kadam
Waqt ne kia kya haseen sitam
Tum rahe na tum, hum rahe na hum...

Restless hearts—the way they met
It was as if, we had never been apart
You were lost, so was I,
Despite having walked the same path.
What sweet tyranny has time imposed,
You are not what you were, I am not what I was...

And if camera ever had a deft palette to go with this sublime poetry, it had to be V.K. Murthy's. The now-legendary association of Murthy and Guru Dutt began on the sets of *Baazi* (1951), Dutt's directorial debut. The cinematographer on the project was V. Ratra, a cousin of Dev Anand. While shooting the song 'Suno Gajar Kya Gaye', Dutt wanted the prelude to be shot at an interesting angle. Ratra had the habit of leaving things to Murthy, his then assistant, from time to time. This was one such occasion, and Murthy grabbed the opportunity. He suggested turning the camera on the huge mirror showing the dancers' and Dev Anand's reflection and then pan out to Dev Anand's back, moving with him till he sits on the chair and the dancer (Geeta Bali) starts singing. The result was striking. Those interested may check out the sequence on YouTube. It showed Murthy's mettle and Guru Dutt promised him that from then on, he would be his chief cinematographer.

While working on *Kaagaz Ke Phool*, Dutt and Murthy used to sit and talk in the afternoons when the shooting was over.

Murthy pointed to a single shaft of sunlight that beamed down from a huge air vent and caught all the dust in the studio. Guru Dutt wanted him to recreate it in the film and gave him ten days to set things up. Murthy tried using a big spotlight, but that didn't create the desired effect. Then one day he spotted a make-up man playing with a mirror, reflecting sunlight on to a wall. This gave him an idea. He obtained two mirrors, about four feet tall—one of them was stationed outside the studio to reflect sunlight indoors, while the other mirror, placed on a platform, reflected that light on to the studio floor in a single shaft of light. This was the landmark shot that was used in the song 'Waqt Ne Kiya'. Guru Dutt himself had a deep understanding of lighting and camera angles. In the documentary *In Search of Guru Dutt*, film-maker Mani Kaul elaborated Guru Dutt's signature foreground and background lighting, which became a norm later. Coincidentally, it was Kaul's uncle Mahesh Kaul who played Suresh Sinha's pompous father-in-law in *Kaagaz Ke Phool*.

Halfway through the film, Sinha's daughter Pammi is, rather unflatteringly, made aware of her father's involvement with his new heroine when her classmates read it to her aloud from a film magazine. She decides to run away from school and meet this 'other woman' in her father's life. What ensues is unique in Bollywood in the sense that we have mostly seen the hero/heroine's rich father or mother trying to dissuade the poor boy/girl from romancing their ward(s), but this was the first time a daughter reaches out to a woman, asking her to stay out of her father's life. Heeding her wishes, Shanti decides to step out of the archlights and goes away to teach children in a remote hamlet. This takes a visible toll on Sinha's work and his films start failing miserably. Thus begins the downward spiral—losing his fame and fortune, Sinha leads a life of obscurity. His somewhat misplaced sense of self-respect prevents him from lapping up the opportunity when Shanti offers to get back to acting if he were to direct again. But keeping away from the studio seemed impossible, and he keeps looking for ways to sneak in to the sets. He finally breathes his last on a film set, sitting on an abandoned director's chair.

Kaagaz Ke Phool is not only indulgent cinema at its best—indulging in the maker's own creative choices, without any heed to audience expectations or market forces—it's also deeply personal and ironic in the way it predicted the future. The film flopped upon release, and its fate left a permanent scar on Guru Dutt's psyche. He never touched the director's megaphone again. On 10 October 1964, Guru Dutt passed away, owing to an overdose of sleeping pills. According to his sister Lalitha Lajmi, he was found lying in a position that seemed to indicate he was just about to say something, when he breathed his last.

Ud ja ud ja pyaase bhanwre
Ras na milega khaaron mein
Kaagaz ke phool jahaan khilte hain
Baith na unn gulzaron mein...

Fly away, thirsty bee, fly
There's no nectar among thorns.
Where paper flowers bloom,
Do not hover in such gardens...

The Legacy of *Kaagaz Ke Phool*

Mainstream Indian cinema has never bothered to look inward. It was too busy cavorting in the hills or beating goons to pulp.

Even the non-mainstream, parallel variant has shied away from exploring the workings of cinema and its makers on celluloid, with some notable exceptions like Shyam Benegal's *Bhumika* (1977) and Sudhir Mishra's *Khoya Khoya Chand* (2007). Even when Raj Kapoor decided to step outside of his own skin and take a look-see at himself, he had to don the garb of a joker and use circus as a stand-in for the film industry.

Kaagaz Ke Phool is one film that peeks into the life of a film-maker and his creative choices and obsessions—to the extent that the entire film seems to track the ebb and flow of Suresh Sinha's filmmaking career—and in doing so, mirrors its own director Guru Dutt's life. Can it get any more self-referential than this? Sinha loses all credibility as a film-maker and languishes on the streets, his glory days behind him. We have all heard stories of riches to rags, of music directors, actors, directors and writers who enjoyed dizzying heights of stardom and died penniless paupers. This is the fickle side of the industry that the titular paper flowers refer to. Over the years, many have claimed that the film was inspired from director Gyan Mukherjee's (maker of Ashok Kumar starrers *Kismet*, *Jhoola* and *Sangram*, and Dutt's mentor) life, but this seems unlikely.

Today, when Guru Dutt's name comes up in social media or online forums, the twin films *Pyaasa* and *Kaagaz Ke Phool* invariably find mention. Though *Pyaasa* got the box office affection it deserved, the other film bombed miserably. Guru Dutt took it personally. *Pyaasa* may have been his magnum opus but *Kaagaz Ke Phool* was a piece of his soul, his grand experiment. Its failure affected him so deeply that Guru Dutt resolved never to direct a film, ever again.

His partner in crime, V.K. Murthy, mentioned in an interview in *The Times of India* that Raj Kapoor consoled Guru

Dutt saying he had made the film fifteen years too early. Said like a true visionary. Around the late 1970s, *Kaagaz Ke Phool* was screened in international film festivals and met with a lot of critical appreciation. Prints of the film were in demand across the globe and it was re-released in India. Film schools and universities discussed and dissected the merits of this work of a true genius.

Guru Dutt's paper flowers had bloomed, finally.

Mera Naam Joker

He made Christ laugh

Release: 1970

Cast: Raj Kapoor, Rishi Kapoor, Simi Garewal, Kseniya Ryabinkina, Padmini, Dharmendra, Manoj Kumar, Rajendra Kumar, Dara Singh

Directed by: Raj Kapoor

Plot Summary: Raju waltzes through life wanting to make people laugh. His only ambition ever was to be a joker. But in the bargain, all he gets is heartbreak — from his teacher, Mary; the Russian trapeze artist, Marina; and even the orphaned Meenu. All of them, willingly or unwillingly, trample over him and his feelings. Raju does manage to become a clown, but at what cost?

It was in the late 1980s that actor-turned-TV presenter Simi Garewal made a documentary called *Living Legend: Raj Kapoor*. It was aired on Doordarshan around the time Raj Kapoor passed away, in 1988. In it, Kapoor describes a scene from *Mera Naam Joker* thus:

> ...this performer has invited all his past attachments, emotional involvements—the girls, the teacher—all of them he has invited. He is a joker and he is giving his last performance. He knows that he's going to die now. He has a kind of ailment and he is not going to live long. We begin with an operation: seven-eight doctors are pulling out the heart of a clown, of a joker. They pull out his heart, and then we find that he has no heart. And he's walking on the ring of the circus, and he asks all from his past, 'Have you seen my heart? Have you seen my heart? Please, have you? Anybody here who has seen my heart?' This scene affects me very much. 'Has anybody seen my heart?' For that matter I feel that (there are) a very fortunate few in this world who have probably the distinction of having people who have seen their heart, to have loved them, to have received love in return...this affects me. Tremendously.[*]

Anybody even faintly familiar with Raj Kapoor's work will vouch for the fact that this magnificent obsession summarizes the man and his work, leading one to believe that he poured the essence of his very being into *Mera Naam Joker*; more than any of his other creations, more than *Shree 420*, more than even *Awara*, *Mera Naam Joker* is the one film that most aptly represented Raj Kapoor's world view.

A little fiddling on YouTube will reward you with an ancient video depicting Raj Kapoor putting up a grand show at

---

[*]'Living Legend Raj Kapoor', *Simi Garewal Official*, 16 October 2012, https://www.youtube.com/watch?v=PnYYfvgx93I

Mumbai's Brabourne Stadium for naval officers.[*] In attendance were the newly appointed Chief of Naval Staff, Sardarilal Mathradas Nanda, Admiral Chatterjee, President V.V. Giri, the Governor of Maharashtra, actors Prithviraj Kapoor, David, Simi Garewal, Dara Singh, Prem Chopra, Sadhna, Babita, Agha, Johnny Walker, Vimmi, Mehmood, Junior Mehmood, Helen, Rajendra Kumar, Jeetendra (introduced as 'James Bondy' Jeetendra), Raajkumar and above all, the stars of the evening, composer duo Shankar-Jaikishan and ace singers Mohammad Rafi and Mukesh. The audience were in a tizzy following the live performances of Rafi and Mukesh, when Rajendra Kumar introduced the song *Jeena yahaan, marna yahaan/ Iske siwa, jaana kahaan* from Raj Kapoor's upcoming magnum opus *Mera Naam Joker*, with a group of sailors providing the chorus. After another round of Rafi's popular numbers, Raj Kapoor appears on stage unveiling another number from his new project — *Jaane kahaan gaye woh din/ Kehte thhe teri raah mein/ Nazron ko hum bichayenge*. Following this, Kapoor himself waltzes on the stage and croons 'E Bhai, Zara Dekh Ke Chalo' in his own voice, ostensibly to account for the absence of Manna Dey, who had sung the original.[**]

As is obvious, *Mera Naam Joker* was launched at en epic scale. Magazine covers, mainstream media, billboards, public functions — nothing was spared. But the plan was not to mount just one big film. The word on the street was, the great showman was conceiving a two-part spectacle. As quoted in daughter Ritu Nanda's book *Raj Kapoor Speaks*, he is known

---

[*]'Raj Kapoor presents Shankar Jaikishan live 1970', https://www.youtube.com/watch?v=M36vPRdeAVc
[**]'Mera Naam Joker-Ae Bhai Zara Dekh Ke Chalo-Manna Dey, *Shemaroo*, 9 June 2009, https://www.youtube.com/watch?v=sqDiqb1GXg0

to have spoken about this in an interview:

> My work is my religion. My obsession. I stand or fall by the yardstick of my creative work. That is why I find questions concerning length, footage and how many parts and so on totally irrelevant, where *Mera Naam Joker* is concerned. Yes, there will be two films, *Mera Naam Joker* Part I and *Mera Naam Joker* Part II. Yes, both parts will be long. Is not human life long? And engrossing? And with never a dull moment?[***]

Enter Chintu Ji

Few films till the 1970s — such as *Kitaab* (1977) and *Mera Naam Joker* — had captured adolescence in all its idiosyncrasies. Although the growing pains of an adolescent are not exactly what the film largely concerns itself with, *Mera Naam Joker* goes into territories no one had ever explored before. Like a teenage boy's obsession for his gorgeous teacher, his raging hormones and certain nightly indulgences adolescents commonly engage in. Rishi Kapoor mentioned on several occasions how he was over the moon when his father asked his mother whether he could borrow little Chintu (his nickname) for an acting job. Without further delay, the boy locked himself up in his room and got busy practising autographs. Although it was hardly his first on-screen appearance (as is well known, Rishi Kapoor was one of the three little children scooting along wearing raincoats in the song 'Pyaar Hua Ikraar Hua' from *Shree 420*), this was the first time he was playing a significant part, and hogging significant screen time. The chubby little blue-eyed boy that he was, Rishi was already winning hearts — his face stared from magazine covers, long before the film was released. As for his

---

[***]Ritu Nanda, *Raj Kapoor Speaks*, New Delhi: Viking, 2002.

performance, it was self-assured enough for one to wonder if it could really have been his first acting role. He was spot on as the adorable little bundle of mush in love with the much older Mary (Simi Garewal), and his performance won him the Bengal Film Journalists' Association (BFJA) Special Award. Amusingly enough, a younger Rishi (seemingly) falling for an older Simi was repeated again, exactly ten years later. The film was Subhash Ghai's *Karz* (1980).

Raju (Rishi Kapoor) has a major crush on his teacher Mary (Simi Garewal), but it really starts to disturb him when he spots her changing behind the bushes while on a school picnic. Consumed with regret, he confesses before God. Mary is also his confidante and he shares his dreams of becoming a clown with her—a joker who is destined to make people laugh. He looks at a Jesus Christ statue and wonders why he never smiles. Mary explains that it is because Christ is burdened by the sins of all humanity. Raju resolves to make Him smile. Soon enough, Mary's fiancé David (Manoj Kumar) swoops in and walks away with her, leaving little Raju with a broken heart, for the first time.

Babu, ye Circus hai

Almost three decades ago, Shah Rukh Khan appeared in a Doordarshan serial named 'Circus' which was about a, well, circus. But how many mainstream Hindi films can one think of that featured a circus prominently? The swashbuckling Fearless Nadia, in the autumn of her career, featured in a film called *Circus Queen* (1959), which was interesting considering she herself worked in a circus before her career in movies. And then of course, there's *Haathi Mere Saathi* (1971) in which Rajesh Khanna launched his own circus. In *Adventures of Tarzan* (1985), the illustrious Hemant Birje is bound in chains and launched as a circus attraction by the evil Dalip Tahil. *Mera Naam Joker* does not merely feature circus as a backdrop, but also talks about those who make their living off it.

As destiny would have it, the grown-up Raju (Raj Kapoor) lands a job as a clown in a circus, owned by Mahendra (Dharmendra). A group of Russian performers are on a tour of India, and Raju strikes a friendship with them, in particular the pretty and petite Marina.

Kseniya Ryabinkina was a promising ballerina at Bolshoi Ballet Academy. Aleksandr Ptushko, known somewhat unfairly as the 'Soviet Walt Disney', recruited her for his classic *The Tale of Tsar Saltan* (1966), in which Kseniya played the legendary Swan Princess. That was her only acting role till Raj Kapoor offered her the part of Marina, something that she was to be known for, for the rest of her life. The erstwhile Soviet Russia/USSR had strong political and cultural ties with India. And it seeped into movies at two distinct levels — there were Indo-Soviet co-productions like *Journey Beyond Three Seas/ Pardesi* (1957), *Alibaba Aur 40 Chor* (1980), *Sohni Mahiwal* (1984), *Ajooba* (1991) — and then there was Raj Kapoor. Possibly owing to the Cold War, Hollywood films didn't enjoy much favour in Russia, and its place was taken by Hindi films. *Awara* (1951) was and still remains a huge cultural phenomenon in Russia. The film landed up on Russian shores only around 1953, and ended up selling over 63 million tickets. Raj Kapoor became a household name, and the songs were on everyone's lips. Even now, almost three decades after Kapoor's passing, the two most recognizable songs in Russia are 'Awara Hoon' and 'Jeena Yahaan, Marna Yahaan', the latter of course from *Mera Naam Joker*.

Raj Kapoor visited Moscow on several occasions, including the Film Festival of Moscow in 1967. Possibly on one of these sojourns, he invited Kseniya Ryabinkina to play the Russian trapeze artist in *Mera Naam Joker*. How Raju and Marina end up communicating without knowing each other's languages, with the 'Da-da's and 'Nyet-nyet's and 'Namaste's, is all a part of Bollywood lore now. The two take a strong liking for each other but Marina eventually has to leave and Raju is again left nursing a broken heart. Kseniya Ryabinkina returned to Bollywood once again thirty-nine years later alongside Rishi Kapoor, in the film *Chintu Ji* (2009), where she plays herself.

Her Facebook page is full of fans asking her about *Mera Naam Joker*, and a number of Indian middle-aged males enquiring after her health. One film, done so many years and three generations ago, in a language utterly foreign to her, still lights up her world.

Return of the Moustache

An urchin wearing a stylish jacket puts up a film poster on the beach. The poster is of a film called *My Darling* and reads, 'Rajendra Kumar Presents...*My Darling*'. Rajendra Kumar (as himself) appears at various points throughout the film. This is one notable instance where an actor stars as himself in a major role in a major film, other such examples being Dharmendra in *Guddi* (1971) and Mithun Chakraborty in *Teesra Kaun?* (1994).

The child putting up the poster is called Meenu (played by Padmini), and Raju, who has by now quit the circus, teams up with him to perform roadshows. Dressed as a boy, Meenu even puts up at Raju's decrepit shack. Although it is quite obvious to the audience, Raju has no inkling that Meenu is actually a girl. But one day, it is revealed to him during one of their shows, when Meenu's shirt rips and a portion of her breast peeks out. Growing up on her own, dressing as a man was her way of coping with lecherous, leering men all around her. Understandably, Raju is shocked at the sudden revelation, while Meenu is in love with him. Wary of getting his heart trampled on once again, Raju packs his bags, but Meenu manages to persuade him, employing her newfound skills as a seductress. They continue performing, but this time they switch to qawwalis, and then graduate to theatre. And theatre, of course, means sprawling dance numbers on stage. Meenu is the dancer and Raju plays a South Indian singer, and since every South Indian singer obviously sports a mundu (dhoti) and a bald head, he wears a bald wig and is clean-shaven. Rajendra Kumar happens to be present in the audience for one of their performances, and is visibly impressed by Meenu's virtuosity. He is impressed enough to offer her a role in his film. The ambitious Meenu jumps at the opportunity, leaving Raju in the fray. Raju sighs again:

...mere kadam jahaan pade
Sajde kiye thhe yaar ne
Mujhko rula rula diya
Jaati hui bahaar ne
Jaane kahaan gaye woh din
Kehte thhe teri raah mein
Nazron ko hum bichayenge...

Wherever my steps fell,
Friends bowed in submission
It made me cry—
The departing Spring.
Where have those days gone...
You used to say, 'In your wait,
Shall I keep watch ...'

In these sad moments, of course, Raju's moustache makes a comeback.

Years later, Raju writes to all the three women in his life (Mary, Marina and Meenu) and invites them to the last show of his life. The evocative scene, as explained by Raj Kapoor in the documentary, involves the clown's heart being ripped off, following which the poor bloke goes around asking his past loves, if they had seen his heart. Tears flow thick and fast, and every throat has a lump in it.

Mera Naam Joker turned out to be one of the greatest flops of Raj Kapoor's career, and it devastated him. The moviegoing audience had clearly rejected the film that he poured his heart and soul into. But Raj Kapoor was hardly the man to sulk and languish in misery. He turned to his young son who was now a teenager, the same Rishi Kapoor who he had borrowed to play a child in his film, and launched him in *Bobby* (1973). The film was a runaway hit and Raj Kapoor had successfully risen from the ashes.

Through the following decades, as is wont with cult films, successive generations obsessed over *Mera Naam Joker* and found new meanings in its pathos. As mentioned before, the film was a watershed in Russia. When former Prime Minister Manmohan Singh visited Russia in 2011, 'Jeena Yahaan, Marna Yahaan' was one of the songs that were played at a luncheon banquet hosted by President Dmitry Medvedev.[*] Alongside *Awara*, *Mera Naam Joker* and its bevy of songs holds a special place in Russian popular culture.

Randhir Kapoor, Raj Kapoor's eldest son, revealed during

---

[*]'Russia's love affair with Raj Kapoor continues', *The Indian Express*, 18 December 2011, http://archive.indianexpress.com/news/russias-love-affair-with-raj-kapoor-continues/889302/

an international film festival in 2011, that *Mera Naam Joker* is now the biggest profit point in his organization—RK Films.

Emotionally though, Raj Kapoor never quite recovered from the debacle of *Mera Naam Joker*. He spoke about it, in the aforementioned documentary *Living Legend: Raj Kapoor*:

> The film that fails is like the child that lags behind. The one that succeeds earns respect, kudos and praise in any case. But the child that lags behind grows closer to you. So there is this film, *Mera Naam Joker* that is very dear to me, because it wasn't a success. Another one was *Jagte Raho* which didn't run either. So they are my two special children. Maybe they had a limp, or didn't have a pretty face or whatever. For some reason they didn't run. Perhaps they were so extraordinary, no one understood them...

Surakksha

Gunmaster G-9

Release: 1979

Cast: Mithun Chakraborty, Ranjeeta, Jagdeep

Directed by: Ravikant Nagaich

Plot Summary: Doctor Shiva and his minions are wreaking havoc, and Agent Gopi aka Gunmaster G-9 (Mithun Chakraborty) is called in to save the day. That's the plot. Yup.

✧

What's the one thing that connects all 'spy movies'? No, it's not the sobriquet 'agent'. It's how the 'Chief' reaches out to the sleuth at the most inopportune moments, namely when he's frolicking with a nubile nymphet who almost never happens to be the heroine of the movie.

What can you say of a film-maker who started his career with *Farz* (1967), and ended it with *Duty* (1986)? In an industry where sequels were uncommon, and character franchises unheard of—unlike now—Ravikant Nagaich created two characters spanning five films and three stars.

The first James Bond movie came out in 1962, the epoch-making *Dr. No*, a cultural phenomenon that irrevocably changed the landscape of English cinema, the English language and male sexuality. Its tropes and formulae impacted action films—phrases like 'shaken, not stirred' and 'The name is Bond. James Bond' became a part of English phraseology, and for the first time in a long time, male sex appeal came to the fore. True to character, Bollywood was quick to spawn a plethora of James Bonds of its own. One of the earliest was M. Mallikarjuna Rao's Telugu film *Goodachari 116* (1967), made within five years of *Dr. No*. The film featured Telugu superstar Krishna, current reigning star Mahesh Babu's father. Krishna stars as Agent Gopi aka Secret Agent 116, whose sojourn in the hills cavorting with his lady love is interrupted by a call of duty, as his colleague Agent 303 has been captured and put out of his misery. Thirty-six-year-old Ravikant Nagaich was the cinematographer of the film. He had been handling photography in Telugu films since the early 1960s. His penchant for special effects and trick photography was well known, which probably explains the initial mythologicals and fantasies like *Sri Seetha Rama Kalyanam* (1961), *Gulebakavali Katha* (1962), *Sri Krishnarjuna Yudham* (1963) and *Shri Krishna Pandaviyam* (1966).

Esteemed Telugu writer and novelist Bhagavatula Sadasiva Shankara Sastry aka Aarudhra, wrote the story that became *Goodachari 116*, and then *Farz* (both 1967). It is unclear as to when it was decided to remake *Goodachari 116* as *Farz*, but both M. Mallikarjuna Rao and Ravikant Nagaich were debuting as directors with the respective Telugu and Hindi films. *Farz* became Jeetendra's breakout film, thus establishing him firmly as the Jack who kept jumping through our consciousness for the next three decades. A number of in-jokes and anecdotes are splattered throughout the story of the *Farz* remake and Agent 116.

Agent 116 began his journey from the aforementioned Telugu film where he was referred to as Agent Gopi. In *Farz*, the agent retains his code but his name is changed to Gopal. Gopal Kishan Pandey, to be specific. Agent 116 aka Gopal, personified in Jeetendra, continued his adventures through *Raksha* (1982), and the decades-delayed *The Gold Medal* (1986). But just like his counterpart—007, Agent 116 was played on-screen by more than one actor. In *Keemat* (1973), Dharmendra played the spy, ably assisted by an ever-frowning K.N. Singh as the Chief of Secret Service. (In *Farz*, the Chief was played by David.) In *Farz*, an important plot point is 116's colleague Agent 303 getting killed by 'desh ke dushman', upon which Jeetendra is entrusted to nab the culprits. In eighteen years, Jeetendra himself would be playing a spy called Bond 303 in a film by the same name, directed by Ravi Tandon, Raveena Tandon's father. The film is full of priceless nuggets such as, 'No Bond. No 303. Chhuttiyon mein, bilkul free,' and 'No job taking. Only lovemaking.' In 1979, Ravikant Nagaich conceived his second and arguably more popular secret Agent Gunmaster G-9 aka Gopi. Just like the one who started it all—Gopi from *Goodachari 116*.

Of Secret Agents and Superheroes

Comicbooks were quite a thing back in the eighties even in small town India. DC and Marvel were available, but what ruled the mindspace were *Tintin* and *Indrajal Comics*. *Indrajal Comics* was an intensely popular comic book label started by *The Times of India* group, abruptly shut down in early 1990s. Used, tattered copies are still sold on Ebay and the streets of Mumbai and Kolkata anywhere between ₹300–1000 a pop. *Indrajal Comics'* gallery of heroes (syndicated from international publishers) became equally famous, starting from The Phantom, Flash Gordon, Rip Kirby, Garth, Buzz Sawyer and also indigenous heroes like Bahadur, Dara and Aditya.

One of the lesser-known characters brought to Indian readers by *Indrajal Comics* was a super-spy Phil Corrigan, who first appeared in a comic strip titled *Secret Agent X-9*, conceived by pulp fiction writer Dashiell Hammett. *Secret Agent X-9* also apparently inspired two film serials in 1937 and 1945, Wikipedia says. X-9 was most likely one of the earliest spies/ secret agents with an alphanumeric code name, a convention that G-9 eventually followed.

Speaking of comic books, way back in the sixties, in the era of *The Lone Ranger* and *The Zorro*, the Wild West and gunslingers became increasingly popular in comics. Clay Boone, a gun smith used to travel through the arid west with his wares—accompanied by his young assistant Bob Tellub. But when the day needed to be saved, Clay donned his mask and assumed the identity of The Gunmaster, as Bob became Bullet, the Gun Boy.

Now if all of this is any indication, our hero Gopi's nom de plume was inspired from a World War II-era spy and a superhero gunslinger from the wild west. But when one Googles the word 'gunmaster' today, *Surakksha* holds pride of place among the search results. Gunmaster G-9 is the most iconic spy in Hindi Cinema, ever.

Prabhujee

Indian audiences (and press-*wallah*s) are known to decorate filmstars with intriguing, often weird, titles. In Bengal, matinee idol Uttam Kumar is still called 'Mahanayak' (the Greatest

Hero), Rajinikanth is known as 'Thalaiva' (Leader/Boss), and there is of course Bhai—Salman Khan. Mithun Chakraborty is probably the only star who has such an ardent following online that he has been adorned with an exclusive title by the netizens: 'Prabhujee'. The term is used, tongue firmly in cheek, to refer to his massy entertainers from the late eighties and nineties. Over the top action (a case in point is the scene from *Military Raaj* where Prabhujee drills a hole in the wall with his finger, sticks a pencil in it and hangs his cap on the said pencil) is the hallmark of such films. 'Over the top' might actually be an understatement. This is what the great Great Bong writes in tribute to the Prabhujee Cult—'Mithunism: The Religion'[*]:

> I once remember Mithun-da running when a villain fires a bullet. What follows is a breathless chase—bullet flying, Mithun-da running, bullet flying, Mithun running. Then when the bullet is gaining on Him, Mithun-da suddenly steps aside and the bullet passes Him by a whisker. Only then does He realize the bullet is going to hit His widowed mother. Now it is Mithun running, bullet flying, Mithun running, bullet flying. And at the last moment, He grabs the bullet and saves His mother.

And here's a sample from another blog called *Deferred Brilliance*[**]:

> The feats Prabhuji has captured cannot be matched by any mortal. Prabhuji redefined complex laws like

---

[*] 'Mithunism—The Religion', *Great Bong*, 9 September 2005, https://greatbong.net/2005/09/09/mithunism-the-religion/

[**] 'A Tribute to GOD himself—Aeeee Salaaaaa Prabhuji!', *Brijesh* 29 March 2010, http://deferredbrilliance.blogspot.in/2010/05/tribute-to-lord-himself-aeeee-salaaaaa.html

'whatever goes up must come down' to his version of 'Whatever goes down must come up and whatever goes up may or may not come down'. Or using simple logic to solve complex problems like in this situation. Mantri: '*Ye kanch bulletproof hai tum mujhe chu bhi nahin sakte*' (This glass is bullet-proof. You can't even touch me). Prabhuji thinks for a moment and then smiles: '*Ye kanch bulletproof hai magar patthhar proof nahin*' (This glass is bullet-proof, but not stone-proof). AND HE BREAKS IT BY THROWING STONES ON THE GLASS AND THEN SHOOTS THE GUY!

This is the kind of imagery that Mithun Da aka Prabhujee evokes, which is somewhat ironic, considering he debuted with Mrinal Sen's *Mrigaya* that earned him his first National Award, and the fact that he went on to win two more.

Surakksha Firsts

The 2015 film *Furious 7*, of the Fast and the Furious franchise, had a breathtaking shot of cars leaping into the air out of a plane. As they are about to hit the ground, parachutes spring off the top of these cars and ensure a safe landing. Thirty-six years before this film, in *Surakksha*, Gunmaster G-9 flies off a cliff with his car, followed by his ill-fated chasers who fall straight down to their deaths. But G-9's is no ordinary car — he pokes a button on the dashboard and out pops a parachute while *Gunmaster G-9* plays in the background.

Ravikant Nagaich also seems to be the first film-maker to introduce the concept of a super-villain, complete with a costume, hi-tech den and henchmen. These villains, more often than not, were played by eminent south Indian actors appearing in cameos. If Supremo from *Farz* was played by veteran Telugu actor Rajanala, *Surakksha*'s Doctor Shiva was portrayed by legendary actor-producer K. Balaji. K. Balaji methodically remade most of the Bollywood hits from the seventies in Tamil, including *Deewar, Don, Dushman, Namak Haraam* and *Johny Mera Naam*.

The film marked the debut of Tej Sapru (son of veteran character actor D.K. Sapru and one of Bollywood's favourite henchmen alongside luminaries like Sharat Saxena, Goga Kapoor, Mohan Joshi, Dalip Tahil and the like). Sapru plays Jackson, an agent who has been captured by an ominous group of no-gooders called SSO, that staged his death and secretly kept him in custody. G-9 rescues Jackson, who has lost the use of his legs due to torture. But does the disability render him out of action? No, Sir! G-9 improvises a special crutch for him, that can transform into a gun at a moment's notice!

Bollywood has always dealt a bad hand to its villains. Besides getting thrashed by the hero at the slightest opportunity, they are shamed by the heroine, and above all, they rarely get to sing and dance! With the glaring exception of Amrish Puri singing time and again in *Tehelka, Vishwatma, Tridev* and *Muskurahat*, and Shakti Kapoor shaking a leg in films like *Rocky* and *Dance Dance*, villains have rarely been known to get entire playback songs and get to dance with an elaborate crew. (And here, I synonymize villains to screen baddies like Prem Chopra, Pran, Amjad Khan and their ilk — not heroes playing 'negative roles' like Shahrukh Khan in *Darr*, Ajay Devgn in *Khaaki*, or Saif Ali Khan in *Omkara*.) But we know *Surakksha* is not your run-of-the-mill Bollywood fare. Jeevan, of all people, gets a Qawwali face-off with G-9 in the song 'Ye Duniya Hai Usiki'. He has no less than Manna Dey crooning for him, and Jeevan breaks into a jig with such abandon that for a while he seems to be giving our Prabhujee a run for his money!

And talking about firsts, what's your earliest memory of a male Bollywood actor sporting a hairband on-screen? Yeah, you got that right. A hairband. Well, circa 1979, Jeevan paved the way for Farhan Akhtar in *Rock On!!* in the aforementioned song. You don't believe me? Check out the song on YouTube.

Shiva Shakti

When Agent Jackson's lifeless body turns up at their doorstep, his wife and son freak out, and so does the CBI. The Chief (Iftekhar) summons Gunmaster G-9 from his night-time sojourns, and hands him the task of looking into it. G-9 soon discovers the body was a decoy, and that Jackson is alive and in captivity under the sinister SSO gang. Earlier we'd seen how Captain Kapoor, pilot of Plane V-G 123 (Suresh Oberoi) helps SSO obtain the secret map to a diamond mine. SSO, as a mark of gratitude, shoots Captain Kapoor who then proceeds to die with a lot of flourish.

Agent Jackson (surprisingly, Jackson doesn't have a code number. He's just 'Jackson') intercepts the SSO goons and hides the map, before they get the better of him and make him their captive. The nail-biting chase between SSO and Jackson is one of the highlights of the film. Jackson, astride a motorcycle, rides to the top of a tall building, and the bike travels in thin air to the next building. (Watch this part of the movie closely to see what I mean.) Cracking clue after clue, G-9 rescues Jackson and the map, upon which, the shrewd and super-smart G-9 (early on, he's introduced by the villain as '*Khatarnaak. Chalaak. Sarkaari jasoos. Khubsoorat ladkiyan jiski kamzori hai*' [Dangerous. Clever. Government spy. One whose weakness is beautiful women], interspersed with shots of G-9 throwing knives into a watermelon) deduces that the map not only shows the diamond mine but also SSO's hideout. All this while, SSO had been sweating itself to get a map of its own hideout—brilliant, no?

G-9 sneaks into the SSO den, only to realize that SSO is an acronym for Shiv Shakti Organization. Whether SSO had any political aspirations (or was inspired by any real-life political party) was not revealed in the movie. The kingpin of SSO finally reveals himself to G-9: the greatest scientist the world has ever seen, the man with the first bionic arm ever in Bollywood, *'Shiv ki teesri aankh'* (the third eye of Shiva), Doctor Shiva. Doctor Shiva introduces G-9 to his lanky killer robot Jango (or is it Django, eh Tarantino fans?) — *'Yeh ek chalti-phirti laash hai, jise maine science ke zariye zinda rakkha hai.'* (This is a walking corpse, that I have kept alive through science.) Upon which, the clairvoyant G-9 quips, *'Waise duniya ke kai deshon mein robots ban chuke hain Doctor!'* (Robots have been made in many countries across the globe, doctor!), and the Doctor patiently explains, *'Lekin insaan ko robot aaj tak koi nahin banaa saka'* (But nobody has been able to turn humans into robots). Doctor Shiva was right. *RoboCop* was still eight years away.

Doctor Shiva also presents his massive fish tank which has giant gold fish fluttering about, and the pièce de résistance: world's first atomic generator, a Death Ray machine. The doctor's *'bees saal ke tapasya ka nateeja'* (the result of twenty years' worth of perseverance), a machine that can create humongous amounts of energy in just seven seconds flat. Power that can artificially create storms, tsunamis and earthquakes. How it does so is pure science, but I'll try to simplify it for you, lay reader. The machine comprises a huge dish laced with diamonds, and a vat of boiling mercury. Sun's rays hit the dish, and passing through the diamonds, reflects on the boiling mercury, thereby charging it. As a result, every atom gains the power of ten suns, and the vat of mercury becomes as powerful as ten million suns! (Stop smirking, Hollywood.)

And throughout this eventful ordeal, is it the spy's resourcefulness or Doctor Shiva's hospitality that Gunmaster G-9 gets to wear three different outfits? Considering he came in with nothing but a t-shirt and a pair of pants on, the dapper suits he sports after that may be attributed to the latter. We get a glimpse of Shiva's largesse when G-9 is welcomed to his quarters by three buxom ladies dressed like they will start playing table tennis any second. They are named Fifteen, Sixteen and Seventeen, and they speak only English.

Femme Fatale
Surakksha has all the bling and chutzpah one looks for in a Bond film. With gadgets, the super-villain, villain's den, qawwali, and Bond girls. Well, maybe the qawwali was a bonus. Girls were present in abundance—G-9 gets to cavort with a bunch of them while swaying to the tunes of 'Mausam Hai, Gaane Ka'. Ranjeeta plays Priya, who for a while hates Gunmaster as he's a playboy, then bays for his blood as she mistakes him for her father's killer, and then, true to her destiny in the script, falls for him.

And then there's Neelam, petty gangster Hiralal's moll. While oozing glamour, she isn't just the villain's arm candy. The goons are in awe of her, she knows how to use a gun, and even has her own *naari sena* of female goons, all sporting the TT attire as described above. Fifteen, Sixteen and Seventeen probably belong to her troop. Halfway through the film, she apprehends G-9 practically on her own, and ties him to her bed, purring, '*Choohe ko maarne se pehle, billi uske saath jee bhar ke khelti hai.*' (Before killing the mouse, the cat plays with it to her heart's content.) Lest we place any doubt on her amorous intentions, she elaborates, '*Kisi ko maarne se pehle main usske saath raat ke akhri lamhe tak jee bhar ke khelti hoon.*' (Before killing someone, I play with them till the wee hours of the night.)

The role was played by Mala Jaggi, one of the millions of talented faces that pop up on Bollywood's firmament, only to be lost in obscurity later. Considering this was just her second film, she was one of the most self-assured actors featured in the movie. Like *Surakksha*'s leading man, Mala Jaggi's debut was also unconventional, and galaxies away from the glam girl she plays here. Her first film was Bengali director Tapan Sinha's Hindi outing, *Safed Haathi* (1977), a children's film in which she appeared as a cruel aunt to the child protagonist.

Gadgets Galore

We have already discussed the car-parachute thing, and a la James Bond, G-9's super-car can also spill fluids in its wake, to cause unwitting chasers to skid. G-9 also owns a rather special cigarette-lighter that, upon pressing a secret button, can put people to sleep; a smartwatch (yeah, back in 1979); and a mini drill.

In *Kill Bill: Volume 2* (2004), our heart goes out to The Bride aka Beatrix Kiddo when she's buried alive by Bill's brother Budd, and we watch and hoot and whistle for her when she punches her way out of the grave. But way back in 1979, when the same stuff happens to Gunmaster G-9 aka Prabhujee, you don't bat an eyelid. You are sure he can make it. You *know* he can make it. Sure enough, before you can spell 'G-9', the man pops the mini drill, and drills his way out of the grave. Easy peasy.

Mausam Hai, Gaane Ka... Gaane Ka, Bajaane Ka

For a film with visibly low production values, jarring camera angles and editing, the music is quite phenomenal. Bappi Lahiri perhaps sings for Mithun Chakraborty for the first time in this film, before going on to become the 'voice of Mithun' for a long time to come. For me personally, three tracks stand out. The Kishore Kumar number 'Maine Pyaar Kiya Toh Theek Kiya' might not be everyone's cup of tea, but makes full use of Kishore's signature histrionics. 'Dil Tha Akela Akela' is more placid in comparison, with romance and longing oozing out of it and borrowed generously from Abba's 1974 track 'Hasta manana'. Even the way it's been shot is at variance with the rest of the film; you can't imagine it's from *Surakksha* until someone tells you. And a personal favourite is the qawwali towards the end, at Doctor Shiva's den: 'Ye Duniya Hai Usiki', partly for Jeevan matching steps with Prabhujee, partly because of the Manna-Kishore combo. And Usha's rejoinder after the mukhda (the opening of a song) takes the song to a different level entirely.

In the movie *Dasvidaniya* (2008), when the dying protagonist Amar Kaul (Vinay Pathak) connects with his long-estranged childhood pal Rajiv Jhulka (Rajat Kapoor), they refer to each other as Gunmaster G-9 and G-10, before breaking into the song 'Mausam Hai, Gaane Ka' in unison.

Mithun Chakraborty aka Prabhujee will be associated with films like *Disco Dancer* and a plethora of other films, but Gunmaster G-9 stands on his own. It will continue to do so.

Chashme Buddoor

Avert the evil eye

Release: 1981

Cast: Farooq Sheikh, Ravi Baswani, Rakesh Bedi, Deepti Naval

Directed by: Sai Paranjpye

Plot Summary: Siddharth (Farooq Sheikh), Omi (Rakesh Bedi) and Jomo (Ravi Baswani) inhabit a bachelors' pad in a quaint neighbourhood in Delhi, in 1981. Siddharth is occupied with studies while Omi and Jomo fool around chasing women and spewing poetry. The two clowns try to woo doe-eyed Neha, but she falls for the old-world charms of Siddharth. Somewhere in this tale, we have Lallan Miyan (Saeed Jaffrey) — the paanwallah with a heart of gold and a supercool Daadi (Leela Mishra).

✧

It was in early 1980, in a park in Moscow, where *Chashme Buddoor* was conceived over scoops of ice cream. Seemingly on an impulse, producer Gul Anand who had just produced *Khatta Meetha* (1978), asked Sai Paranjpye to make a film for him. He was deeply impressed by Paranjpye's first feature, *Sparsh* – a sensitive tale of a blind man played masterfully by Naseeruddin Shah. But he wanted her to make a fun film. At first, she dismissed it as a typical Bollywood filmwallah fancy and promptly forgot about it once she was back in India.

Sai Paranjpye clarifies, 'I didn't actually forget about it. It will be more truthful to say that I didn't take it seriously. These filmy people, I had heard so much about their big talk and so on. So, I did nothing. Didn't write a single word. And then, dot on the day Gul said he'd call me, he called!'

Sai apologized and started putting together the new film.

Dhuaan Dhuaan

Back in the 1970s, Sai Paranjpye worked for Doordarshan as a producer in Delhi.

She reminisces in a telephonic interview:

> I was in Television then, working as a producer in Delhi Doordarshan, and I used to do a lot of tele-plays which were very popular at that time. There were not too many plays, but somehow my tele-plays caught the public's fancy and were appreciated and replayed again and again. So I had written a tele-play of about one hour called *Dhuaan Dhuaan*, making fun of the idle youth of the time — not that anything has changed now — of three good-for-nothing college students who just enjoy life, smoke cigarettes, have fun, chase girls, and do precious little else in life. It was a good-natured, fun look at the adventure of these three, all woven into a coherent story-line. It begins with their smoking and chatting, and then they see a girl and chase her and it ends in nothing as usual. It's a sort of a pipe dream — *Dhuaan Dhuaan* is

about their pipe dreams, talking big, making big plans that end in nothing.

Paranjpye narrated the story of *Dhuaan Dhuaan* to Gul Anand. He liked it very much, but had his reservations about all three characters being portrayed as slackers—he wanted at least one 'hero' character. She rewrote the story, with Siddharth Parashar as a serious, studious type and weaved in the romance and a few more characters, thereby fleshing out the story. She had the script ready in about a couple of weeks.

But something had to be done about the title. There were two working titles at various stages of development of the film—*Dhuaan Dhuaan* and *Diva Swapna*.

Paranjpye clarifies,

> About *Dhuaan Dhuaan*, Gul put his foot down and said, 'No way, because distributors are going to say, "Our money will go up in smoke", so no *Dhuaan Dhuaan*. I said okay. Then *Diva Swapna* was also too sort of...so you know we talked about it and then I remember...we were standing outside, waiting for the lift in his building and suddenly it struck me...I said, 'How about *Chashme Buddoor*?' and he said, 'Fantastic' and nearly went jumping into the lift all the way down. We were on the twelfth or the thirteenth floor...and it became *Chashme Buddoor*! But unfortunately, my Marathi brethren who were so unfamiliar with any Urdu phraseology, they said, 'Sai, tuzha Chashme Bahadur...' hahaha...so some people referred to it as 'Chashme Bahadur'. As for *Sparsh*, they would say 'Sparsha' because in Marathi we say 'Sparsha kela...tu Sparsha kahila.' It would sort of make me cringe, but what do you do—I mean—they mean well.

Recruiting the Crazies

Ravi Baswani is not a Sindhi, as his surname would have us believe. He was born in a Punjabi Jat family, of Dr Balram Singh and Shringar Kaur, hailing from Bulandshahar. Their family name was Baswan. When Balram Singh Baswan's passport landed on the desk of a Bengali clerk in the passport office, he considered the surname to be a ghastly lapse of spelling and took it upon himself to rectify it. The decidedly more popular Sindhi surname of Vaswani and the absence of 'V' in the Bengali world view did the trick. You see, our wise clerk thought 'Baswan' was a corruption of what he really considered to be 'Baswani' (Vaswani), and he went ahead and made the necessary changes. The passport became the basis for Dr Balram Singh Baswani's medical diplomas, and the name stuck. Ravi Baswani forgave us Bengalis and continued with his father's 'revised' family name.

Ravi had an interest in theatre since early days, and made his acting debut at at the age of six! A graduate from Delhi's Kirori Mal College, he went on to form a troupe of his own called, curiously, 'Non-Group'. Naseeruddin Shah came to Delhi with the script of a new film called *Sparsh*, and that's when things started getting interesting. Ravi knew Naseer as a fellow stage actor—one look at the script, and Ravi wanted in. Soon enough, Non-Group was handling the props for the film. Although Ravi Baswani wasn't mentioned explicitly, Non-Group was thanked in the credits for *Sparsh*.

One year later, Sai Paranjpye was casting for *Chashme Buddoor*, and Ravi's name came up. What happened next, is encapsulated in this priceless story, that was widely circulated on the internet in 2013, on the verge of *Chashme Buddoor*'s re-release. It was in the form of a worn-out letter, that read:

Dear Ravi,

Hi. Brace yourself – here goes. How about doing a role in my new film Dhuan Dhuan? It's a super duper comic role with miles and miles of footage. A star crazy, movie crazy pal of the hero, Farooq Sheikh. Ask Sudesh for detail of story and role. Anyway, I know you will never refuse the role once you read the script, but as there is no time you have to say 'Yes' (hopefully) immediately. Trust in my good judgement and all that.

If it is yes, come to Bombay [now called Mumbai] *for a 'do' on the 3rd Sept. Rajdhani will be paid to and fro. For stay, either your own arrangements or my pad (most welcome). No extra allowance. If you can't come to Bombay it's ok, but I must have a very quick, no, immediate reply so that I stop talent scouting. You will get Rs. 3000/- (another low budget thing) – approx. one month's work. Then dubbing in Bombay later. Shooting Oct/ Nov. Send me a cable.*

Love,
Sai

Any film buff would know by now that this letter was from Sai Paranjpye to Ravi Baswani. Ravi played the affable and loony Jomo aka Jai Lakhanpal. There's an amusing story about the Lakhanpals, which is just one in a long line of in-jokes prevalent in Sai Paranjpye's brand of cinema.

When Jomo/Jai (Baswani) lands at the doorstep of Neha Rajan (Deepti Naval), he announces, '*Mashoor director D. Lakhanpal ka naam toh aapne suna hi hoga!*' (You must have heard about the famous movie director D. Lakhanpal!)

Neha shakes her head. 'Nahin.' (No.)

Undeterred, Jomo continues, '*Toh main unka bhai, Jai*

Lakhanpal. Delhi talent-scouting ke silsile mein aaya hoon...' (I am his brother, Jai Lakhanpal. I am here in Delhi to scout for talent.') What follows is too gory and heart-rending to relate on these pages.

Like many *Chashme Buddoor* fans, these dialogues are probably etched in your brain. On one of the countless viewings of the film, you think you just spotted something familiar in the credit rolls, and hit the pause button. There it is! Listed under Assistant Director, the name 'Dinesh Lakhanpal' stares at you.

Khushbudaar, jhaagwala... Chamko!

I was trying my best to get in touch with the crew of *Chashme Buddoor*. Sadly, I was a year too late for Farooq Sheikh. He passed away in 2013. But Deepti Naval was still active in Hindi films. In fact, they had just gotten together for one last gig, *Listen Amaya* (2013). Both their performances were widely appreciated by critics everywhere.

Reaching out to Deepti Naval seemed utterly impossible. I didn't have any 'industry contacts' as such. So, I turned to the only person I could think of: a veritable giant of Hindi Cinema, one that Deepti Naval has shared many a film with, and someone who I had interviewed a few months ago — Naseeruddin Shah. It took a lot of courage for the simple act of texting him to ask for her number. This is what transpired:

Sun, 21 December, 12:14 p.m. – 'I am writing about *Chashme Buddoor* now, as part of my book. Can you help me get in touch with Deepti Naval? Forgive me if this sounds inappropriate. — Amborish'

Sun, 21 December, 1:45 p.m. – My phone buzzes, and ten lonely digits pop up. He had sent the number. Just the number.

Sun, 21 December, 1:51 p.m. – 'This is surreal. Thanks a ton. — Amborish'

I had spent a pretty mundane childhood, and a mundaner (if that's a word) grown-up life. It was like drifting through episode after episode of an interminably long saas-bahu soap. Back then, it would have seemed quite outlandish to me, that a day would come when Naseeruddin Shah would be sending me Deepti Naval's number. But when that day came, it was equally inconceivable.

Exactly a week later, I was sitting across the table and there she was, in all her luminous glory. The years hadn't been able to steal away all that much. Miss Chamko was still as heavenly as ever.

Deepti Naval says,

> Everything was written down. There is a scene in Talkatora Gardens where Siddharth proposes to Neha, she says, '*Main soch ke bataungi.*' (I'll think about it and tell you.) He says, '*Kab bataogi?*' (When?) She replies, '*Ye tutti-frutti khatam ho jaane ke baad.*' (Once I'm done with this tutti-frutti.) *Waiter aata hai aur kehta hai ke 'Interval ke baad laata hoon.'* (The waiter comes and says, 'I'll bring it after the Interval'.) All that was written down on the page. It was not so much left to the actors. I remember that very well, noticing the fact that it is all written down. It was all there in Sai's head.
>
> She knew the little details like how Neha goes, you know, in her mind, singing at the bus stop and all that. Of course, the actors bring in their own persona, to interpret a certain role and which we all did, and the freshness, a lot of it, you know sort of, attributed to the actors

because we were fairly new faces. He (Farooq Sheikh) had done *Noorie*, I had done *Ek Baar Phir*.

The movie was full of performances with a spontaneous quality that finds place in precious few films of the 1980s. The heartwarming relationship between the boys and Lallan Miyan (Saeed Jaffrey), the inordinately cute Daadi (Leela Mishra), the romance of the lead pair (Deepti Naval and Farooq Sheikh), and of course, the trio of punters at the centre of it all—Omi, Jomo and Siddharth (Rakesh Bedi, Ravi Baswani and Farooq Sheikh respectively). Successive generations of youngsters have been pleasantly surprised at how the depictions of a bachelors' pad and lifestyle are so accurate. But there was also a measure of innocence and naiveté, and Farooq Sheikh was at the heart of it all.

An Actor and a Gentleman

Farooq Sheikh would have ended up as a lawyer. He was born in a lawyer's family—his father was one. He even attended Siddharth Law College, Mumbai, but the seeds of acting were sown during his undergraduate days at St. Xavier's College, around 1969. More often than not, him and one of his classmates—a young Shabana Azmi—would end up winning the best actor and best actress awards. Sheikh was actively involved in the theatre scene and also got involved with the Indian People's Theatre Association (IPTA) movement. Subsequently, he trained as a lawyer but couldn't make peace with the profession. Film-maker M.S. Sathyu came calling and *Garm Hava* (1974) happened. In a career just shy of four decades, Farooq Sheikh appeared only in a bit more than fifty films, despite having worked with a wide range of directors like Satyajit Ray, Muzaffar Ali, Hrishikesh Mukherjee, Yash

Chopra, Basu Chatterjee, Kalpana Lajmi, Ketan Mehta, Dibakar Bannerjee and Ayan Mukherjee. One would believe this proves his selectivity in picking projects, which is not to say that he didn't do his share of bad films, or roles. There was *Toofan* (1989) where he played the ever-sacrificing friend Gopal, or two excruciatingly bad Bengali movies *Agni Kanya* (1990) and *Shukher Asha* (1995), and a plethora of action movies where he played either the victim or the brother/friend. But it was Muzaffar Ali (*Gaman, Umrao Jaan*) and Sai Paranjpye who allowed him to showcase his potential. In Paranjpye's *Katha* (1983), he excelled as the scheming upstart who uses his friend like a doormat. But it was *Chashme Buddoor* that made him a household name.

In a lot of ways, Sheikh's character in *Chashme Buddoor* reflected his own persona. Straight as an arrow, but with a taste for the finer things in life. When Siddharth bags his job, he shops around for the best clothes and shoes he could afford. But he is also a thorough gentleman. During the legendary 'Chamko' scene, he is conscious about being alone in the room with a woman. Also, he seems least interested in his roommates' misadventures with women. In real life, Farooq saab was an infallible cavalier — he would ask after the well-being of everyone, from his colleagues to his cook. In the cynical little cocoon that film personalities inhabit, nobody has to speak a word of malice about this man.

Ye Dhuaan Sa Kahaan Se Uthta Hai

A faint hint of a ghazal wafts in, as we focus on a coconut shell loaded with some zillion dead cigarettes. The ghazal sounds clearer, and we hear strands of Mehdi Haasan's voice, *Dekh toh dil ke jaan se uthta hai/ Ye dhuaan sa kahaan se uthta hai.* A cigarette butt is puffed, then passed on from hand to hand, until it reaches a set of toes which transfer it to its destined end—the lips of the protagonist Siddharth Parashar. This rather singular opening sets the mood for *Chashme Buddoor*. We dive into the world of Siddharth, Omi and Jomo. Jomo, as discussed earlier, was played by newcomer Ravi Baswani, and Omi by Rakesh Bedi.

I catch Rakesh Bedi right before his play at Rangsharda Natyamandir one January evening.

> The DOP of the film was Virendra Saini, who happened to be my batchmate at FTII[*]. He was in cinematography and I was in acting. He gave me a call and told me about this role. I just went and heard the character and was totally floored by it. I took the script and whatever I could improve on it by contributing a little bit of sher o shayri,[**] I did.
>
> A few years before this, I graduated from FTII, and I had a lot of funny memories of my hostel life, and I am not saying that all of it was there in the film, but the attitude, the behaviour, the girls—how when a girl comes, what happens to the chemistry of the men in the room—some of it was there. *Abhi toh khair zamana bahut tez ho gaya, lekin us zamane mein kya tha, ke ladki ko hostel mein leke aana hi bahut badi baat hoti thi. Ye sab humne kiya bhi tha, pakde bhi gaye thhe...phir main yahaan par bhi jab rehta thha—humlog chaar-paanch log saath rehte thhe—main,* David Dhawan, director Raman Kumar (the maker of *Saath Saath*), cameraman Sunil Sharma (collaborated on *Saath Saath* as well), *aur bhi kuch log thhe. Wahan pe bhi*

---

[*]The Film and Television Institute of India
[**]'sher' means couplets; 'shayri' as in poetry

humaara bachelors' pad thha, landlady ka bagal mein ghar thha—toh yahaan par bhi, jo masti hoti hai bachelor life ki— sans the drugs—*sab humne kiya hua tha. Ye sab dramebaazi mere system mein thi. So, jab mujhe Sai ne bulaya, toh maine bhi kuch apne inputs dene shuru kiye. Aur sone pe suhaaga yeh thha, ke saari shooting Delhi mein ho rahi thhi...* (Life is much faster nowadays. But back in the day, even to get a girl inside the hostel was considered a huge deal. We had done all of that and got caught in the act, too. And then when I was living here—four of us used to stay together: me, David Dhawan, director Raman Kumar, cameraman Sunil Sharma, and a few others. All this drama was in my system. It was a bachelors' pad and the landlady lived next door. We did all of the fun stuff bachelors do—sans the drugs—we did it all. So, when Sai called me, I started sharing some of my own inputs. And ironically, the shoot was happening in Delhi!)

Chashme Buddoor was majorly shot in Defence Colony, and Bedi was born and raised in Delhi. He used to stay in Greater Kailash. So, Delhi's lifestyle, youth lingo and so on, were very familiar to him. Thus, a lot of his personal experiences shaped his depiction of Omi. Near Rakesh Bedi's bachelors' pad in Mumbai, coconut trees would be found aplenty. Out of respect for the smokers in the household, Bedi would slice open a coconut and carve an ashtray out of the shell. Every few months, there would be a new ashtray of this novel breed, as the old ones would flay or burn around the edges. For nine years he lived in that house. Bedi says—'When I went for the shooting, I carried some ashtrays with me. And I told her, "See—we used these kind of ashtrays..." Sai was so excited, so thrilled to see that thing, you know. People still ask me,

"Where did that ashtray come from?" It was my brainchild, my prop which I took with me!'

Sai Paranjpye, the Taskmaster

> *Kya jaaniye ke chhati jale*
> *hai ya daag-e-dil*
> *Ek aag si lagi hai kahin*
> *Kuch dhuaan sa hai!*

> Who knows what burns,
> The breast or a heart-sore
> There is, however, a fire somewhere
> And there is smoke.

> *Ban kar, sanwar kar woh nikle makaan se*
> *Yahi shor hoga yahaan se, wahaan se*
> *Qayamat qayamat kise kehte ho*
> *Woh dekho qayamat chali ja rahi hai!*

> There she goes, all dressed-up
> A clamour rises all around
> What would you know what Doomsday is
> Behold her—there's your Doomsday walking right past!

Above are some of the lines attributed to Omi, the sprightly shayri buff. When I ask Rakesh Bedi about the source of all the poetry, this is what he had to say:

> *Maine bahut* improvise *kiya…halaa ki Sai ne bahut likhe thhe, lekin maine bhi kiye. Kyunki mujhe shuru se hi* poetry *ka ek* knack *hai, main khud* poetry *likhta bhi hoon,* language *ka bhi ek pakad hai, Urdu ke alfaaz se bhi waakif hoon. Toh maine kaafi* improvise *ki usmein* poetry*. Kai dafaa aisa bhi hua ke, koi sher usne likha hua tha par uska wazan* correct

nahin hai, toh uska wazan theek karne ke liye ek adh word *ko yahaan se wahaan....*

I improvised quite a bit...although Sai wrote most of it, but I did too. I always had a knack for poetry, I write Urdu poetry, I know the language. So I improvised a lot of poetry there. It also happened that she'd composed the poem but the weight of those couplets was not right, so I shifted a few words here and there to fix it.

But about general improvisations during the shoot, Deepti Naval elaborated that it was all Sai's vision.

All of it was written. I don't remember whether improvisations happened. Everything was written.

But Sai, let me tell you...Sai had detailed stuff on her (Neha)...in her screenplay. She knew the reactions, everything was there on the page. In fact, the little that we did, it seemed as if that was improvised, because it was thought of in such a natural way, it was written down like that—it seemed as if all of it had happened right there... I mean, it doesn't look like too scripted. That was the beauty of that screenplay which Sai had written.

Even the magic of the 'Chamko' scene was all Sai Paranjpye. She had detailed instructions for Deepti. Step by step. 'She knew exactly. She said, "You're going to smile at him, but not too much smile" <laughs>, "so give him half a smile," which I did very well, because she said, "Oh my God, you know exactly what I mean," and I said, "Yeah, I know this part."... The scene is very well crafted, it's one of the most beautifully crafted, easy and natural scenes, of that kind of cinema,' Deepti Naval tells me.

Sai also had these great hat-tips to commercial cinema, throughout the film. Ravi Baswani's 'fictionalized' encounter at Neha's house was full of hilariously recreated songs from the 1960s featuring the two of them, instead of the original actors. Also, there was a scene where Siddharth and Neha deconstruct the process of how a hero and heroine break into a song when they fall in love.

Deepti Naval tells me about the scene:

> Like me and Farooq Sheikh singing in the garden. We're talking about how it's just like in the movies, music starts playing in the background, and they actually start singing... and then they actually start singing.... So conventional Hindi Cinema stuff was used by Sai with the same references, instead of simply breaking into a song; she said, 'That's too typical—there's the voices and the music, and the hero-heroine start singing!' So it was used very cleverly, it was very intelligent of her to use those factors of commercial cinema and make them appear like these people are only talking about it. You know, it's mentioned like that. So when you mention something and you make the setting for it, it then acquires a lot of credibility because of that.

But Sai Paranjpye was also quite the taskmaster. She would insist on a certain kind of integrity and authenticity, which could sometimes attain alarming proportions, despite the intent.

Rakesh Bedi shares one such story:

> Everyone was scared of Sai's anger. She used to get angry fairly quickly... If you remember, I am sporting a small moustache in the film, '*Talvaar*-cut' (as sharp-edged as a

sword) it was called those days. I'd grown the moustache for the film and was maintaining it. Meanwhile I had to go to Bombay for another shoot, and continuity was an issue. I had already shot for the film, and I had shot without the moustache. Now I had to come back to Bombay again and shoot without the moustache. So I had to shave it off. But then I also had to go back (to *Chashme Buddoor* shooting) after a few days. I knew if Sai were to spot this, she will lose her temper again — what should I do? I drew the moustache with a pencil, and also let it grow beneath it. A few days went by. Sai didn't notice. Nobody got to know. One day me and Farooq were shooting — I wiped my mouth with a handkerchief and half of the moustache disappeared!

Farooq, obviously amused, said, '*Zara aaina mangwaaiye aap!*' (Get a mirror!) Rakesh got a mirror and realized the blunder. He had to spill the beans to Farooq. They had a good laugh over it, but Rakesh continued 'drawing' the moustache, and nobody knew anything about it. As a matter of fact, Rakesh is still unsure whether Sai Paranjpye ever got to know about it, in all these years.

In 2013, *Chashme Buddoor* was remade by David Dhawan as *Chashme Baddoor*, starring Ali Zafar and Tapsee Pannu. The film raked up a lot of money, and its music topped the charts. Strange thing is, it's just been five years since then, but today when one mentions 'Chashme Buddoor' (spelling notwithstanding), it's always about the 1981 film involving three boys in a barsaati (one-room apartment on a terrace) and Miss Chamko, that one instantly thinks of. And order is restored in the universe.

Silsila

When the reel and the real collide

Release: 1981

Cast: Amitabh Bachchan, Rekha, Sanjeev Kumar, Jaya Bachchan, Shashi Kapoor, Kulbhushan Kharbanda, Deven Varma

Directed by: Yash Chopra

Plot Summary: Amit (Amitabh Bachchan) and Shekhar (Shashi Kapoor) are brothers, but destiny lands a blow when Shekhar dies in a crash and Amit has to get married to his widow Shobha (Jaya Bachchan). But Amit's old flame Chandni (Rekha) has come back in his life, through his acquaintance with Dr. Anand (Sanjeev Kumar), whom Chandni is now married to. Amit and Chandni rekindle their relationship as Shobha and Dr. Anand watch silently, from the fringes.

For years, Yash Chopra's cinema has been equated with Swiss Alps and chiffon sarees. Our national obsession with assigning labels to people has been satiated by tagging him with an over-simplistic 'King of Romance' sticker.

Yash Chopra's first directorial venture *Dhool Ka Phool* (1959) was about an illegitimate child adopted and raised by a Muslim, ostracized by the society for sheltering an infant whose religious identity is uncertain. At a time when India was coming to terms with the socio-economic realities of freedom, his debut film was soaked in Nehruvian socialism. And to prove he wasn't a flash in the pan, his next film too was on religious fundamentalism: *Dharmputra* (1961). His third film had the most epic ensemble cast ever assembled on Indian screens: *Waqt* (1965) starring Raaj Kumar, Sunil Dutt and Balraj Sahni, among others. Without revelling in the success, Chopra plunged into one of the darkest films he ever made, a film noir-esque *Ittefaq* (1969).

Deewar (1975) in particular remains a sizzling gangster saga in the garb of Bollywood kitsch. To call him the 'King of Romance' may be doing disservice to a prolific creator like Yash Chopra. His meditations on male-female relationships were mostly mistaken for mush, given the packages they came in. But *Daag* (1973), *Kabhi Kabhie* (1976), *Silsila* (1981), *Chandni* (1989) and *Lamhe* (1991) remain enduring human stories.

Take *Silsila* for example. One will be committing nothing short of a crime by calling it simply a romantic film. While romance is a very important aspect of the film, *Silsila* is about human relationships more than anything else. The story of two brothers, seemingly loveless marriages, ill-fated lovers and infidelity. Chopra had earlier made a film about a man having to choose between his two wives (*Daag*) but this was the first time he was making a film on infidelity. Released in an era of unbridled on-screen violence, *Silsila* didn't do well at the box office, but is considered a classic today. There are other reasons cited for its fate, but we will get to that later.

The Cast

When *Silsila* was conceived, Yash Chopra had visualized Amitabh, Jaya and Rekha in the lead but considering what was (reportedly) going on in their personal lives, coupled with the fact that Jaya Bachchan had all but quit films after *Nauker* (1979), *Silsila* was announced with Amitabh Bachchan, Padmini Kolhapure and Parveen Babi portraying the main characters. Kolhapure was apparently playing the wife Shobha, and Parveen Babi was to portray Chandni, the lover. Parveen Babi may have pulled off the 'other woman' role with aplomb, but Padmini Kolhapure as Amitabh Bachchan's wife seems to be a terrible idea in retrospect—she was in her late teens and Bachchan was more than twenty years her senior! Anyhow, Kolhapure couldn't commit to the dates and Smita Patil stepped in. So, with this cast, Chopra planned the first shooting schedule.

Before *Silsila* could begin filming, Yash Chopra was in Kashmir to oversee the shoot of *Sawaal* (1982), starring Sanjeev Kumar and directed by Ramesh Talwar, a film for which Chopra was the producer. During the same time, Amitabh Bachchan was in Kashmir shooting for *Kaalia* (1981). Sensing an opportunity, Yash Chopra made him read the script of *Silsila*. Bachchan asked him whether he was happy with the casting and Chopra, hesitantly, replied in the negative. The ideal cast was Bachchan, Jaya and Rekha, according to him, but nothing could be done as the shoot was about to begin. Amitabh Bachchan said, 'Let's go back to Bombay tomorrow and speak to both of them.' They flew back to Bombay together the next day. Not a single word was exchanged during the journey; both wondered what was about to happen now.

Both Rekha as well as Jaya Bachchan were only too happy to say yes. Chopra also made the two ladies promise that there won't be any trouble on the sets. He is also said to have revealed in a BBC interview that he was on tenterhooks throughout the shooting of the film. But it's a testament to the professionalism of the three principal actors of *Silsila* that despite what transpired in their personal lives, they didn't allow any of it to tamper with the film in any way. As a matter of fact, generations of film fans have debated whether it actually *helped* in creating the intensity on screen.

After the two leading ladies had been cast, the ones they replaced were to be informed of the change. Being part of *Kaalia*, Parveen Babi was also shooting in Kashmir when all this was unfolding. Yash Chopra always found such situations awkward to deal with, and instructed his assistant director Romesh Sharma to inform her and apologize on his behalf. Within days, as fate would have it, Yash Chopra bumped into Parveen Babi at the Srinagar airport. Parveen assured him that it was okay. She understood that what he was making was a once-in-a-lifetime film, and whatever decisions he was taking were in the interest of the film.

Dealing with Smita Patil went differently. Shashi Kapoor had already been cast as Amitabh Bachchan's older brother. Kapoor, four years older than Bachchan, had so far always played his kid brother, in *Deewar* (1975) and *Trishul* (1978), while in *Suhaag* (1994) they were twins. *Silsila* was the first film in which he played the elder brother. Yash Chopra requested him to break the news to Smita Patil that the cast has changed, and she was no longer a part of the project. Smita Patil took it sportingly but felt Yash Chopra could have spoken to her in person. Later, they met in Rajkamal Studios where Smita Patil was shooting for a film, and they settled things amicably.

An apocryphal story about casting Sanjeev Kumar goes that he initially turned the role down, under the impression that he will have to play second fiddle to Bachchan. Yash Chopra insisted on a narration and during the process, Kumar realized that he would have some powerful scenes with Jaya Bachchan. He and Jaya Bachchan shared an impeccable working relationship and they had made some wonderful movies together — *Parichay* (1972), *Koshish (1972), Anamika* (1973), *Naya Din Nai Raat* (1974), *Nauker* (1979) and of course, *Sholay* (1975). He signed the film, and delivered an underrated but brilliant performance as Rekha's husband, Dr. Anand.

His is the most refined performance of *Silsila*. Right after one of the most evocative romantic numbers ever made, *Ye kahaan aa gaye hum/ Yun hi saath saath chalte,* even before you are out of the stupor, Sanjeev Kumar's furious snarl snaps you out of it. His wife and her lover sing love songs and spew poetry at each other, getting all snuggly in each other's arms, and then suddenly the husband bursts out, 'What the hell is going on?' Only later does it dawn on you that Dr. Anand/ Sanjeev Kumar is in the operation theatre where the lights have gone out, and he is annoyed. Priceless.

As he realizes what his wife is up to, Dr. Anand sits Shobha (Jaya Bachchan) down to tell her what is going on, and then tells her a fairy tale. A fairy casts a spell on the prince and leads him away, while the princess is left shedding tears at her misery, back at the palace. Instead of crying, Dr. Anand says the princess should fight for her rights. Shobha then asks who he is, in this tall tale? This is what he has to say to that:

Hum uss nagar ke Raja hain. Raaton ko bhes badal kar hum praja ka haal maloom karte hain. Logon ko nyay dilaate hain. Hum par har zimmedaari hai, Bhabhi...nagar ki, mahal ki, kartavya ki, parampara ki. Aur hum parampara nibhaa rahein hain...

I am the king. I disguise myself as a commoner and walk around my town, to know how my subjects are doing. I deliver justice. I have duties...towards my city, my palace, my responsibilities, my traditions. And I am carrying them out...

Only Sanjeev Kumar could have mouthed the above dialogues the way he did. One look at his face and you will know why he is one of the best actors we have had, since the dawn of Hindi cinema.

In another scene, Dr. Anand is leaving town for work and is standing in the airport lounge with his wife Chandni (Rekha), not wanting to leave as he fears that by the time he returns, she will have eloped with Amit (Amitabh Bachchan). Though she obviously doesn't have much left to say to him, he tries to prolong the conversation as much as possible by making mundane small-talk. He reminds her to pay the telephone bill, about the gardener's wife being ill, tells her he has left some blank cheques for her to encash if she needed money, asks her to check his mail, all this while not forgetting to tell her that he will put up at The Taj, so that she knows where to find him.

'*Mujhe yakeen hai jab main ghar wapas lautunga toh tum mujhe yahin khadi milogi,*' he adds. (When I am back, I know I will find you standing, waiting for me right here.)

These moments simply sparkle. In India, intense acting is all about thunder and lightning. Few actors know how to use silences well. Jaya Bachchan is one of them. In *Silsila*, she uses this skill with a lot of panache. A wife who watches silently as her husband drifts away, slowly but surely. A wistful look here, a soulful glimpse there, she underplays Shobha to perfection. In one powerful scene, the fiery wife in her leaps out and comes face to face with her rival. We watch them from a distance, converging at each other. It's almost like armies coming together in a battlefield. The wife asks her nicely to let him go. The lover refuses outrightly. The wife throws some caution and warns her—if it's a war she wants, that's what she will get.

Physics and Chemistry

Since its early days, romance has been an inseparable part of Hindi cinema. No relationship has been explored in as many different ways (or, for most part, in the exact same way) as that between a man and a woman. But in all these years, the number of on-screen pairs who had the chemistry to set the screen ablaze, can be counted on one's fingers. Whether because of personal rapport, or a great working relationship, or simply because they were two great actors who people loved to see together over and over again, some pairs have always worked better than others. Ashok Kumar–Devika Rani and then Ashok Kumar–Nalini Jaywant, Dilip Kumar–Vyjayanthimala, Guru Dutt–Waheeda Rehman, Dharmendra–Hema Malini, Rajesh Khanna–Sharmila Tagore, Rajesh Khanna–Mumtaz, Jeetendra–Sridevi, Jeetendra–Jaya Prada, Rishi Kapoor–Neetu Singh, Farooq Sheikh–Deepti Naval, Naseeruddin Shah–Shabana Azmi, Sanjay Dutt–Madhuri Dixit, Aamir Khan–Juhi Chawla, Govinda–Karisma Kapoor, Shah Rukh Khan–Kajol and so on. But two pairs stand out for their sheer chemistry, so much so that the passion seem to spill over from the screen. They were Raj Kapoor–Nargis and

Amitabh Bachchan–Rekha. The whirlwind romance between Raj Kapoor and Nargis is public knowledge and the passion between them was visible in films like *Awara* and *Shree 420*.

One would tend to believe the single most important reason that Amitabh–Rekha are considered in this list, is *Silsila*. Of course, they looked great in *Mr. Natwarlal* (1979), *Suhaag* (1994), *Muqaddar Ka Sikandar* (1978), *Do Anjaane* (1976), *Khoon Pasina* (1977), *Ram Balram* (1980) and *Alaap* (1977). Heck, their two-minute cameo in *Chashme Buddoor* remains one of the highlights of the film, and leaves you gasping for more. But their sheer chemistry during the romantic interludes in *Silsila* is unparalleled. The scenes pulsate with passion and sensuality rarely seen in Indian cinema. In fact, the tension is so palpable on TV and laptop screens, one wonders how it would have looked like on the big screen, in a dark theatre. Despite the film not doing well, what most people remember about *Silsila* is its music and Amitabh–Rekha's on-screen romance. One can't blame people for wondering whether this kind of passion spilled off screen. Reportedly, Yash Chopra seemed to indicate in a 2010 BBC interview[*] that it did. Or could it be Mr Bachchan's peerless craft, coupled with Rekha's deeply-held admiration of him (she expressed it in no uncertain terms on the show *Rendezvous with Simi Garewal*)[**] that created the magic? And they looked mesmerizing in the film—Amitabh Bachchan has never looked so impeccably handsome, and Rekha was dreamy!

Yash Chopra's obsession with the name 'Chandni' is another urban legend that has never been entirely explained. The first time a character called Chandni appears in Yash

---

[*]The BBC interview with Yash Chopra no longer exists online.
[**]https://www.youtube.com/watch?v=6L1MbL_azrc

Chopra's cinema, is in *Daag* (1972) where Rakhee plays Chandni. Then passing through Rekha in *Silsila* and Farha in *Faasle* (1985), the name's journey culminated in the eponymous film, *Chandni* (1989), starring Sridevi.

The Music

Javed Akhtar, who shot to fame writing scripts as an integral part of the Salim-Javed duo, had always had a penchant for poetry. Yash Chopra struck a friendship with them during the shoot of *Trishul*. He noticed Akhtar's flair for poetry and encouraged him to start writing lyrics. An opportunity presented itself with *Silsila*. Chopra's usual collaborator Sahir Ludhianvi had passed away a few months before this.

After some amount of cajoling, Javed Akhtar wrote his first song, *Dekha ek khwab to yeh silsile huye*. The music director duo of the film, Shiv-Hari, Santoor maestro Pandit Shiv Kumar Sharma and renowned flautist Pandit Hariprasad Chaurasia, were also making their debut as composers with the film. They went on to compose for many Yash Raj films after this — *Chandni* (1989), *Lamhe* (1991), *Darr* (1993), etc.

The most popular song in the film remains that eternal Holi anthem, 'Rang Barse', originally written by ace poet Harivansh Rai Bachchan, Amitabh Bachchan's illustrious father. Amitabh Bachchan played a major role in the music of *Silsila*. He sang both 'Rang Barse' and 'Neela Asmaan' — legend has it that the tune of 'Neela Asmaan' was originally composed by Amitabh Bachchan and Shammi Kapoor while shooting for *Zameer* (1975), and Bachchan sought his permission to use it in the film, which Shammi was only too glad to provide. 'Neela Asmaan' is another song that packs a punch and is remembered as much for the intermittent poetry by Mr Bachchan, as for the masterful singing by Lata Mangeshkar.

The End

For years, many attributed the failure of *Silsila* to the impression that it messed with the institution of marriage. But the reality may have been quite the opposite. Today, watching *Silsila* after so many years, what sticks out as a sore thumb is the conclusion of the film. It ends with everyone realizing their mistake, and the truant lovers reuniting with their respective spouses. Contrary to popular perception, the principal characters actually bend over backwards to not only accommodate, but also uphold the institution of marriage. What's jarring about this, though, is that it comes across as somewhat fake. Lovers who spent a large part of the film trying to get into each other's arms even at the risk of rocking their marriages, suddenly see the error of their ways in the last twenty per cent of the film. What's more, the wronged spouses who were earlier painfully made aware of their partners' indiscretions, now take them back, no questions asked.

If Amit and Chandni ran away for good, leaving Shobha and Anand behind to lick their wounds, it would have been a conclusion truer to the rest of the story. It may even have been received better by the audience. It's not that Indian moviegoers never welcomed unconventional endings. Yash Chopra himself successfully pulled off a radical conclusion in *Daag* (1972), one that was accepted by the viewers.

Early on in the film, Amit — in his million-dollar baritone — recites the following immortal lines to Chandni. One just marvels at the film *Silsila* could have been, had he delivered on his promise.

Dil kehta hai duniya ki har ek rasm uthha dein
Deewar jo hum dono mein hain, aaj gira dein

Kyun dil mein sulagte rahein, logon ko bataa dein,
'Haan, hum ko mohabbat hai, mohabbat hai, mohabbat!'

The heart wants me to break all rules of the world
Destroy these walls that separate us today
For why should we suffer in silence?
Come, let us tell everyone
'Yes, we are in love! In love! Love!'

Jaane Bhi Do Yaaro
Hum honge kaamyaab

Release: 1983

Cast: Naseeruddin Shah, Ravi Baswani, Pankaj Kapur, Om Puri, Satish Shah

Directed by: Kundan Shah

Plot Summary: A pair of bumbling photographers, Vinod (Naseeruddin Shah) and Sudhir (Ravi Baswani) get sucked into the corrupt nexus of builders, bureaucrats and journalists. Naive as they are, the two try to expose the nexus, but realize they have been taken for a ride. Murder, a dead body on a roller skate, a hilarious stakeout and an epic staging of Mahabharata forms the rest of the story. If you haven't seen *Jaane Bhi Do Yaaro* (*JBDY*) yet, now is the time to redeem yourself.

∽

It was an unusually warm February morning. Heart thumping louder than a steam roller, I pressed the doorbell. The man himself answered the door as I stood stupefied, only my sense of decency holding my jaws together. He was having breakfast and pointed me to a chair, and I parked myself on it, hoping that my shaking knees wouldn't show. It was inconceivable that I, a wannabe writer who rather pompously calls himself a film buff, was sitting at the house of someone who I had grown up watching with a good deal of awe. I have always felt, in a strange way, that I knew him, but more on that later.

But in a few more minutes, that awkwardness would disappear, and I would soon forget that I was chatting with Naseeruddin Shah, in the flesh. I had the cheek to imagine that I was talking cinema with a fellow film lover. How unbecoming of a fan! But in a sweeping contrast to the 'grumpy old man' persona pushed by the ever-so-judgemental media fraternity, Naseer saab comes across as extremely open and approachable.

Doordarshan's Progeny

I refer to my generation as the 'Doordarshan Generation'. Where I come from, theatres were not greatly inviting places. Further, as a rule, we middle-class Bengalis scoffed at mainstream films with a vengeance. The fact that it was (the eighties) the golden age for trashy cinema in Bollywood, didn't help matters either. So, Doordarshan and VHS cassettes were the primary sources of entertainment. Sunday evening screenings were a family event, and since DD made it a point to air the so-called 'arthouse films' along with the mainstream fare from the 1960s and seventies, we grew up on a steady diet of both kinds of cinema. *JBDY* was shown during one of these evening screenings and since it had Naseeruddin Shah in it, I immediately tagged it as an 'art film', and expected a lot of intense looks and silences. But I was stumped when everyone started calling it a comedy film and sat cozily around the TV set with wide grins wrought on their faces whenever it aired.

I laughed so hard, my sides hurt. But I couldn't help noticing that *JBDY* didn't look and sound like the other comedies we were so used to watching. It was funny as hell, but it was not gift-wrapped in glittery paper. Though it made us guffaw aloud, there were bits we didn't really understand.

It so happens that many of those associated with the film shared my sentiment. Naseeruddin Shah says, 'No one had any clue as to what we were making, apart from perhaps Kundan and Renu Saluja, the editor. They were the two constantly positive influences. None of us dreamt that the film would be seen even thirty-five years later.' The crew had a very difficult time shooting for the film. Hungry, cynical and irritable, the team was just too perfect a fit for a black comedy about the dark underbelly of society.

The film was shot on a budget of ₹7 lakhs, a modest amount even then. The funding was through National Film Development Corporation (NFDC). They shot in the wee hours of the morning, to avoid any disturbances. Food was ordered for a limited number of people but there were always more mouths to feed than expected, so a lot of water had to go into the daal. Actors brought in their own props—Shah brought his own still camera to the shoot and left it behind on the platform while filming at the Marine Lines station, and only realized the lapse when he had hopped on to the train. Kundan Shah later made up for it and bought him a new one. In the film, one can see Vinod (Naseeruddin Shah) brandishing the camera and talking about publishing the photographic evidence they have against Tarneja. Sudhir (Ravi Baswani) points to the camera and warns him, 'Bag *mein rakh le*!' (Keep it inside the bag!)

Ravi Baswani got to feature in his debut *Chashme Buddoor* (1981) owing to his prop work in Sai Paranjpye's *Sparsh* (1980), and it was *Chashme Buddoor* that got him the role in *JBDY*. Sudhir Mishra, who was the assistant director on the project, took him to meet Kundan Shah on his old Lambretta scooter. Kundan Shah narrated the script and Ravi jumped at it.

It was like a team on a mission, a bunch of FTII and NSD[*] graduates who believed in a certain kind of cinema, one that could hold up a mirror to the world. Kundan Shah was at the helm, assisted by Sudhir Mishra and Renu Saluja who also doubled up as the editor, her then husband — a one film-old Vidhu Vinod Chopra as the production controller, Binod Pradhan as the cinematographer and Pavan Malhotra handled production and costumes. The story and screenplay were written by Kundan Shah and Sudhir Mishra, while the dialogues were written by Ranjit Kapoor, actor Annu Kapoor's brother, and Satish Kaushik.

Once Upon a Time in Hyderabad

After graduating from FTII, Kundan Shah and his compatriots put together a commune for struggling artists and wannabe film-makers in Hyderabad, with an objective to try and find some satisfactory work. But such work was hard to come by. After making some documentaries, the team disbanded, concluding that it was a fool's errand. But two of Kundan's friends remained, Ravi Ojha and Rajendra Shaw. But when work dried up entirely, the two opened a photo studio.

Ravi Ojha dropped by Kundan Shah's house on a trip to Bombay, and they ended up spending the night drinking and chatting. Ravi regaled him with misadventures from their new studio, and Shah cracked up like there's no tomorrow. By the time the night was through, he had decided to make

---

[*]National School of Drama

a film on two photographers opening a photo studio.

At the time, Kundan Shah was writing a script inspired by Akira Kurosawa's *One Wonderful Sunday* (1947), a charming little film where two lovers set about to spend a Sunday on all of thirty-five yens they have in their pockets. Shah had intended to give it a comedic twist, but now the story that would become *JBDY* had started taking shape in his head.

Meanwhile, another now-legendary incident took place that found its way into the film. The drainage pipe in Kundan Shah's building ran next to the water tank, and it started leaking. The muck was dripping on to the water tank, and they had no option but to drink the polluted water. A discussion with the architect revealed that ten bags of cement were required to repair the drainage pipe. Cement was being rationed those days, and one had to seek permission from a Rationing Officer. Shah met the official, a certain Mr Parker who was sprawling with his legs up on the desk before him. Parker smirked at his request and said, 'Half of Bombay drinks gutter water. What's the problem?' The resulting shock and anger was imprinted on the script of *JBDY*.

Shah had also been trying to bag a job as an assistant director on the sets of Richard Attenborough's *Gandhi* (1982). The task was basically to control the crowd — as Attenborough and his core crew didn't know the local language, they were looking for locals who could help. And the money wasn't bad either — ₹10,000 a month, quite a sum in the early eighties. But this meant he would have to abandon the script he was working on, and plunge headlong into the epic. Kundan had almost got the job, but his friend Saeed Mirza won't have any of it. He reprimanded Shah for even thinking about it and urged him to go write his script. *JBDY* also, therefore, owes its existence to Mirza.

Writing the Cult

For writing the dialogues, Shah wanted help. Vidhu Vinod Chopra, who was already on board, recommended Ranjit Kapoor, a writer-actor-director from theatre. Ranjit also happened to be the brother of Annu Kapoor, and is known for his work in landmark plays like *Hum Rahe Na Hum, Woyzeck* and *Sher Afghan*. Kapoor was willing to listen to the story, and roped in his partner in crime, Satish Kaushik, to be a part of the narration. Kaushik was a struggling actor back then, spending a lot of time on stage. Kapoor was in awe of Kaushik's penchant for comedy and comic timing, and invited him to the session with Kundan Shah.

Halfway through the narration, Kapoor indicated that he was in, but he wanted Satish Kaushik to be a co-writer. It was Kaushik's turn to be shocked—he jumped with a start and tried to explain that all he had ever written was his signature. But Kapoor was convinced that Satish Kaushik's comic timing will be a boon for the film.

Kapoor firmly believed that just like every serious film has comic relief, a madcap comedy like *JBDY* needed some 'serious relief'. This is where the bits with 'Hum Honge Kaamyaab' came in. Although the film evokes laughter every minute, its heart is consumed in darkness. Kundan Shah and Co. had some unpalatable truths to say about the world around them, and as Oscar Wilde (or Bernard Shaw, depending on who you want to believe)[*] once wisecracked, 'If you want to tell people the truth, make them laugh, otherwise they'll kill you.'

For generations who have savoured *JBDY* and its zaniness,

---

[*]If you are interested to know, here's the story of the quote: https://quoteinvestigator.com/2016/03/17/truth-laugh

the high point of the film remains the 'Mahabharata scene' during the climax. The whole scene was written in a matter of hours. What was needed, was a comic climax with all the principal actors in it. Considering the limitations on budget, getting everyone on stage seemed a good option. A pavement bookseller in front of Santacruz station provided the inspiration, and a play on the Mahabharata was obtained, all for fifty paise. Ranjit Kapoor once stated in an interview that the dialogues in the booklet were used as is, with minor modifications for comedic effect. The improvisations of the cast did the rest. What ensued was utter chaos.

Ranjit Kapoor also wrote a song for the film, which Satish Kaushik hummed in a YouTube interview.[*] If his rendition was anything to go by, it is a pity that the track was never even recorded. It went, *Jaane bhi do yaaro/ Jaane bhi do…/ Jo hona hai/ Ho jaane do…* (Let it go, friends/ Let it go…/ Whatever is going to happen/Let it happen…) However, the song wasn't the only thing that never made the cut to appear in the final film. Anupam Kher was cast in a crucial role. *Saaransh* (1984) hadn't released yet, and this might well have been his official debut. The role that Kher was slated to play was named 'Disco Killer', a colourful but buffoonish paid assassin whom Ashok (Satish Kaushik) hires to kill the photographer duo. A ten-minute extended scene was shot in Disco Killer's lair exploring his methods (in addition to quoting his price, he doesn't forget to mention that he also offers festival discounts!). But since the film was becoming too long, the scene, and Kher's role, had to be snipped at the editing table.

Naseeruddin Shah says, 'The amount that was thrown away could have made another film. At least an hour's footage

---

[*]See https://youtu.be/5N7mTn09bNc?t=7m5s

was chucked out. We went nuts shooting that film which was so tough. None of us will be able to go through that again. All of us were pretty strapped. We were broke.'

The role of Ahuja, portrayed by Om Puri, was initially supposed to have been played by Vinod Nagpal, who was known for his role in Doordarshan's 'Hum Log', and had appeared as Deepti Naval's music teacher in *Chashme Buddoor* and many years later in *Khosla Ka Ghosla!* (2006) and *Luv Shuv Tey Chicken Khurana* (2012). But because Nagpal wasn't available, it went to Om Puri, who was previously seen only in intense, even angry, roles. When Ranjit Kapoor recommended him for the role, everyone questioned it. Om Puri had appeared in an out-and-out slapstick comedy role before in the play *Bichhoo*, but this was the first time he was doing something funny on screen. The popularity of Ahuja went on to encourage other film-makers to use him in comic parts for the next three decades.

Pankaj Kapur was also offered the role of Ahuja. He too was brought in by Kapoor to portray the role. They had collaborated on the stage earlier.

Bol Sorry!

Pankaj Kapur told me, sitting across his huge Victorian style desk,

> I used to live in Delhi at that time and I had done three plays with Ranjit as a director and me as an actor. So, we had a team and we had done some wonderful work on stage. He was writing Kundan's film. I didn't know Kundan. I knew Vinod Chopra because Vinod Chopra and me, and 4–5 of us had written a script together in Delhi, *Khamosh* (Vidhu Vinod Chopra's first feature as

director) which hadn't been made yet. We were working on another script. So, I had known Vinod because he had come to Delhi and that's how we met and we became friends. Ranjit and Satish Kaushik were writing the dialogues of this film and I got a call from Ranjit saying, '*Ek role hai* yaar ...*toh tu aaja* Bombay.' (There is a role for you. Please come to Bombay.) I was, I think, doing some work for *Gandhi* at that time and he said, 'You come and meet Kundan.' And I did. They offered me what Om played in the film, 'Ahuja'. So, I was supposed to play Ahuja but they could not find anybody for Tarneja. So, he again called me up. He said, 'Yaar *yeh* problem *ho gaya hai...Tarneja ke liye hum ko koi nahin mil raha hai*, would you mind switching to Tarneja?' (There's a problem, we are not getting any actor for the role of Tarneja.) I said, 'It's a role...as long as you give me a good role and my director is okay with that, I don't have any issues.' In those days, I never used to think like that. Any role is a role...okay, fine! So, that is how I got switched to Tarneja. And every day I used to sit in Kundan's house to discuss the character and for weeks we could not discuss the character because every day he would sit down and calculate the money he had spent in the entire day.

Initially, this irked Pankaj no end. Who was this director who didn't even have time to sit down and talk? But over time, he realized that Kundan was trying his level best to keep the film within budget, so that the film would eventually see the light of the day. How Tarneja donned his pair of glasses is also a story; Pankaj explains,

Because of a certain flyover, they decided to shoot in April, on a given day and it was my scene. I was supposed to make a speech. There were no costumes. They just brought a kurta-pyjama for me from somewhere and I looked very young! I couldn't go with that. So, in order to give maturity to my face I said, 'Let's buy a pair of specs.' So, Renu Saluja, the editor, went with me to buy a pair of specs and that's how I have specs in the film and that is how the first day of the shoot happened! So, this is how the journey of *Jaane Bhi Do Yaaro* began.

Despite the hell everyone had to go through during the shoot, what made the task doable, was the commitment of every crew member to make it work, come what may. The sequence at the Commissioner's beach house was actually shot in a bungalow in Alibaug, and all that could possibly go wrong, did go wrong. It became so bad that at one point, Kundan Shah threw up his arms and decided to go back. But Pankaj Kapur and Sudhir Mishra would have none of it.

'Electricity issues, generator issues, bulb fuse *ho gaye, actors ke theatre performances nikal aaye, koi beemar pad gaya*!' (...bulbs blew up, actors were giving theatrical performances, people were unwell...), reminisces Kapur, 'You know every possible thing that could go wrong went wrong in that schedule. Kundan said, "*Achcha baad mein aayenge.*" (Okay, we'll come back later.) Sudhir Mishra, who was his chief assistant director, and I, we both stood on his neck and said, 'Nahin! Let's complete it and go from here.' Very few people will remember it today. You know what I mean? All these things, only those who are involved will remember, rest of them would tend to ask, "Were you the one who said that?" But because I remember doing it...so.... not to take any credit for that, but I am just saying, we were so friendly...I mean Kundan could have overruled us and said, "Get lost! I am not doing it." But he heard us and he thought that we were making sense possibly. That's how we could complete that schedule.'

Films in a Film

Bunch of film-crazy youngsters get together to make their kind of film. It's only logical that it will be full of in-film pokes and winks. The fact that the lead characters Vinod Chopra (Naseeruddin Shah) and Sudhir Mishra (Ravi Baswani) were named after the production controller and assistant director of the film, has been discussed and dissected by many.

But Naseeruddin Shah says, 'Lot of meaning has been attached to it now, the fact is we were so bloody fed up...it was four o'clock in the morning or something, and we were miserable and tired and hungry and we had to shoot this scene. So, I said, "Hey yaar Kundan, if he asks my name, should I say Vinod Chopra?" He said, "Yeah yeah, just say it" and that was it! I said Vinod Chopra, he said Sudhir Mishra and we had a big laugh over it and that's how it happened. Didn't mean anything.'

Vinod and Sudhir stumble upon a murder while clicking what they thought was an innocuous picture of a monkey in a park. This bit was similar to Michelangelo Antonioni's *Blow Up* (1966), so the park was christened 'Antonioni Park'. In the very first scene, Vinod mentions having taken a loan of ₹2,500 from 'Kundan Shah'.

Ahuja and Tarneja hold a 'secret meeting' at Tarneja's bungalow, which is so heavily guarded that even a trespassing mouse is shot by the guards. But our heroes hilariously sneak in, taking photos of their meeting. Vinod steps up to Tarneja's man Friday Ashok (Satish Kaushik) and tells him he has an 'urgent' trunk call.

Ashok: *Kiska phone hai*? (Who is calling?)
Vinod: Secret call, sir!
A: Secret call? Oh! Code word *kya hai*? (What is the code word?)
V: *Albert Pinto ko gussa kyon aata hai*? (Why does Albert Pinto get angry?)
A: Ah! *Samajh gaya samajh gaya...daadhiwale ka phone hai na*? (I understand...is it the bearded one who's calling?)
V: *Maine phone par dekha nahin, aap chal kar dekh lijiye*! (I haven't looked inside the phone...please come and take a look!)

Needless to say, *Albert Pinto Ko Gussa Kyon Aata Hai* refers to the eponymous movie, and the 'Daadhiwala' is its director, Saeed Mirza. What follows is one of the most surreal and hilarious scenes in all of Hindi Cinema, where the two men prance about in the same room with phone lines tangled around them, talking to each other — over the phone!

The role that Bhakti Barve did, editor Shobha, was based on Shobhaa De, then Shobhaa Rajadhyaksha, who was the editor of *Stardust*. The part was initially offered to Aparna Sen, Bengali actress and film-maker. Legend has it that while Kundan Shah was narrating the script to her, she dozed off! Zeenat Aman was briefly considered, but she didn't seem right for a modest film like theirs. So, the search began again.

Naseeruddin Shah recalls, 'I was shooting for *Katha* in Poona [now called Pune] and Kundan turned up there and said, "Yaar, I can't find anybody, what shall I do?" So I said I was going to see a play and we went to see a play of Bhakti's called *Hands Up* where she was playing a, you know, a very flamboyant woman. And she was really good. So that's when Kundan decided that she's the one.'

Playing a Dead Body

When Kundan Shah was narrating the part where the two friends would run away with Commissioner D'Mello's (Satish Shah) dead body, Naseeruddin Shah was flummoxed. Especially with the part where they disguise the 'dead body on skates' in a burqa. They leave the body and turn away for a second, and it starts rolling away on the skates.

'I said, "Kundan, how are you going to shoot this? You have conceived an animation film! You need a world skating champion to do this—standing still and then starting to move!",' Shah says.

But Satish Shah pulled off the role with aplomb. For the duration of the climax, he had to basically play a dead body, keep falling over with a static expression on his face. But he made it count, and it remains one of his best performances ever. Even with the supposedly 'deadpan' (pun intended) expression, Satish Shah decided to react to what was happening and effect minor changes in his expression. When he was made to wear a bindi and a saree a la Draupadi, he maintains a coy expression that made the proceedings even funnier than they were already. Throughout his stint as a dead body, he kept making such subtle improvisations.

They say *Jaane Bhi Do Yaaro* was a satirical response to what was happening in India at the time. They also say it's time a sequel was made, because we too live in interesting times. But I beg to differ. We do not need another film like *JBDY* anymore, as we are living in a satire of our own making. Just take a good look around you.

Mann mein hai vishwas, poora hai vishwas...

Katha
Grandma's tales

Release: 1983

Cast: Naseeruddin Shah, Farooq Sheikh, Deepti Naval

Directed by: Sai Paranjpye

Plot Summary: Rajaram Purushottam Joshi (Naseeruddin Shah) is in love with his neighbour, Sandhya Sabnis (Deepti Naval). The tranquility of their little chawl is shaken when Rajaram's friend Vasudev Bhatt (Farooq Sheikh) moves in. As their worlds collide, Rajaram risks losing everything he holds dear.

∽

The child pulls the quilt tighter around him, and looks at his grandmother, rapt in attention. Grandma raises her eyebrows and gesticulates dramatically, 'Once upon a time...'

And a tall tale begins. Tales that we have all consumed with far more attention and alertness than any class at school or college. Grandmothers should be teaching, kids would learn more. *Katha* begins with just such a grandmother and her grandchild. She tells him one of the oldest tales in the book: that of the hare and the tortoise. They challenge each other to a race. Who wins? The desultory tortoise who plays by the book, or the swift hare who's cunning and sharp? Well, we all know how the tale ends. Or at least that's what we have been told as kids. But through *Katha,* dear cynical cine-goer, Sai Paranjpye explores what would happen if they were to run this race in the real world.

Rajaram Pu. Joshi
Naseeruddin Shah once asked me about *Katha* during an interview, 'Don't you think it's *too* sweet?'

I think most of Sai Paranjpye's films, at least in those early days, existed in their own individual realities. Her first film *Sparsh* (1980) inhabits a gloomy, sombre world, one with a lot of cynicism (personified in Naseeruddin Shah's Anirudh Parmar, a blind man), but also with a capacity for hope (in the form of Shabana Azmi's Kavita Prasad, who brings light into his life). *Chashme Buddoor* (1981) is all sunshine and birdsong. The exuberance and impishness of youth, romance in its most innocent (hence corruptible) form. A world where even eve-teasers look innocent and loveable. *Katha* (1983), on the other hand, is a clash between this cynicism and naiveté.

Rajaram Purushottam ('Pu.') Joshi (Naseeruddin Shah) lives in that celebrated Mumbai tenement called a chawl, surrounded by a coterie of neighbours and a web of bittersweet exchanges that characterized the 'middle class'. Among such neighbours, is the nubile Sandhya Sabnis (Deepti Naval), who Rajaram fancies but is unable to proposition. Sandhya regards him as a friend, someone she looks up to. Their quaint little world shakes up with the coming of Vasudev Bhatt, a jerk of the first order, one blessed with a silver tongue. He spends the rest of the span of the movie trampling all over Rajaram, sweeping Sandhya off her feet and juicing Rajaram's boss dry. Like I said, a jerk of the first order.

Katha was adapted from a Marathi play entitled *Sasa Ani Kasav* ('The Hare and the Tortoise'), written by Shambhu Sathe, a professor of economics who also wrote plays. Sai Paranjpye says:

> I didn't like the way the play was written or the way it developed but I thought the theme was just brilliant! The theme being that in today's day and time, this fable no longer applies. It is not the slow and the well-meaning and the prodding tortoise who wins, but it is the smart aleck, quick thinking, the glib hare...rabbit, who wins the race, you know. So, that is a beautiful commentary on the day at that time and even it holds true today and for times immemorial it will still hold true. So, taking that theme...I knew it very well and I asked for his permission. I said, 'Look, I am going to just take this theme and develop it in my own way.' So, he gave me the permission. He was very magnanimous. Then I wrote this...the chawl of course was his. His story also unravels in a chawl.

Rajaram works for a company called Footprint Shoes, and lives in a chawl somewhere near Churchgate. He is an innately good person who places other's interests before his own. So much so, that a seemingly incapacitated neighbour referred to simply as 'Bapu' (Vasudev Palande) keeps summoning him from time to time to carry out mundane tasks, paying absolutely no heed to what Rajaram might have to say. Most of the neighbours in the film are called by names like 'Bhau', 'Maai', 'Tatya'—all familial affectionate terms reserved for family members in a Marathi household. Everyone counts on Rajaram for errands, but he's treated as a nobody. The doe-eyed Sandhya fails to see the admiration and longing in his voice. He's 'Rajaram Ji' for her — he would protest, obviously hurt by this respectful distancing: '*Kitni baar kaha hai mujhe Rajaram Ji mat kaha karo!*' (I have told you a million times not to call me Rajaram Ji!)

'*Kya karoon, aapke personality mein hi "Ji" hai...*' (What to do? Your personality has 'Ji' in it...)

But nevertheless, she is friendly and at ease with him, and they do end up spending a lot of time together now and again. The stillness of this sweet little tenement is shaken up when Vasudev 'Bashu' Bhatt is thrown into the mix.

Anyone remotely familiar with Naseeruddin Shah's filmography would note that 1983 was a singularly important and interesting year. Here's what happened that year: *Woh Saat Din, Jaane Bhi Do Yaaro, Ardh Satya, Masoom, Mandi, Haadsaa* and of course, *Katha*. So, he was at the top of his game when Sai Paranjpye approached him for the role of Rajaram Purushottam Joshi. Out of the two leads in the film, his was the more sorted, simpleton of a guy — while the scheming, conniving, sweet-talker role was being given to Farooq Sheikh. Conventionally, Naseeruddin Shah has been known for dark, on-the-edge characters. And Sheikh was the boy next door with good morals. But here, Paranjpye seemed to have twisted things up a bit.

'When I approached them, I had already worked with Naseer in *Sparsh* and with Farooq in *Chashme Buddoor*. So, when I gave the script, they were delighted and Farooq said, "Yeah, so I play the good guy?" I said, "No no no, you are not the good guy, you are the naughty guy! You are the smart aleck." So they said, "But, that's strange casting!"

I said, "Listen you guys, you're actors and brilliant actors at that, don't you want some kind of a challenge...you just want to play stereotyped roles?"'

Need she have said more? Shah donned the skin of Rajaram Joshi perfectly, etching not only the naiveté but his moments of helplessness and pain deftly. One doesn't exactly relate Kishore Kumar's songs with realistic or arthouse cinema, but *Katha* contains arguably the best Kishore song ever shot on someone like Naseeruddin Shah: 'Maine Tumse Kuch Nahin Maanga' (I asked for nothing from you...).

Rajaram wears his morality and idealism on his right arm. When Bashu admits having stolen from him, and has the cheek to ask why he doesn't lock his stuff, Rajaram says things like, '*Main taala sanskriti ke viruddh hoon. Mera bas chale toh duniya ke saare taale tod ke rakh doon. Taalon ka matlab hai aadmi ka aadmi ke prati avishwas!*' (I hate this culture of locks. If it were up to me, I'd break all the locks of the world. Locks signify a lack of faith on your fellow humans.)

Bashu Bhatt

Why would someone named Vasudev Bhatt insist on being called 'Bashu' of all things? Just to sound cool? Well, that's what Bashu himself would have you believe, but that is hardly the case.

Avant garde film-maker Basu Bhattacharya had produced Sai Paranjpye's feature directorial debut, *Sparsh* (1980). Even his staple music director Kanu Roy was roped in to compose music for the film. But there was a long delay in the release of the film. And legend has it that Bhattacharya had something to do with it, and that's what led Sai to name her somewhat shady character after him—'Bashu' (Bengali way of saying 'Basu') Bhatt, short for Bhattacharya. But there never has been any official confirmation of this.

Katha was probably the only instance Farooq Sheikh was given an opportunity to portray a grey character. It was evident that he was enjoying himself to the hilt, being given this wide a berth to play. Twirling a key ring (an annoying habit very common among youth of the day, especially the street-smart variety), fixing his hair from time to time and sporting a hint of a swagger, he mouths lines like, '*Jab tak mere rehne layak jagah nahin mil jaati, tumhare saath reh lete hain* yaar!' (Till the time I don't get a place to stay in, I am staying with you man!) or '*Chai tum badi strong banate ho* yaar...*ekdum ghaati!*' (You make extremely strong tea...absolutely undrinkable!)

But when he needs things done by people, Bashu's techniques are straight out of Dale Carnegie's *How to Win Friends and Influence People*. He woos everyone, right from the Grandma to Sandhya and her parents, to Rajaram's boss and even his family. The only people slightly sceptical about him are the boss's daughter (played by Winnie Paranjpye) and Rajaram himself. Everyone else seems ready to hand over the keys to everything they own to him, at a moment's notice.

There's a scene where Bashu tells Rajaram the kind of work he has been doing for a living, all these years. Here Sheikh slips in and out of characters, and especially shines as an 'Advertising and Publicity' professional selling 'Chakachaundh Aushadhi Tel' ('*Ande par bhi baal ug ayenge!*' [Even eggs will grow hair with this]). The scene is actually representative of the movie, how Bashu keeps stepping in and out of roles to hoodwink different people. If you haven't seen *Katha* before, Farooq Sheikh will dazzle you.

Ms. Sabnis and Hibiscus Flower
While Rajaram is busy making tea and humming *Dekho maine*

dekha hai ye ek sapna/ Phoolon ke sheher mein ho ghar apna (See I've been seeing this one dream/there will be a home of ours in the city of flowers), Sandhya pops out of nowhere, asking for milk. During their conversation, a hibiscus flower drops out of her hair straight on to a couple of paavs he had kept away. Rajaram picks it up in a jiffy, managing to hide it from her. Later, he is seen securing it carefully inside his diary.

During the song 'Kaun Aaya', she is again seen meddling with the same hibiscus flowers. When Sandhya has been betrothed to Bashu, Rajaram pines for her, wriggling and slithering in his bed. And that's when Kishore's baritone wafts in. During the song, Sandhya appears in his waking dream and sways to the music, a hibiscus flower between her lips.

Sandhya Sabnis is one of the truly emancipated women in popular Hindi cinema of the 1980s, if *Katha* may be bracketed thus.

Deepti Naval says, 'Sandhya Sabnis coolly walks into some sleazy motel...wearing glasses, thinking "Nobody can recognize me now" and gets into bed with this guy...'

From the very first moment Bashu set foot in the chawl, it was evident that Sandhya wanted him. Bashu does all the wooing eventually, but she doesn't seem to be in need of wooing. She has already fallen for him. Later, when he takes her to a motel, she walks in (with some hesitation, pretending to run away and Bashu brings her back) knowing fully well what it entails. But in her mind, she was 'doing it' with someone she's engaged to be married with. Little did she know that her 'fiancé' will be in Dubai in a few days!

In the final showdown scene with Rajaram, she spills the beans and also says she isn't sure whether she's pregnant. In the end, after their marriage, someone eavesdrops at their door, and Sandhya seems to be the more outgoing one of the two. Despite her 'homely' charm, all the blushing and hiding behind curtains, Sandhya was a woman of the eighties, and an urban one at that.

Deepti Naval tells me about one particular scene, the one where she goes, '*Bade swaad hote hain Purohit ke samose.* (Purohit's samosas are the best!) And I had to be, you know, a little flirtatious, but I was shy. Sai said in front of the whole unit, "Oh My God! You're shy? You're shy?" I was so embarrassed, I said, "No, I'm not shy." It was a revelation for her, that a girl who's come from New York, and in this scene where everyone is having a ball and she has to be kind of coquettish…she is shy? I remember that.'

In the middle of *Katha's* schedule, Deepti Naval had to go to London for a film, and she had permed her hair. When she was back on *Katha's* sets and was all set to do the scene on the beach with Farooq Sheikh and the tonga, she found herself struggling to contain her newly permed hair so that a wig could be fitted over it. But fitting a wig above the huge mountain of hair seemed a herculean task. They had to shoot in the available sunlight and precious time was ticking away. Paranjpye came in, fuming with rage, and fired away at Naval, in front of the whole unit. Deepti Naval was almost in tears, the whole unit including Farooq Sheikh was standing in utter silence. Nobody knew what to do. Finally, her hairdresser came up with the obvious answer: that they could spray, get the hair wet and fix a wig over it! The day was saved, but later Paranjpye told someone how even in the face of the firing from her, Deepti Naval was calm and never uttered a word.

While she enjoyed doing Neha Rajan in *Chashme Buddoor*, Sandhya Sabnis was a bigger challenge. Deepti Naval, before entering into the movies, was in New York studying. She had no clue what a chawl resident from Teen Batti would behave like.

I used to walk from my home to the subway station and take a train to my college, and I would pass Andy Warhol's house. I was studying Art and I was going to Art school, and I was a different person. For me Sandhya was not familiar at all. I was not Sandhya. Right?... Of course I know enough Sandhyas, but in my subconscious, not in my immediate environment. I had just come back from America, and had just done one *Ek Baar Phir* which I could relate to very well because it was about a free sensitive girl falling in love with another sensitive struggling artist. I arrived on the sets and Sai was waiting for me. She said, 'Oh you arrived.' She was doing scenes with somebody else, and then said, 'Okay now Deepti, tell me, we are going to do this one scene of yours, what do you say?' I said, 'Sai, two things. All the girls here, no matter what colour saree they're wearing, they're wearing white petticoats underneath. And when they are sitting, they're sitting like this. If they are shy, they're a little swingy, like this, but their heads are a little bent like this, I noticed.' She said, 'Amazing! You've just entered, you haven't even been here twenty minutes, and you've already noticed this!' So, I won't be able to say that we complemented each other because Sai knew what she wanted. I had never done anything like this before. That was the first picking-up-from-somebody-else's-mannerism, *ek* character *ko* observe *karke uska kaisa* mannerism *hai*, I did it for the first time in *Katha*. You know the way she goes, hammers in the nameplate and says, '*Sahab ke bhasha mein rob hai, rubaab hain.*' That was the first time I thought I'm not playing something that comes to me naturally. I'm playing a character and I need to understand who she is.

That girl in *Ek Baar Phir*, I didn't even have to think twice. I could have been that girl. Neha Rajan from *Chashme Buddoor*, I could have been that girl also. But Sandhya was different. She was a character that I was playing.

Word on the street is, *Katha* is being remade. I am all for remakes and finding newer ways to telling an old story, but some stories firmly belong to a time and place. Imagine 'updating' a *Pather Panchali* or a *Modern Times,* or *Do Bigha Zamin*. I am not comparing *Katha* to any of these films, but their souls are entrenched in an era, a point in time. An interview with Amol Palekar comes to mind, that I had watched on YouTube* some time back. The interviewer asks him why films like *Chhoti Si Baat* (1975) or *Baton Baton Mein* (1979) cannot be made now. Palekar said it is just not possible, simply because it's a different time — the world has moved on. He quoted an example — in *Baton Baton Mein,* the hero Tony Braganza and heroine Nancy Pereira travel in a local train everyday, and Tony sits and makes a sketch of her. Today, where even getting on and off a train is so difficult, it's inconceivable that a young man would do the same. It's a different world, with a different language, a different pace. Life changes, so does cinema.

---

*'Guftagoo with Amol Palekar', Rajya Sabha TV, 21 October 2015, See https://youtu.be/CxX-cR316X8?t=16m50s

Chameli Ki Shaadi

Naari nark ka dwaar hai

Release: 1986

Cast: Anil Kapoor, Amrita Singh, Pankaj Kapur, Amjad Khan, Bharati Achrekar

Directed by: Basu Chatterjee

Plot Summary: Charandas (Anil Kapoor), a rookie pehelwan (wrestler), has taken a vow of chastity. But the petite Chameli (Amrita Singh) takes his breath—and his vow—away, and Charan decides to woo her. Unschooled in the matters of the heart, he takes a Guru in Advocate Harish (Amjad Khan). Chameli is only too eager to be swept off her feet but her friend Anita (Komal Mahuvakar/Rupini) is sceptical of Charan's future prospects. Also, Chameli's father, the bumbling Kallumal Koyelewallah (Pankaj Kapur) will have none of this nonsense.

Om Prakash Sharma was probably one of the few Hindi fiction writers whose fan following spread as far as China. Every week, he received thousands of fan mail at his house in Pahari Dhiraj, Delhi. As far as Hindi detective fiction was concerned, he was considered second only to Devaki Nandan Khatri, the legendary creator of *Chandrakanta*. In fact, Sharma was heavily influenced by the style of *Chandrakanta Santati*. He didn't have a college degree, but his mastery over the language was such that he could effortlessly keep his readers glued to his text. Another writer who influenced him heavily was Saratchandra Chattopadhyay. Though Sharma was known primarily for his detective novels, he also wrote historical and literary novels. One such non-detective, literary work was *Dhadkanein*, about a small town slacker called Charandas who falls in love with the local koyelewallah's (coal merchant) daughter.

In the early 1980s, Satyen Pal Choudhary, one of film-maker Prakash Mehra's financiers, invited Sharma to Mumbai to discuss adapting *Dhadkanein* to a film. Sharma granted them permission to make the film, but turned down the invitation to travel to Mumbai. In some time, director Basu Chatterjee paid him a visit at his Meerut residence and revealed that it was he who was directing the film, Prakash Mehra being the producer. Chatterjee narrated the script and the dialogues written by him. Sharma held great regard for Basu Chatterjee as a film-maker. Assured that his work was now in the right hands, Om Prakash Sharma finally breathed easy and gave the project his wholehearted support and blessings. *Chameli Ki Shaadi* was released on 21 February 1986.

Khalifa Mastram

For decades, the name Mastram has been synonymous with soft porn literature in the Hindi heartland. These pulp novels would sell in railway stations, dingy book stalls, bus stations and footpaths, and contain details of sexual escapades of Mastram. To this day, nothing is known about the real identity of the anonymous author. Mastram again came into prominence in mid-2014, when a film of the same name, a fictional biopic of the author, was released.

It is for the reader to decide whether the irony was intended, but in Om Prakash Sharma's *Dhadkanein*, one of the characters was called Khalifa Mastram. He is a practising celibate and a misogynist. He takes Charandas under his wing and inspires him to take a vow of celibacy. In *Chameli Ki Shaadi,* this character was called Ustad Mastram Pehelwan, played by veteran actor Om Prakash. Charandas subscribes to Mastram's philosophy—'*naari nark ka dwaar hai*' (Woman is the doorway to Hell) but destiny dealt him a fateful blow by presenting Chameli before him.

Kallumal Koyelewallah

Pankaj Kapur is one of the warmest individuals I have had the honour of interviewing. The directions to his house in his SMS were precise as an arrow—I had no difficulty finding his apartment. As his associate ushered me in, I ogled at the small waiting room full of movie posters, especially the one of his directorial debut *Mausam* (2011). Within minutes, Pankaj Kapur called me in. One look at him, and I was awed. Can't quite express what I felt. A diminutive man with a tall presence and a gruff voice, famously amplified in *Maqbool* (2003). He was sitting on the other side of a very Victorian-looking desk, with a host of reading and writing paraphernalia on it. Pankaj Kapur reminisces,

> *Chameli ki Shaadi*…it happened very strangely! I did a film called *Ek Ruka Hua Faisla* with Basu Chatterjee. It was a stage play, which Basu Da decided to shoot and

make into a film. It's actually based on *12 Angry Men* which was adapted as *Ek Ruka Hua Faisla* and Basu Da decided to make a film on that and he did.

We had done some twenty-five shows before Basu Da saw it and decided to make a film on it. During the making of the film, he was also planning for *Chameli Ki Shaadi,* which he planned to direct. I was a young twenty-eight- twenty-nine-year-old and he asked me to play Amrita Singh's father. We never used to think in those days. We were only interested in acting and the characters we were playing, and I said, 'Okay Dada, fine Dada, I am there for you.' And then we worked on the look of the character.

Pankaj Kapur was barely thirty-one in 1985 when *Chameli Ki Shaadi* was shot, and Amrita Singh was twenty-seven, yet he was meant to slip into the role of her father. However, he was no stranger to playing older men — he had already played a sexagenarian in *Ek Ruka Hua Faisala* (1986). Being an NSD alumnus, all he cared about was playing meaty characters. Preferably a different one every time.

Hindi film industry those days didn't use scripts. Once the project was locked in, a writer was hired and he would hastily write dialogues on the set. So, many actors didn't get to see a script before they had agreed to join a project. But of course there were exceptions. Basu Chatterjee was one.

'The good thing with Basu Da, always from day one, was that he always had a bound script to work on,' Kapur says, 'Even in those days, Basu Da had a complete script to work on! So, the script was given to me. Otherwise, I practically refused a lot of films because I refused to work in a film where there was no script. Dada gave me a complete script and I went through it and I thought it would be interesting to make something out of this character...to make this character interesting and that is how the whole thing happened. And because I come from a small town, I have been exposed to such characters.'

Kallumal Koyelewallah was probably Pankaj Kapur's first attempt at comedy on screen, after *Jaane Bhi Do Yaaro* (1983). But there it was more sinister, as his was a villainous character. In *Chameli Ki Shaadi,* he adopted a more loony and wayward style, which he used later in *Phatichar*, one of his best comic roles ever. *Phatichar* was a serial on Doordarshan about a fictional tramp who flees the book his creator intended him to be a part of. The tramp then raises a ruckus wherever he goes, owing to his naive and rather unique world view. In Om Prakash Sharma's book, here's how Kallumal has been described:

'*Aiye aapko Kallumal se milayen. Kad saade-char feet. Ji haan, saade-char feet. Ausat kad se bahut chhota kad, hum usey piddi kehte hain. Rang saanwla, badan gol issliye tanik betuka thha. Shiksha chhati fail.*' (Meet Kallumal. He is about four and a half feet tall. Yes, four and a half feet. A height that's below the average height of humans, we call them piddi. Dark skinned, with a round-shaped body, he looked a bit absurd. As for education, he had failed the sixth grade.)

Pankaj Kapur personified this guy in the film, and added his own idiosyncrasies. Kallumal mumbles to himself as he walks along. When his friend Natthilal reveals that Chameli and Charandas have been dating on the sly, his wife Champa (Bharati Achrekar) and daughter get into an argument. To everything his daughter says, Kallumal (in the background, corner of the frame) goes, 'Aaha...aha....Wah! Wah!'. Neither mother nor daughter pays any heed to him. When Champa blames it on him saying he shouldn't have let Chameli go to school, he protests: '*Mujhe toh tumne bina maa–baap ke samajh rakkha hai na! Jab chaha jhaad diya? Himmat ho toh usko jhaado, jisne ye kasoor kiya hai…!*' (What do you think I am, scolding me all the time? Catch the one who is responsible for this, I dare you!)

Champa: *Kisne kiya hai kasoor?* (Who's responsible for this?)

Kallumal: *Indira Gandhi ne kiya hai! Pakdogi usey? Ussi ne kaha hai auraton ko padhane ke liye!* (Indira Gandhi! Can you get hold of her? She's the one who keeps insisting on women's education!)

…and Bharati Achrekar's wails!

'Prem ka matlab hai okhli mein sar dena'

It is such a pity that Amjad Khan is remembered largely for his spectacular debut in *Sholay*. I mean of course, it is undoubtably one of his best performances. *One* of them. He also featured as Nawab Wajid Ali Shah in Satyajit Ray's *Shatranj Ke Khiladi* (1977), Sage Vatsyayan in Shashi Kapoor's *Utsav* (1984), Don Heera Lal in *The Perfect Murder* (1988), etc. And then there's *Chameli Ki Shaadi*. He delivered a nuanced act as lawyer Harish, Charandas's new mentor when he decided to switch Gurus after falling in love.

Harish Babu ghostwrites his love letters to Chameli, professing Charandas's undying love. Every little obstacle he faces, Charandas turns to the lawyer for advice. Harish doesn't let him down, sees him through all troubles. Khan's portrayal of Harish is reminiscent of veteran actor David's roles in Hrishikesh Mukherjee's films—as an impish catalyst in the plot. He would lie and deceive, even arm-twist a bit, all for a good cause—in this case, uniting Charandas with his lady love. He endears us to Harish and makes it one of the most identifiable parts he ever played.

Charandas, brother of Bhajandas, is as simple and naive as they come. Commanded by his guru Mastram Pehelwan, he vows not to marry before he's forty years old. Within hours, he sees Chameli and forgets his vow. He lives with his dear bhabhi and bhaiyya (sister-in-law and brother), who implore him to start earning a living, but he seems only keen on pehelwani. It is another matter that despite the odd swagger he invents for Charandas, Anil Kapoor doesn't look anything like a wrestler or a bodybuilder. Anyhow, Charandas falls for Chameli—hook, line and sinker. He stands outside her school for a glimpse of her, but doesn't know how to take the first step. For advice and guidance, he turns to Harish Babu, lawyer and love guru extraordinaire. Anil Kapoor had already established himself as a promising action star with films like *Mashaal* (1984), *Andar Baahar* (1984), *Yudh* (1985) and *Meri Jung* (1985). *Chameli Ki Shaadi* may have been an experiment in proving his versatility, with the added credibility of being a Basu Chatterjee–Prakash Mehra project. He had earlier appeared in a minor role in Prakash Mehra's *Hamare Tumhare* (1979) and went on to work with him on *Thikana* (1987) and *Zindagi Ek Juaa* (1992).

Chameli also has a mentor of her own—her friend and confidante Anita. Unlike Chameli who has been stuck in the eighth grade for four years, Anita has moved on to college. Anita, played by Komal Mahuvakar, is credited as a special appearance. Mahuvakar has a unique history and filmography. She was launched as a child artiste by Hrishikesh Mukherjee in films like *Mili* (1975), *Kotwal Saab* (1977) and *Khubsoorat* (1980). Growing up, she started getting supporting roles in a plethora of eighties' films—*Awara Baap* (1985), *Pyar Ho Gaya* (1986) and *Nagina* (1986). But towards the late 1980s, she joined the south Indian film industry and became very popular. She was rechristened 'Rupini', and she worked in films of all the major south Indian languages opposite huge stars like Mammootty, Rajinikanth, Kamal Haasan, Mohanlal, Sathyaraj, Vijayakanth, Dr Vishnuvardhan, Ravichandran, Nandamuri Balakrishna and Venkatesh.

Anita 'advises' Chameli in responding to Charandas's love letter, which was actually written by Harish lawyer. She is also witness to their first date in an uptown restaurant. As fate would have it, one of the waiters—Natthilal—happened to be an acquaintance of Kallumal Koyelewallah. Natthilal spills the beans to him and all hell breaks loose. Chameli is grounded, and Champa brings in her brother—one of the feeblest 'toughies' ever seen in Hindi films, Chhadami (Annu Kapoor). Chhadami vows to teach the young lovers a lesson. Chhadami also happens to be one of the few bad guys in the annals of Hindi Cinema who is thrashed mercilessly (on separate occasions) by both the male as well as female leads.

Chameli: Ahead of Her Times

Chameli talks about her desires openly. She wears her attraction for Charandas on her sleeve and stands up to her parents when they want to get her married within their biradari (social class). When a family 'well wisher' rats her out, she doesn't just protest, she attacks him physically. Also, she has no qualms admitting that she has been failing the same class for the past four years, or telling her friend that she doesn't care so much for studies and wants to get married soon.

As far as popular Hindi cinema from the 1980s goes, this is quite huge. Most heroines were models of good behaviour, good students, almost stoic, and never spoke out loud about their desires. In that sense, Amrita Singh's depiction of Chameli is a large departure from your run-of-the-mill heroines of the period. I mean, what self-respecting Hindi film heroine would ruthlessly bash their uncle, because he had spoken ill of her beloved? When Charandas arrives to meet them at a posh restaurant, Chameli tells her friend, '*Woh aa raha hai, woh aa raha hai! Shaadi ki baat aaj hi pakki kar lete hain*!' (He is coming, he is coming! Let's fix the marriage today itself!) In another instance, while telling her friend about Charandas for the first time, Chameli says, '*Mere mohalle ka ladka hai. Waise toh mohalle mein bahut ladke hain, aur mujhe taankte bhi rehte hain. Lekin mujhe toh yahi ladka achha lagta hai... Sach maan Anita, main toh jab bhi usse dekhti hoon na, mere mooh se aah nikal jaati hai.*' (He is a boy from the same locality as mine. There are of course several boys in my locality, and they keep ogling at me too. But I like only this boy...Believe me, Anita, whenever I see him, my heart beams with pleasure.)

In today's day and age, when a film like *Queen* (2014) comes out, we cannot help going ga-ga about how progressive the lead character is. To a lesser extent, *Chameli Ki Shaadi* had achieved it way back in 1986. And Amrita Singh's performance totally nailed it.

Andheri Raat Mein Diya Tere Haath Mein

It's not what you think it is

Release: 1986

Cast: Dada Kondke, Usha Chavan, Dina Pathak, Amjad Khan, Mehmood

Directed by: Dada Kondke

Plot Summary: Gulloo (Dada Kondke) is a naive simpleton living with his mother. A band of thieving gypsies arrive at their village, and Gulloo takes a fancy for Gillauri (Usha Chavan). Also new to the village is Sultan (Amjad Khan), an Arab Sheikh. Gulloo and Sultan become friends but Sultan seems to be hiding secrets of his own. The evil moneylender Thakur (Mehmood) sucks the villagers dry and Gulloo ends up in his crosshairs.

✧

For the longest time, *Andheri Raat Mein Diya Tere Haath Mein* was a horror film as far as I was concerned. The imagery of a lady holding a lamp in the dark helped. It left me wondering what the fuss was all about. Until one fine morning, it came to me—a truly 'wow' moment, if there was one. The sheer brilliance of the title and its maker shimmered before my eyes. Little was I to know that the title was just a tip of the iceberg.

Aristophanes, the playwright from Ancient Greece, wrote a celebrated comedy called *Lysistrata*, about Grecian women who refuse to have sex with their husbands unless they agree to end the Peloponnesian War. Talk about making love, and not war! The play and its dialogues were laden with thinly veiled sexual innuendos. We have visibly aroused men appearing on the stage and pleading their women to show mercy. Such desperate men include a Herald and a Magistrate, among others. Sample these lines from the play:

> Herald: ...I am a Herald, of course, I swear I am, and I come from Sparta about making peace.
>
> Magistrate: (pointing) But look, you are hiding a lance under your clothes, surely.
>
> Herald: (embarrassed) No, nothing of the sort.
>
> Magistrate: Then why do you turn away like that, and hold your cloak out from your body? Have you got swellings in the groin from your journey?[*]

More recently, the moustachioed Groucho Marx was (in)famous as the king of sexual innuendos. He had a brush with the Censors for his film *Monkey Business* (1931), and some of the lines in the film had them cry foul murder. One such dialogue was, 'I know, you're a misunderstood woman who's been getting nothing but dirty breaks. Well, we can clean and

---

[*]See http://www.public.iastate.edu/~jmusal/lysistrata.html for full text.

tighten your brakes, polish your frame and oil your joints, but you have to stay in the garage all night' which was toned down to 'I know, you're a misunderstood woman who's been getting nothing but dirty breaks. Well, we can clean and tighten your brakes, but you have to stay in the garage all night.'

And then there was Mae West and her legendary misquote 'Is that a gun in your pocket or are you just glad to see me?' from *She Done Him Wrong* (1933), which she really ended up saying in *Sextette* (1978). Her actual line from the former film was 'Why don't you come up sometime and see me? I'm home every evening.'

Closer home, innuendo comedy has been prevalent in many regions of India. Stand-up comics, kavi sammelans (gatherings of poets) and other performances have made liberal use of double entendre, and in many instances, direct references to carnal acts. Chirkin's shayri, popular among many north Indians, is laden with sexual and often scatological humour. Marathi lavni and qawwali are known to contain suggestive lyrics and poetry.

So Krishna Kondke, popularly known as Dada Kondke, was carrying forward an illustrious tradition when he was termed the uncrowned king of double entendres and sexual innuendos in Indian cinema. He often found himself in the crosshairs of the Censor Board, owing to alleged obscenity in his dialogues. Probably, Kondke is also the only such film-maker to come out of this battle unscathed. He always had his way with the Censor Board. His logic was simple: those below eighteen years won't get the joke, and those above are adult enough to have a good laugh.

Andheri Raat Mein Diya Tere Haath Mein was the pinnacle of Kondke's brand of comedy. The title is proof enough. He had also registered another title with the Indian Motion Picture

Producers' Association (IMPPA), that never came to fruition: *Main Deti Hoon Tu Leta Jaa.*

But despite all the innuendos and nudges and winks, Dada Kondke's characters retained a simplicity quite unparalleled in Hindi cinema. He was the definitive Marathi superstar, and even today, twenty years after his death, his popularity in Maharashtra shows no signs of waning. People from all parts of the state used to flock his office at Tardeo, Mumbai to meet him, get a picture with him, invite him for their family functions or sometimes just to get a glimpse of him. Kondke patiently catered to every whim, he turned down no one.

The film opens with Mehmood emerging from a palanquin and addressing the screen, '*Hum kab tak dete rahenge aap ko? Aur aap log kab tak lete rahenge? Arre hum toh dete dete thak gaye, lekin aap log lete lete nahin thake.*' (How long should I keep giving it to you? How long should you take it? I'm tired of giving it to you, but you are not tired of taking it!) The camera zooms out and it is revealed that he is addressing the villagers who keep borrowing money from him.

Usha Chavan, Kondke's frequent partner in crime, plays the gypsy girl Gillauri who falls for Dada Kondke's simple charms. They meet at the temple, where both of them turn up with coconuts as offerings to God. She hands him hers, to crack at the altar, and hilarity ensues: '*Yeh badawala tumhara hai…Nahin yeh mera hai, woh tumhara hai.*' (The bigger one is yours…No this is mine, that is yours.) As Dada Kondke fumbles with the coconuts, you can't help but chuckle at the supposedly innocuous scene.

There's a scene where Gulloo, who is a tailor, teaches Gillauri how to sew. Threading a needle forms the heart of the scene. Gulloo gesticulates as she struggles to put the thread in:

> '*Ye sui...ab dhaaga daal de andar.*' (Here's the needle... now insert the thread into it.)
>
> '*Seedha daal de*! (All the way inside!)
>
> '*Dekha...andar gaya ki nahin.*' (Is it in? Are you sure?)
>
> '*Bolo kyon gaya? Thook lagaya tha!*' (You know why it went in? I spit on it!)

In another instance, Gulloo is supposed to note the Gypsy girl's 'measurements' with the tape in order to make a choli (blouse) for her. Of course, while scanning her bust, his measuring tape snaps and he has to make do with his bare hands, upon which Gillauri breaks into a delightful song *Sun lo re mori arji/ Meri choli sila de, o darji* (Listen to me, o tailor/ Weave my blouse for me, please).

Thakur gets a massage from his minions and moans appropriately. Mehmood quips in his inimitable style, '*Yeh tum log Thakur sahab ki maalish kar rahe ho, ya Thakur sahab ko Thakurain samajh ke maalish ka mazaa uda rahe ho?*' (Are you people massaging the Thakur, or deriving pleasure out of it — imagining him to be the Lady Thakurain being serviced by you?)

When Sultan (Amjad Khan), an 'Arab' from the Middle East arrives, it creates a flutter in the village. He lives in a tent and rides a camel. A magical camel that eats money and defecates gold biscuits. He loves parading his ride and its abilities in front of the wide-eyed crowd of villagers. Consider this conversation between Sultan and the temple priest:

> Priest: '*Ek baat kaan* mein kehni hai!*'
> (I have to whisper something in your ears.)
> Sultan: '*Kis mein kehni hai?*' (In my what?)

---

*The word 'kaan' (ears) is uttered in an obviously suggestive fashion.

Priest: '*Kaan mein!*' (In your ears!)
Sultan: '*Abe to kaan bol na! Main samjha...*'
(Then say that clearly! I thought you said...)

Unless you have seen the film, dear reader, it will take a while to crack the depth of this conversation. But you will get there eventually.

Soon enough, our country bumpkin Gulloo endears himself to this Sheikh and they become fast friends. As a gift, he sews clothes for the camel and brings them to Sultan. Another terrific exchange follows:

> Gulloo: '*Uunth ka kapda see ke laya hoon...*' (I'm carrying stitched clothes for your camel.)
> Sultan: '*Chal khol ke dikha!*' (Take them off and show me!)
> Gulloo: '*Khol ke dikhaun?*' (Take them off?) (Starts undressing)
> Sultan (horrified): '*Abe woh nahin, uunth ke kapde!*' (Not those ones! The camel's clothes!)

It will be nothing short of a blunder to dismiss all Kondke's jibes in the film as off-colour humour. He doesn't shy away from social and political commentary. Time and again, Gulloo would stop and talk to 'Bapu' and lament what his country had come to. While showing Sultan around, the latter wonders rather naively why the village temple, mosque and church were not in the same place, instead of being so distant from each other. Gulloo laughs and wisecracks, what will happen to the politicians then? The bank manager reiterates to Sultan that theirs was a bank dedicated to rural people. The name of the bank happens to be 'Urban Bank'. When Gulloo is unable to untie a knot, Sultan says,

'Lagta hai ye gaanth Reagan ne apne haathon se maari thhi...'
(Reagan must have tied these with his own hands!)
'Kya maari thhi?' (Tied what?)
'Gaanth!' (The knot!)

Coming back to innuendos, the songs in the film are also filled with delightful double entendres: for instance, *'Chu chu chu chu...teri chu chu chunri ko chuhaa khaa gaya'* (Your skirt was bitten off by a mouse) or *'Kas ke na dalo toot jaayegi... choodi yeh kaanch ki!'* (Don't push so hard...the glass bangles may break!)

Dada Kondke's ouvre may have sent the Censor Board into a fit and baffled the critics, but his stardom was undisputed. The Marathi audiences lapped up whatever he had to offer, and to them he was a veritable icon.

But his Bollywood sojourn did not go very well. His first Hindi venture, a remake of his Marathi film *Ram Ram Gangaram* (1977), was called *Tere Mere Beech Mein* (1984). It failed at the box office, and so did his next, *Andheri Raat Mein...* But somehow the latter remained in public consciousness, more so because of the mind-boggling title. To this day, Dada Kondke is known to Hindi film audiences as the guy who made *Andheri Raat Mein Diya Tere Haath Mein*.

Kondke's associates were known to reprimand him for being so accessible to people. They told him, if he was a star he might as well start acting like one. Kondke later said in an interview,[*] 'Tell me why should I act like a star? The day I do so, it will mean that I've fallen on very bad days.'

---

[*]Heptanasia Mumbaikar, 'The comic spirit', 14 March 1998, http://www.rediff.com/entertai/1998/mar/14dada.htm

Superman

Duryodhan in tights

Release: 1987

Cast: Puneet Issar, Dharmendra, Ranjeeta, Ashok Kumar, Jagdeep

Directed by: B. Gupta

Plot Summary: Zenko (Dharmendra), a scientist on a distant planet, ships his infant son to Earth right before their planet is destroyed. The child is adopted by a kind couple (Ashok Kumar and Urmila Bhatt), and grows up to be Shekhar (Puneet Issar). Shekhar is secretly Superman, a hero having unearthly superpowers. Whenever anyone needed saving, he slips into his costume and wig, and carries out his duties as a hero. The villainous Verma (Shakti Kapoor) invents a locket that would render Superman powerless.

∽

India had its first Superman movie less than thirty years after Jerry Siegel and Joe Shuster had created the eponymous superhero, in pre-Word War II America. The two kids conceived the character in 1933, and the first comic book appeared in 1938. In just twenty-two years, Hindi Cinema came up with not one, but two Superman adaptations. And both of them had Jairaj starring in them.

Jairaj was known for his action roles and managed to stay in shape to play swashbucklers and superheroes through three decades: right from the 1930s to the 1960s. Most would remember him as Zeenat Aman's Karate trainer from *Don* (1978), and the police commissioner from *Sholay* (1975). In a surreal coincidence, there were two movies on Superman being made in 1960, and both featured Jairaj as the protagonist. One was titled, of course, *Superman*, directed by Mohammed Hussain but very little about the film is known today. The other film was being helmed by Manmohan Sabir and initially had the same working title as the other film, but was later changed to avoid any confusion. Ironically, it was one of the most bewildering titles ever: *Return of Mr. Superman*! The film is available on YouTube in all its VHS-styled glory.

For the next twenty-seven years, we let Superman be. He was free for Hollywood to tinker with. A plethora of cine-serials were made in the 1930s and forties, followed by full-length feature films. Not the least of which was Richard Donner's seminal *Superman* (1978), a landmark film as far as superhero films go. Donner's *Superman* was like *The Godfather* of Superhero movies. Oh, and just like *The Godfather*, this one had a Marlon Brando too! Good old Brando is fabled to have read the dialogues off the chest of the 'super'-baby. Typical of Hollywood in the 1970s, the movie was well made and full of quirks that one doesn't associate with superhero movies and summer blockbusters anymore. To this day, Christopher Reeve is as synonymous to Superman as Sean Connery is to James Bond, or Jagdish Raj to a police officer.

Gene Hackman delivered a chilling performance as criminal genius Lex Luthor, and Terrence Stamp's stare makes one believe in the power of heat vision.

Superman II, III and an utterly unnecessary *IV* were conceived in the next decade, none of which matched the brilliance of the first film. But in 1987, in the same year *Superman IV: Quest for Peace* was released in the US, Bollywood decided to give Superman a second chance, championed by a gentleman called B. Gupta.

Your Eyes are Playing Tricks on You
IMDb lists B. Gupta's debut as *Aas Ka Panchhi* (1961), where he was credited for special effects. If that may be the case, Mr Gupta proved his mettle rather swiftly. Within a year, he was handling visual effects for the comedy epic *Half Ticket* (1962). In just about six years in the industry, Gupta graduated as a director with the Helen-starrer *Jadoo* (1966), while still continuing to provide visual effects for films as diverse as *Shikari* (1963), *Lootera* (1965), *Jaani Dushman* (1979), *Bees Saal Baad* (1988) and *Khiladi* (1992).

Back in 1972, B. Gupta set about making *Dr. X*, a science fiction spectacle on a budget, based on H.G. Wells' *The Invisible Man*. His choice for leading man was the latest B-town sensation following the success of *Mere Apne* (1971): Vinod Khanna. But in retrospect, it can only be surmised that budget constraints prevented him from signing Khanna, a star by then. Vinod Khanna had debuted with Sunil Dutt's *Man Ka Meet* (1969), a launch vehicle for his brother Som Dutt. Khanna had been the villain, while Som Dutt was showcased as the hero. But in four years, the tables had turned. Since Mr B. Gupta couldn't afford the villain of *Man Ka Meet*, he turned to the hero instead. As told to film critic and author

Raja Sen in a Rediff.com interview,[*] Gupta elaborates how Som Dutt demanded ₹50,000 but settled for ₹20,000, on condition that Gupta feed him chicken every day on the sets!

When Richard Donner's *Superman* (1978) came out, B. Gupta was fascinated by it and the special effects professional in him was intrigued. He longed to make a Superman movie of his own. He believed his skills in trick photography granted him the wherewithal to make one. His dream was to be realized in a decade or so.

Puneet Issar, Man of Steel

Ghazal maestro Jagjit Singh is primarily known for his non-film work, but the first movie that brought him into national prominence was *Prem Geet* (1981), which marked his debut as a music director. The song 'Hothon Se Choolon Tum' became an overnight sensation. *Prem Geet* was directed by Sudesh Issar, who was known for his association with Raj Khosla. Issar was a long-term confidante of Khosla, and assisted him in films such as *Ek Musafir Ek Haseena* (1962), *Woh Kaun Thi?* (1964), *Mera Saaya* (1966) and *Mera Gaon Mera Desh* (1971). In the early seventies, Sudesh Issar branched out as a film-maker and debuted with *The Cheat* (1974), starring Vinod Khanna in the lead, and then went on to make a number of films, primarily with Vinod Khanna, Shatrughan Sinha and Raj Babbar.

When stars used to walk in and out of Sudesh Issar's house in Mumbai, his son used to listen intently to their conversations. The young Puneet was obsessed with actors and acting. In due course, he got himself enrolled in Kishore

---

[*]'*Yeh desh hai* superheroes *ka:* Making Dharmendra play Marlon Brando', 29 June 2006, https://specials.rediff.com/movies/2006/jun/29slid3.htm

Namit Kapoor's Acting Studio and learned the chops. His first real acting assignment would just have been a minor blip in his career had he not shared screen space with the mighty Amitabh Bachchan. He was playing the villain's henchman, normally a blink-and-miss part. But the turn of events he unwittingly set in motion would literally shake the nation and eventually make him a celebrity of sorts, within a short span of time.

The film was *Coolie* (1983). It was being shot in Bangalore [now called Bengaluru] as the requisite permissions to shoot in Mumbai could not be obtained. It was Monday, 26 July 1982.

As the day progressed, a number of action scenes were canned, as Bachchan would later elaborate in his blog.[*] When Puneet Issar was told he had a scene with Amitabh Bachchan, he was understandably excited. He was to punch the hero, who was then to swirl, as if on impact, and hit a table close by. Legend has it that there were multiple takes—Bachchan kept egging Issar to make the blow look as 'real' as possible, as the young actor was seemingly holding back. The final swing had the Big B hit the aforesaid table with so much force that the sharp corner of the table ruptured his spleen. All hell broke loose—Bachchan was airlifted to Mumbai, and operated upon. The next week went by in a haze—he slipped into a coma and the whole nation was in a mad frenzy, praying for him. All this while, Puneet Issar was a sorry soul blaming himself—here was this newcomer who sent the greatest star, a national sensation and an icon, to the hospital.

On 2 August, the Day of Resurrection for all Bachchan fans the world over, Amitabh Bachchan regained consciousness, and was well on his way to recovery. Issar later elaborated

---

[*]https://srbachchan.tumblr.com/post/25089103363

in an interview* how he sheepishly went to meet Bachchan at the hospital. The first thing Big B did was to reassure him that it was not his fault, and then went out to the balcony, with his arms around Puneet Issar, and assured the millions assembled, that all is well and the kid was not responsible.

Coolie released on 14 November 1983 and was a runaway success, and Puneet Issar's phone just wouldn't stop ringing. An actor who started his career as a henchman signed his next film *Purana Mandir* (1984) as lead hero, another immensely exciting film that we will discuss in another chapter. But what was to make him a household name across the length and breadth of India, was his role as Duryodhan in B.R. Chopra's magnum opus 'Mahabharata' (1988–1990). To many, he's still Duryodhan.

Sometime during the intervening years when Issar was signing on low and medium budget projects as hero, *Superman* came his way. Here was an opportunity to play a superhero, showcase his ample physique and hopefully establish himself as an action star. The metrosexual hero (read Shah Rukh Khan)** hadn't arrived yet, it was still the era of post-Bachchan 'macho men'***. Week after week, there was a deluge of '*Jalaake*

---

*https://www.youtube.com/watch?v=V2GX1trOcQY

**The term 'metrosexual' kept cropping up across mainstream media articles in the late nineties, referring to Shah Rukh Khan and his urbane appeal. In fact, SRK addressed himself as one in a 2009 report by *DNA*; see http://www.dnaindia.com/entertainment/report-metrosexual-what-s-that-1294534

***Amitabh Bachchan didn't see the same level of euphoria in the late eighties as he had experienced with the release of his earlier films—except a few spurts like *Aaj ka Arjun*. He only got his groove back with *Mohabbatein*, but as a patriarchal figure, a strict old man. Growing up during that period, I recall that there was much chatter in the press about who will be the 'next Bachchan'—Sanjay Dutt, Anil Kapoor or Sunny Deol.

Raakh Kar Doonga's' and '*Main Badla Loonga*'s', and *Hawalaat*s and *Hifazat*s. The idea of an Indian Superman, on the face of it, sounded great.

Jor-El Singh and Lara Kaur

The movie opens with washed-out shots of Krypton from Richard Donner's film, as the credits play out. Zenko, the Indian version of Jor-El (Superman's Kryptonian father) is reprimanded by the 'councilmen' led by Murad Sr.—Raza Murad's father—for his warnings that '*mom ki tarha pighalkar yeh planet saari kaynaat par phail jaayega*' (the planet will melt like wax and spread all over the universe) if they didn't evacuate the planet immediately. All the 'aliens' seemingly wear designer bathrobes in bright hues of pink and blue. So, the councilmen rebut Zenko's theory—the one who does it more definitively, doesn't look like a regular actor, so I bet my money that it's B. Gupta himself. Zenko, rather disappointed, convinces his wife (Ranjeeta Kaur) to ship their baby off to 'Prithvi' as their own 'plaanet' (Dharam Paji had this sweet way of saying 'planet') is about to explode. What follows, is a mishmash of Donner's *Superman* and Kubrick's *2001: A Space Odyssey* (go figure!), accompanied by an epic Raza Murad voice-over that briefs the kid what his powers will be, and also announces that he'll be known as Superman.

The super-baby lands on dharti (earth), and decides to wail in the shrillest way possible. As if on cue, he is discovered by the childless Captain saab and his wife (Ashok Kumar and Urmila Bhatt do an Indian Jonathan and Martha Kent), who then proceed to adopt him immediately. Little Shekhar— that's what they name the baby, shows early signs of super power by twisting a garden hose—and dancing to Michael Jackson's 'Beat It'. Growing up, Shekhar has a classmate, who'd eventually turn into a supervillain, the Lex Luthor-ish Verma (Shakti Kapoor) who always seemed to be suspicious of Shekhar's strength. Meanwhile, Shekhar is shocked when he overhears his father telling someone that he's adopted. Captain saab sees Shekhar brooding and is filled with remorse, immediately performing the 'dil-ka-daura' death scene. Shekhar broods even more, sets out on a quest carrying his biological father Zenko's nishaani (souvenir)—a pencil torch from his 'plaanet'. We see a washed-out Christopher Reeve walking through the snow. Frustrated, Shekhar flings the pencil torch (he's supposed to be out in the open but we see a ceiling and curtains behind him), there's smoke and lightning, and out pops Zenko aka Dharam Paji's apparition. Zenko then explains the complex logic behind Shekhar's super powers:

Pareshaan mat ho bete. Tum iss dharti ke rehnewaale nahin ho. Tumhari paidayish jis planet par hui hai, wahan ke waqt ki raftar dharti ke waqt ki raftar se mukhtalif hai. Isi liye dharti par iss waqt tumhari umar sirf bais saal hai, hala ke humse bichade hue tumhe hazaaron saal ho chuke hain. Yehi tumhare bepanah taaqat ka sabab hai. Tum dimaagi aur jismaani taur par dharti pe rehnewaale logon se kahin zyada taaqatwar ho. Tumhari zindagi ka maqsad dharti par achhai ki hifazat karna, aur burai ko khatam karna hai. Isi liye humne tumhe dharti par bheja tha. Bete, iss tarah himmat mat haro. Humari duwayein tumhaare saath hain. Kaamyabi tumhaare kadam choomegi. Jeet tumhari hogi. Dharti par rawangi ke waqt jo super power *humne tumhe di thi, uske istemaal ka waqt aa gaya hai. Dharti par ho rahe har zulm-o-sitam ka khatma kar do.* **Ahimsa aur nafrat ke pujariyon ko nestonabood kar do.** *Insaniyat ke dushmanon ke dil mein deshshat paida kar do, taki nek insaan sukh aur chain ki* *zindagi jee sake. In vehshi darindo se swarg jaisi dharti—jo ab tumhari Maa hai—paak bana do bete. Humne tumhe udne ki shakti di thi. Ab tum jaa sakte ho.*

Don't worry, son. You are not from this earth. You belong to a planet where time passes at a different rate. And this is why though you are but twenty-two years old on earth, it has been thousands of years since you left us. This is also a testament to your boundless powers. Both physically and mentally, you are far stronger than earthlings. Your goal is to protect goodness on earth and destroy evil. That is why we sent you there. It's time you used the superpowers we gave you while setting off for earth. Finish all injustice on earth. **Vanquish the worshippers of hatred and non-violence**. Unleash terror in the hearts of those who oppose humanity, so that good human beings may live in peace. Save the earth—which is your mother now—from evil and wrongdoers. Make it holy again. We have granted you the power to fly. You may go now.

I hope you read through the entire speech reproduced above, in the interest of Good Cinema. The reason I have highlighted one specific line is that I couldn't believe it at first. Kept listening over and over again. But it was 'Ahimsa' (non-violence) every time. He asks his son to destroy *'ahimsa ke pujari'*, meaning peaceful people, which was the opposite of what he wanted to say. Anyhow, after this extended speech, we see Christopher Reeve flying out, and some aerial shots of some American city. And what is the first thing that Shekhar does, now inspired by his father's invocation? Enters a ladies' hostel and peeks on women changing clothes. But no, he's there to meet his old classmate Geeta, who now works for the

Daily Times. Soon, he bags a job at the paper. So, if Geeta's Lois Lane, who's Jimmy Olsen? Well there's Jagdeep, a bumbling reporter who curiously answers to the name 'Topol' (remember *Fiddler on the Roof*?). In a major departure from Superman mythology, the Perry White character here is a female. The editor of *Daily Times* is played by Sonia Sahni.

Superman-Lois' first adventure has to be a plane hijack, right? So Geeta and Topol are on a plane, and while the plane is being hijacked, Topol gets hit on by Ms. Musclewoman from Zambia (Preeti Ganguli). A session of toilet humour ensues. There's a calm announcement, 'Please note, our flight has been hijacked. Please bear with us.' As the hijackers take control of the plane — surprise surprise! — Zenko's ghost reappears, and magically manoeuvres the aircraft down towards the runway. When it hits the runway, we see our Indian Superman touching his shoulder to the side of the plane, as it slowly rolls to a stop. Had he been carrying the plane on his shoulders all along? We'll never know.

On another occasion, Shekhar and Geeta are attacked by Verma's men — Shekhar is shot but later shows us that he clandestinely grabbed the bullet. The goons are in a sky blue Premier Padmini, but when Shekhar chases them, we realize that the car has miraculously changed to a red one. Bob Christo was driving and he was the one who shot Shekhar, but this new car has a brand new set of goons with no sign of Bob. When confronted by the bad guys, Shekhar excuses himself to take a leak, and disappears behind a tree only to emerge from the other side as...Superman. And he, well, saves the day.

One of the highlights of the film is when Shakti Kapoor aka Verma aka Chairman of the Underworld is struggling to find a way to kill Superman. He says, '*Jin purani kitabon ko padhkar Superman ne taaqat haasil ki hai, un kitabon ke andar usska tod bhi zaroor hoga...aur main woh tod haasil karke rahunga.* I shall kill him!' (The old books that Superman read and acquired his powers from, in those very books the ways to break those powers will also be certainly present...and I will get those means by hook or by crook. I shall kill him!) What follows is a priceless scene of two and a half minutes where Shakti Kapoor and Bob Christo read book after book in the library (looks like Verma's personal library), in a quest to find the 'antidote' to Superman. You got that right. I can bet that if one were to add up all the instances where villains are seen reading books, the sum total won't be as long as this one. They read everything from *The New Book of Knowledge* to encyclopaedias to picture manuals. Finally, Verma finds the 'tod'. It is something called 'Clefton Stone', a stone that will take away all of Superman's powers (Superman fans, does that ring a bell?). Verma & Co. design a necklace with the stone, make him wear it and throw him into a pool. What's to happen now? Zenko to the rescue again! A certain Marlon Brando would have fired his manager, if he'd noticed the number of times Dharmendra makes an appearance in the film.

Epilogue

With the exception of the one interview with Raja Sen alluded to above, very little about Mr B. Gupta is known today. When I set about to track him down, it looked near impossible. A bit of research on Google (where else!) revealed he has an office in Santacruz in Mumbai. I called the number, but realized the office has moved. The name of a housing society in Santacruz emerged, the address was not available. But Google Maps showed a garment shop which mentioned the building as a landmark. The only thing left to do then was to follow the GPS on my phone to the shop, and pray that I find the building. Sure enough, the housing society was right there. But Mr B. Gupta had passed away, apparently. His daughter had sold the flat off and lived elsewhere now. What a pity! We Indians suck at recording and archiving things — a staggering number of film-makers and stars, and their work have been forgotten. All we know about a film-maker who had the cheek to make a movie on one of the world's most iconic superheroes, is just his first initial and a surname. Sad.

Shahenshah
One Calcutta morning

Release: 1988

Cast: Amitabh Bachchan, Meenakshi Sheshadri, Amrish Puri, Pran, Kader Khan, Aruna Irani

Directed by: Tinnu Anand

Plot Summary: Vijay Srivastav (Amitabh Bachchan) is a bumbling, corrupt cop by day but moonlights as a costumed crimefighter, known as 'Shahenshah'. While inspector Vijay gladly accepts bribes and hobnobs with shady criminals, Shahenshah takes it upon himself to destroy crime kingpin JK's (Amrish Puri) evil empire.

January 1968
The streets of Calcutta [now called Kolkata] were on fire. Youngsters had taken to the streets professing their allegiance to Maoist ideology. Curfews were announced every other day.

In these turbulent times, on a late winter morning, a

sprightly youngster sat on the steps of Satyajit Ray's Lake Temple Road residence. His appointment was at 8 a.m., but he was there by 7:30, to be sure that he's on time. He had travelled all the way from Bombay in the hope that the mighty Ray will take him under his, rather gigantic, wings.

When he told his father he wanted to be a director, his father, legendary writer Inder Raaj Anand, offered him the option of three cinematic giants to train from: Raj Kapoor, Federico Fellini or Satyajit Ray. Anand had been working with Raj Kapoor and his father Prithviraj Kapoor for many years.

At the exact stroke of 8, he stepped up to the door and rang the bell. The door opened and Ray himself answered.

July 2014

Forty-five years later, on a cloudy July morning, Tinnu Anand had me sitting in his trailer on the sets of a new TV show he was working on. I found him with make-up on, fake blood dripping from his forehead. He looked surprisingly comfortable with it. It didn't take me long to push him back to that chilly Calcutta morning, four and a half decades earlier. His eyes still glisten talking about that day.

'The man opens the door—six-feet-four, towering personality, great voice! He says, "Come in, come in", and he calls out in Bengali "Tinnu *eshechhe, chaa ene dao*"' (Tinnu is here, bring some tea). Ray excused himself and started clicking away at his old typewriter as Anand looked on, slightly puzzled. After forty minutes when he had started feeling disappointed about the whole encounter, Ray stood up and handed him those pages he'd typed. It was the screenplay of *Goopy Gyne Bagha Byne* (The Adventures of Goopy and Bagha, 1969) neatly typewritten in English since Anand hardly knew any Bengali. Ray had been up since 4:30 a.m., typing away the synopsis of the film. Anand says, 'Whenever I am lonely or when I am feeling cold, I wrap those eight sheets of paper around me, and I feel Mr Ray's warmth even today.'

Tinnu Anand went on to assist Satyajit Ray on five films: *Goopy Gyne Bagha Byne, Aranyer Din Ratri* (Days and Nights in the Forest, 1970), *Pratidwandi* (The Adversary, 1970), *Seemabaddha* (Company Limited, 1971), *Ashani Sanket* (Distant Thunder, 1973) and the documentary, *Sikkim* (1971).

When he came back to Bombay, contrary to what he expected, people started shunning him. It was assumed that he would be inclined only to make 'serious' cinema.

But when Tinnu Anand finally wielded the camera, he made a thriller called *Duniya Meri Jeb Mein* (1979). In another two years, he made his breakout film, *Kaalia* (1981). The film became a phenomenon, one of Amitabh Bachchan's most iconic films of the early 1980s. And before the decade was out, Tinnu Anand and Bachchan were to team up again, for *Shahenshah*. The very people that once dismissed him as a wannabe 'arty' film-maker were now biting their tongues. *Kaalia* and *Shahenshah* — could it get more mainstream than that?

Mid-1983

Shahenshah had just been announced amidst much fanfare. *Kaalia*, the earlier collaboration between Tinnu Anand and Amitabh Bachchan, had been a phenomenal success. Having struck gold at the box office, Anand was now hot property. He was a sought-after director. Obviously, the press and the public lapped up the *Shahenshah* announcement.

Tinnu Anand had been toying with the concept of *Shahenshah* for the longest time: an Indian superhero who walks the streets of Bombay in the dead of the night and fights criminals. Superman was the original inspiration for this vigilante—the dual persona of Clark Kent and Superman finds an echo in the cowardly inspector and the courageous Shahenshah. But this hero was devoid of any super powers, nor did he don a mask. He did sport a grey beard though, and a unique costume—black latex pants and jacket, and a distinctly recognizable chainmail sleeve that dodges bullets and more.

'A fifteen days' schedule was to be held at Bangalore. I think Bachchan was shooting for *Mard* at the time, and once the shooting got over the next day, he would join my unit in Bangalore,' Tinnu Anand reminisced as we waited for his next shot to be ready. He lit a cigarette and continued, 'We were going to shoot in Bangalore and Mysore, and at that time Dimple (Kapadia) was the heroine of my film. I got a distress call from Mysore, asking me to come to Bangalore, because that's where Amitabh was. He was about to travel to Madras [now called Chennai] to have a check-up. Something had happened on the sets of *Mard*.'

While shooting in Bangalore, Amitabh Bachchan was afflicted by a rather strange disease. His legs gave way and his throat lost the ability to gulp down water. It was a rare condition called Myasthenia Gravis, a neuromuscular disease that causes progressive weakening of the muscles. Mundane activities that we take for granted—swallowing, walking, talking are adversely affected. Bachchan was immediately transported to Madras, and subsequently, to Bombay. Everything he was working on, was put on hold. Including *Shahenshah*.

It was a major setback for Tinnu Anand, who was just three films old. *Shahenshah* was launched on a big scale, the Press was told about it and payments made. Creditors lined up on his doorstep.

'The shooting schedule got cancelled. I came back to Bombay, and of course we could not meet Amitabh.' Tinnu Anand explained, on that rainy afternoon in Film City, 'And then on a Sunday, there was an interview with Khalid Mohammed in *The Times of India*, where the biggest shock came to me. Amitabh had said, "Because I have not started *Shahenshah*, the question of making it does not arise. I'll try to complete my incomplete films."'

This gave rise to a unique course of events. Tinnu Anand began making ad films with Maruti, a new company then, the costume of Shahenshah was given to another film and at least two major stars showed willingness in reviving the project.

The Costume

Akbar Shahpurwalla set up Kachins, a men's wear brand in Bombay in 1973. That year, the nation was gripped by Amitabh Bachchan's stardom. *Zanjeer* had released and had single-handedly landed him on the top of the league — he was the Man of the Year. As Bachchan blazed a trail across the middle of tinsel town, Akbar Shahpurwalla, with Kachins, was starting to make some headway into designing costumes for films. By 1975, Bachchan and Kachins were collaborating. It started with *Sholay* (1975) and continued with *Kabhi Kabhie* (1976), *Do Anjaane* (1976), *Amar Akbar Anthony* (1977), *Khoon Pasina* (1977), *Don* (1978) and many others.

Eventually when *Shahenshah* was conceived, Kachins was the logical choice for costume design. Shahenshah, the vigilante, needed a superhero costume — a uniform. As the project was launched, a rough draft of the suit was put together. The initial costume consisted of leather tights and a jacket. It didn't have the iconic chainmail arm.

When *Shahenshah* was seemingly shelved, and there was

little hope that it would ever see the light of the day again, the 'uniform' made a detour.

Tinnu Anand explains, 'The costume which we had designed for Amitabh, the designer gave it away to Jeetendra for a film in Madras. Same costume, black leather—not the Arm—and the rope which he wears around his shoulder. That was the biggest shock that I received, because it was entirely my concept—the rope, the black leather and boot were conceived by Akbar of the famous Kachins fame.' When Anand confronted Akbar about this, he was told that since Anand's film was 'not being made', he gave it to Jeetendra, who was also his client.

Aag Aur Shola: The Chain Master

The 'Madras Film' referred to above is *Aag Aur Shola* (1986). Jeetendra plays a Robin Hood-ish character who went around thrashing a particular band of hooligans, led by Shakti Kapoor. He's clad in the same leather, the same boots as Shahenshah, only this time the beard isn't grey. And instead of the rope, there's a flimsy metallic chain that he swings around his fingers.

Vishal, the character played by Jeetendra, was almost a cameo. Although he makes some brief, violent appearances in the first few reels, we delve into Vishal's back story only in the second half.

Vishal was in love with Aarti, who had a greedy uncle (Suresh Oberoi). He tries to force her into a marriage to the highest bidder. She runs away to Vishal. There is a face-off with the uncle, in which he ends up killing her and Vishal ends up killing him. Aarti dies in Vishal's arms, but not before urging him to 'protect all lovers'. You get the drift. This highly engaging and heart-rending tale is told in twenty minutes flat.

The rest of the film concerns itself with the saga of Raju and Usha, star-crossed lovers played by Ashish Chanana and Mandakini respectively. The film was supposed to be a launch vehicle for Ashish Chanana, whose short-lived acting career included films like *Deewane* (1991) and *Mehendi Ban Gayi Khoon* (1991). Ashish now runs an animation and VFX studio in Mumbai, and his work seems to have featured in Hollywood biggies like *Avatar* and *Alien*. He was something of a prodigy, having designed an electric car when he was at school.

Usha's no-gooder sibling Nagesh (Shakti Kapoor in pristine form), of course, doesn't approve of the union. Vishal, true to the promise extracted by his dying girlfriend, takes it upon himself to get the two married and protect them. Two hours into the movie, in a particularly poignant scene, Vijay makes a declaration and the audience, as if by epiphany, gets to know his 'other' name. As he and Nagesh challenge each other over the young couple's fate, Vishal roars: '...*Aur agar issi mahine ki 18 tareekh ko maine, teri bahan ki shaadi tere marzi ke khilaaf Raju se na karwa di, toh ye Vishal jise duniya "Chain Master" kehti hai, apne chain ko tere kadmon mein phenk kar, saari zindagi teri ghulaami karega*!' (If I fail to get your sister married to Raju against your will on the eighteenth of this month—me, Vishal, who the world knows as 'Chain Master'—will lay down my chain at your feet and serve you as long as I live.)

Vishal smuggles Raju and Usha away to a neighbouring village where their wedding is to be held. As the ceremony begins, Vishal stands guard at the border of the village. Nagesh's gang of bikers arrive and there's an elaborate exchange of blows and kicks, but they are no match for him. Nagesh himself decides to join the party, riding a bike armed with Samurai swords. A certain Quentin Tarantino revenge drama of 2003-04 immediately leaps into memory. But *Aag Aur Shola* came in 1986, a good two decades before *Kill Bill*. Anyhow, Vishal and Nagesh engage in combat, a major part of which they spend flying. At the end of a three-minute battle of epic proportions, Vishal, the Chain Master, kills Nagesh and breathes his last in the arms of the newly married Usha and Raju, with the last words '*Ussne kaha thha!*' If you actually end up seeing the whole movie, at this point I'd suggest a Chocolate Sundae. Strongly recommended.

What if..?

What if Jackie Shroff were to don the costume of Shahenshah and walk the streets of Mumbai, grey beard and all? Or if Jeetendra were to speak those immortal lines: '*Rishtey mein toh hum tumhare baap lagte hain, naam hai Shahenshah!*' (I'm your daddy, and my name is Shahenshah!)

Well, in those early days when the project was mothballed, every star worth their salt wanted to get on to the bandwagon. An Amitabh Bachchan vehicle was like a touchstone everybody wanted to rub.

Tinnu Anand chuckles when speaking of that phase. 'When Bachchan dropped out of the film, because of so much money having been spent, we went to Jeetendra to play Shahenshah. Jeetendra through his PRO announced that he is being approached to play Shahenshah, whereas we had never said anything to the Press.

'...and then Jeetendra called and said he would not like to work on a role that his friend was (supposed to be) playing. Then we went to Jackie. Jackie Shroff heard the story in Subhash Ghai's house. Subhash arranged for a meeting between me and Jackie. He was excited, very excited. He said it was a good script. Then the next day, announcement in the trade papers: "Jackie Shroff playing Shahenshah". And then two months later, again I get a call saying, sorry, Jackie will not be able to play it because he feels he can't step into the shoes of Mr Bachchan!'

Tinnu Anand is called in for his next shot, and I step out to make a few calls. Mobile phones are not allowed inside a shooting set.

Maruti Udyog

It was 1984–85 or thereabouts. Sanjay Gandhi conceived the small car revolution in India, with the advent of Maruti. It changed how cars were looked upon in India—shiny metal giants that were the sole reserve of the rich. Maruti made it possible for the burgeoning middle class of India to own cars of their own. This was when, fed up of waiting for *Shahenshah* to be revived, Anand indulges in doing ad films for the car brand.

'I got back to doing ad films. (I was) in Delhi making ten ad films for the Maruti people. So I am going to the factory in Gurgaon every day. On the eighth or the ninth day, I was passing by Amitabh's tree house in Gulmohar Park, and I wanted to say hello to him. He was in Bombay, but his brother was there.'

Amitabh's brother Ajitabh Bachchan alias Bunty received him very cordially. Soon, Anand was pouring his heart out to him. The damage done to him, the money that he had to pay out, the creditors knocking at his door. Bunty wrapped his arm around Tinnu Anand and told him, if Amitabh were to get well and back in action again, after completing the two incomplete films (*Mard* and likely, *Aakhree Raasta*), the very next film he would do would be *Shahenshah*. And eventually he did come back, and *Shahenshah* was revived again.

Costume 2.0

The first thing to be decided now was the new costume. Going back to Kachins was not an option, at least as far as Tinnu Anand was concerned. That's how Bada Saab came into the picture.

Bada Saab was conceived by Kishore Bajaj, back in 1976. It started off with a rented tailoring house and a single sewing machine. Within a decade, they had established themselves in the movie business, designing for films such as *Mangalsutra* (1981), *Shaukeen* (1982), *Pasand Apni Apni* (1983), etc. In 1982, they reached a major landmark by designing for *Disco Dancer*. Today, Kishore Bajaj has expanded his business to hospitality, luxury, retailing and real estate sectors. *Shahenshah*'s credits read, 'Amitabh Bachchan's costumes by Kishore Bajaj of Bada Saab.'

Tinnu Anand elaborates, 'My inspiration came from an ad, a fencers' ad in a magazine—where the fencer was wearing this kind of an arm. Then it became a cult thing because of the heaviness of it. Because it was heavy, it used to sag and Amitabh had to wave his arm for it to come to shape, so that became his signature action in fights.

'We had to give him a different identity than the police inspector (Shahenshah's alter ego). The inspector's always shabbily dress—he wears his cap at an angle, never wears the uniform with respect. But here's a man (Shahenshah) who wears his uniform with great respect. The police uniform comes with a baton also—it should be effective, but it's never used. But here Shahenshah's arm becomes that baton.

'You know, Amitabh was just coming out of an illness and wearing such a heavy arm made of steel! The first day he wore it, he didn't come out of the dressing room for about 7–8 minutes. We were waiting outside. When I went in, I saw him looking at himself in the mirror. He was floored, millions of others were subsequently floored with that costume too! It is the greatness of Amitabh the actor, that he pulled it off wearing that heavy arm. We made another such arm that was much lighter, one made of aluminium. But he refused to wear it, he said the feeling of the costume was in that heavy arm.'

Tinnu ji also says that he was surprised to see the 'same arm' sported by a villain in the latest Captain America film. He was referring to Winter Soldier's prosthetic arm in *Captain America: The Winter Soldier* (2014). Notwithstanding that, the fact remains: *Shahenshah* was the first iconic costumed superhero in Bollywood, complete with an alter ego and secret identity.

The Epic Tinnu Anand Voice-over

It will probably go down in history that a director had dubbed as many as six voices in his own film. If one were to watch (listen, rather) closely, one may spot that he spoke for Mahesh Anand, the CBI Officer, a goon at Pravin Kumar's den, the waiter at the bar, the truck driver and a shooter named Rana in the film.

Tinnu Anand explains, 'Not only in *Shahenshah*, my voice was used in a number of places in *Kaalia* also. But they'd be used when the character actors themselves didn't have strong voices or in some cases, where the actor had died. I also used to do voice-overs for my friends back in Calcutta, during my struggling days. Now all that is paying off, a lot of commercials are coming my way for voice-overs.'

The Legend of Mukhtar Singh

Does the name Mukhtar Singh ring a bell? Seasoned Bachchan fans will instantly recollect the opening scene of *Kaalia*, where the slacker Kallu (Amitabh Bachchan) is telling a story to a bunch of kids: '*Haan to bachchon, Mukhtar Singh ka naam suna hai tumne?*' (So, kids, have you heard of Mukhtar Singh?)

'*Mukhtar Singh woh aadmi hai jiske naam se sheher ki police bhi kaampti hai aur public bhi. Bazaar se nikal jaay, toh aisa lagta hai ki sheher mein curfew lag gaya — bazaar khaali ho jaata hai, dukaane band ho jaati hain…*' (All the people and all the cops are terrified of Mukhtar Singh. When he passes by the market, it seems as if there's a curfew in the city — shops close down, the whole market is empty.)

And he proceeded to tell a fable of his encounter with Mukhtar Singh and his 'alsesan' dog. This is the point where a stray dog from the mohalla barks at him, and the brave Kallu runs in mortal dread. The film ends with Kallu, who is now Kaalia, telling the Mukhtar Singh story to Parveen Babi.

But what many won't remember, is the fact that Mukhtar Singh returns again to an Amitabh Bachchan-Tinnu Anand film, seven years later. In the opening, post-credits scene of *Shahenshah*, we see the protagonist inspector Vijay Srivastav touting a gun at the mirror and yelling, '*Hilna nahin apni jageh se Mukhtar Singh! Suna hai jis bazaar se tum guzarte ho, bazaar khali ho jata hai, dukaane band ho jaati hain, aisa lagta jaise sheher mein curfew lag gaya ho! Aur log toh kya, suna hai policewaale bhi tumhare naam se kaampte hai?*' (Do not move, Mukhtar Singh! They say if you pass by the market, it becomes empty, shops close down…it's as if there's curfew in the city. And not only the people, even the cops are scared of you?)

And once he reaches the police station, the *Kaalia* scene is replayed, only this time the audience is a bunch of constables.

> Vijay: '*Mukhtar Singh ka naam suna hai tumne?*'
> Constable: '*Arre saab Mukhtar Singh ka naam kisne*

nahin suna? Yahaan ki public toh kya, apun policewaale bhi kaampte hai us se. Woh jis ilaake se guzarta hai, wahan curfew lag jaata hai. Dukaane band ho jaati hai, bazaar khali ho jaata hai!' (Who hasn't? Not only the people, even the cops are terrified of him. Wherever he goes, curfew is imposed, shops close down, markets become empty.)

Vijay: '*Haan haan wohi Mukhtar Singh! Aaj uski shaamat ayi thi jo humse ulajh pada bazaaar mein...*' (Yes that's the one! It was foolish of him to clash with me at the market today...)

...and another tall tale begins. Only this time, there's no dog. It's Mukhtar Singh himself who interrupts the session. Mukhtar Singh (Praveen Kumar, fresh from his successful stint as Bheem in B.R. Chopra's *Mahabharat*) who later becomes Shahenshah's first victim, and the first recipient of those immortal lines, '*Rishte mein to hum tumhaare baap lagte hai, naam hai Shahenshah!*'

˄

The young man squatting at Satyajit Ray's doorstep that winter morning, had finally come full circle. For just like his giant of a guru, he too was making films he believed in.

ashes to ashes
ashes to ashes
ashes to ashes
ashes to ashes

Raakh

Sizzling ember

Release: 1989

Cast: Aamir Khan, Pankaj Kapur, Supriya Pathak, Chandu Parkhi, Jagdeep, Naina Balsaver

Directed by: Aditya Bhattacharya

Plot Summary: In a dystopian Indian city some time in the future, Aamir Hussain's (Aamir Khan) girlfriend is raped right in front of his eyes by gangster Karmali and his henchmen. Aamir can't deal with this and spirals into despair and eventually, violence. Inspector PK is looking for a way to crush Karmali, whose influence pervades the highest echelons of power. PK can't touch him, and this eats him away from the inside. Aamir and PK join hands to bring Karmali to justice, and the body count starts piling up.

Aamir Khan's *PK* was undoubtedly the biggest money-spinner of 2014, and possibly of 2015 as well. But a quarter-century ago, in another lifetime, Aamir was part of a small but powerful film featuring another PK. A film so raw and unyielding, that it's impossible to stay unaffected once you've seen it.

It's all fuzzy but as a ten-year-old, I remember Aamir's picture, peeking out of the darkness with a gun in hand. It was from the film review section of a Bengali newspaper called *Aajkal*. *Raakh* was reviewed and the critic was all praises about the film. Till then, all one had seen of Aamir was *Qayamat Se Qayamat Tak* (*QSQT*; 1988) which had released about a year back and he was an overnight sensation. But what I saw on that paper was inconceivable—the 'chocolate boy'—a term used by the media back then to refer to charming young actors who played romantic leads—as a tough guy wielding a gun. *Baazi* was still seven years away, and *Sarfarosh*, eleven years.

Bandra Boys

Around the summer of 1981, two teenagers from Bandra got together to make a short film about growing up blues of a, well, teenager. It was a silent film, that showed snippets in the life of a teen—his experience with violence, with sex, his parents. So, one of these kids who conceived the film was Aditya Bhattacharya, avant-garde film-maker Basu Bhattacharya's son. He wanted his friend, the other guy, to play the protagonist. Reluctantly, the boy agreed. That is how Aamir Khan's first brush with serious acting happened. Before this, he had appeared as a child artist in his uncle Nasir Hussain's films, but never harboured any dreams of pursuing acting as a career.

The film was called *Paranoia*. It was Aditya's brain-child, a film with little or no plot, a montage of scenes in the life of the protagonist. The film had an illustrious cast—Aamir's father was played by Victor Bannerjee, while the mother was played by veteran Marathi actress, Deepa Lagoo (Dr Shreeram Lagoo's wife), and his girlfriend was Neena Gupta. Celebrated cameraman Ashok Mehta agreed to do the cinematography. But while making the film, the boys ran into some financial trouble. So they turned to another veteran actor for help.

Aamir Khan explains to me, sitting across the table in his sprawling sitting room with a giant French window overlooking a placid sea: 'Behind his (Aditya's) bungalow there is a building, attached to his bungalow. In that building, on some seventh or eighth floor, Dr Shreeram Lagoo used to live. So both Aditya and I went to his house one day and said, 'Sir, give us some money. We want to make a film' and all that. So he gave some ten thousand bucks to Babla (Aditya's pet name) to make the film. So we made the experimental film. It is after going through the experience of *Paranoia* that I realized that this is where I want to be. I want to be in films. That experience made me clear in my head, that, for the rest of my life this is what I want to do. Whether it is acting, whether it is filmmaking, just to be part of this whole process is what excites me. So that was *Paranoia* which made me make up my mind.'

But encouragement also came from another quarter that reinforced this idea in him. Besides finances, *Paranoia* faced some other challenges as well. Aditya was convinced that Aamir could pull off the role, but not only was Aamir not confident about it, his parents Tahir and Zeenat Hussain wanted to keep him as far away from the profession as possible. They wanted him to pursue a more conventional, job-oriented career path. So even when Aamir relented to do the role, he had to be secretive about it. He used to sneak out early in the morning, saying he had to go play a hockey match or some such.

Once *Paranoia* was completed, Aditya held a screening at Dimple theatre in Bandra. Shabana Azmi happened to be among the audience, and she stepped up to Aditya asking who 'the boy' in the film was. Aditya introduced Aamir to her. Not having met him before, she complimented him on his performance. Rinki Bhattacharya — Aditya's mother, Bimal Roy's daughter — clarified that he was Tahir saab's son. Shabana was doing a film produced by Tahir Hussain at the time, called *Khoon Ki Pukaar* (1978). She said, 'Oh! I'll tell him you are such a good actor!' Aamir Khan requested her not to tell him as he didn't know his son was doing the film. Shabana agreed, leaving him with, 'But you should act.' Ironically, in a few years, her husband Javed Akhtar would spot Aamir assisting Nasir Hussain on *Zabardast* (1985), and quip, '*Ye aapka assistant kyon hai? Isko toh aapka star hona chahiye.*' (Why is this guy your assistant? He should be the hero in your film!)

Raakh: Genesis

While all of this was unfolding in Aamir's life, there was something else simmering in Aditya's. Aditya had had a brief stint with acting when Shyam Benegal spotted him with Sanjana Kapoor (Shashi Kapoor's daughter and Aditya's then girlfriend), and offered him a role in *Mandi* (1983). But he knew filmmaking was his calling, and there was an idea that was slowly taking shape in his mindscape.

As Aditya explained in a Skype interview, 'It was the eighties, which was probably the most violent time in our city's lives. All that gangland stuff and shootouts and violence — it definitely had me imagining what it would be like if something bad happens, how would I react then? So it was a fantasy of sorts, but then there is a part of me that was influenced by the things I was reading, day in and day out.'

Raakh is the story of a youngster whose life is turned upside down when his girlfriend is raped by gangsters right before his eyes. He reports it to the cops, but the rapists were all 'respectable citizens' who could not be touched. Consumed by rage, he decides to take matters in his own hands, and kills them off—one by one. But each kill changes him in ways he couldn't quite understand. His life goes from 'ashes to ashes', hence the title. The film was unrelentingly gritty, dark and violent. Khan hadn't done quite something like it before, and didn't do anything so violent till *Baazi* (1995) came along, almost a decade later.

He says, 'According to me, finally it turned out to be quite surreal. But when Aditya wrote it and when he used to narrate it, it was a very realistic, heart-wrenching story about a boy who is madly in love with this girl, goes through a traumatic experience—his girlfriend getting raped in front of him—and then can't come to terms with what has happened and just needs to take revenge. And after he kills the first guy he feels sick. So, essentially it's the story of this guy whose life is going to ashes. You know. One thing after the other.'

When it came to writing the dialogues, Aditya faced a bottleneck as he wasn't as proficient in Hindi/Urdu as he was in English, and he couldn't afford established writers of the day. With this predicament, he turned to Aamir's cousin, who he knew had dabbled in writing. Nuzhat Khan was happy to oblige.

Nuzhat Khan

Nuzhat Khan was at that point helping her father, Nasir Hussain, put together the story and screenplay of *QSQT*. Aditya knew about this and requested her to write the dialogues. Most of the dialogues had already been written by him in English, she was supposed to prepare the dialogues in Hindi/Urdu.

Nuzhat explained in a telephonic interview:

> See, Aditya is a friend of Aamir—my cousin—and they were in school together for about a year or so at some point, and that's how I knew of him. He used to come over occasionally with Aamir and so I got to know him a little bit better and I can't remember how exactly he decided to bring me on but he said, 'Look, I am making this film and I have got it but I don't understand...I don't have the language...I don't have Urdu and these are all Muslim characters, so would you work on the dialogues with me?'
>
> He had scenes where there were English dialogues... or some kind of uncertain stuff where he said, 'I want to say this' or 'this is what is going on and what would somebody say at this point?' But he had a very, very clear idea of what he wanted to say. I didn't change any original dialogue. It was more of an intonation of what he was saying, into Urdu.

The movie opens with these haunting lines, in a very young Aamir's voice. Trust me, they stay with you after you have seen the film in its totality.

> *Saat Sitambar. Uss din khoon ke ilzaam mein meri giraftari hui thhi...*
> *Ikkis saal ki umr mein meri zindagi raakh ban chuki thhi.*
> *Itni si meri kahaani hai...*

> The seventh of September. It was the day I got arrested for murder.

At the age of twenty-one, my life had turned to ashes.
And that is my story.

Aamir's voice-over keeps returning throughout various crucial places in the film, adding to its noir-ish feel. There's one point where Aamir's (Aamir's real name was used in the film, as Aamir Hussain) father barges in his room and breaks into a lengthy tirade—much like fathers of teenagers' fathers are prone to do time and again—'*Pata nahin kis type ke logon se milte ho. Mujhe toh sab ke sab charsi lagte hain. Tum kuch lete toh nahin ho? Tumhara kamra hamesha bandh kyon rehta hain? Andar akele akele kya karte rahte ho? Raat bhar ghumte ho! Aisa kaun sa kaam hai jo sirf raat ke andhere mein ho sakta hai…choron ki tarah?*' (God only knows what kind of crowds you move around with. All of them seem like junkies to me. Why don't you have something? What do you keep doing all day, locked up in your room? You keep roaming the streets in the dead of the night. What kind of business can only be conducted in the dark, like thieves?)

When the mother walks in to pacify him, his voice mellows. '*Aamir, main tumhara dushman nahin hoon…Tumhe samajhne ki koshish kar raha hoon.* Let's be friends.' (I'm not your enemy, Aamir. Just trying to understand you. Let's be friends.)

That last phrase 'Let's be friends' was a masterstroke. It's so obviously hollow, it'll make you cringe. It sounded fake, and that was the desired impact. A middle-aged father in a desperate attempt to reach out to his teen son, blurts out these lines like clockwork, like something he's supposed to say in moments like this. Nuzhat Khan elaborates,

> Here's this man who is trying to connect but has no idea how to connect with his son and is trying to be…to

sound 'cool' you know, which is what we are supposed to do...we are supposed to be friends...So, yes, that was the idea...to be a sort of thing that a kid would roll his eyes to and say, 'what are you saying?'

Look...*Raakh* was a very intense story and I connected with that. I did not have that much experience directly with filmmaking to have been able to see how this is going to look on screen...at that time, we were all very young and I was working on *QSQT* which was a completely different kind of storytelling style — and this was, I think, a very uncomfortable space for all of us...I mean simply because of the subject matter. I think we were these very young people dealing with rape and murder and revenge and hoping that it would kind of hold up!

All those involved with *Raakh* were in their early twenties and thirties — young film buffs who wanted to tell a story. It was Aditya's debut, film-maker-cinematographer Santosh Sivan's first Hindi film (before this, he'd worked on two Malayalam films), editor A. Sreekar Prasad's second Hindi film (he went on to make a celebrated career editing Mani Ratnam's landmark films), and composer Ranjit Barot's debut (later worked on, among other projects, *127 Hours*). Partho Sen-Gupta, now an internationally acclaimed film-maker, served as art director.

Partho Sen-Gupta, Boney Kapoor and *Mr. India*

Partho Sen-Gupta has a singular, most interesting filmmaking career. He learnt the ropes assisting veteran art director Bijon Das Gupta in major mainstream films like *Saagar* (1985) and *Mr. India* (1987), and served as an art director on *Raakh*, Sudhir

Mishra's *Main Zinda Hoon* (1988) and the TV series 'Zabaan Sambhalke' (1993–94), then lands up at La Fémis, France's elite film school, makes a few French films, shoots his first Hindi film *Hava Aaney Dey* (2004) with a French crew, and his second feature in Marathi, *Sunrise/Arunoday* was made in 2014, and it received rave reviews from film festivals across the world.

Sen-Gupta enthusiastically commented on my Instagram post about *Raakh*, a collage that I put up: 'That brings back memories. I was the Art Director on *Raakh*,' later adding: 'I also did the cops' costumes which were recycled Mogambo's army uniforms dyed black (I worked as assistant director on *Mr. India* just before).'

Wow!

Sen-Gupta was in Sydney at the time, so I had to fall back on technology again. Skype to the rescue.

'It was a period which was very difficult for us. We were all young and wanted to do a different kind of cinema, we were impressed by the likes of Scorsese, we were watching all these movies on VHS tapes—scoffing a little bit on guys like Saeed (Mirza), Kundan (Shah) and all these guys who, by then, had sort of turned against the idea in a way. They were all our heroes who had gone on a different path now. Which I understand now—after twenty-five years, now I do understand what happened, but at that point of time we didn't.'

Their wide-eyed dream at the time was to make something that would change the concept of cinema in India. A film that would go against the grain, shake things up. *Raakh* was born out of that thought. And being film buffs, who could resist the influences and the hat-tips?

Sen-Gupta continued, 'When I look back today, there is

a lot of inspiration from *Taxi Driver* (1976) — a lot of shots, stylization that came from *Taxi Driver*. We were naive, we wanted to do this film that changed everything.'

Traces of *Taxi Driver* and Travis Bickle can be seen throughout the film. Actually, the Travis Bickle character seems to have been split into two in this film.

In Aamir's quest for vengeance, he finds an ally in a tainted cop. One who has monsters of his own — a cop named PK, played masterfully by Pankaj Kapur. Kapur's performance remains the highlight of the film, and attracted one of the three National Awards *Raakh* got. PK wants to nab mobster Karmali, his and Aamir's common enemy, but the long arm of the law becomes a deterrent instead of helping him. He is suspended for unruly behaviour, as his inability to act eats him away from the inside. His loneliness, the paranoia, the seething rage is reminiscent of Travis Bickle in *Taxi Driver*. He trains Aamir, whose self-righteousness in resolving to kill the Karmali clan also, in part, has shades of Travis setting out to 'clean the streets'. In fact, towards the end, when they are going for the final kill, PK laments that he shouldn't have dragged Aamir into his vendetta as he is a kid, and asks him to not go. It's Aamir who reminds him of their understanding and says with chilling intensity, '*Chalein*?' (Shall we?)

But the setting here is not Bombay. Not the Bombay of 1980s, anyway. It is made clear at the beginning of the film: 'Few years from today... A big city in India.'

When asked why he didn't set the story in Bombay, Aditya says, 'I think the other big influence, you could say, was *Blade Runner* (1982). Like a dystopian society. I wanted to have a different kind of police uniform, wanted them to be a little badder than they were. What happened was, sadly, we didn't have any money, so apart from the police station, we didn't have much changes in the settings.'

In addition to the moody, dark lighting and cinematography, *Raakh* had a distinct look to the police force. In this dark world, the policemen are different, the police station is different. The cops are all draped in black. But you have seen those uniforms before.

'The whole film was actually shot in magic hour,' Partho Sen-Gupta says, 'So we used to hang around all day at Aditya's home, smoking cigarettes and other things. We waited for evening to arrive and we used to go and shoot. Of course, there were large parts of the movie which were shot in what I would call as "sets". Like the police station. The whole thing has been shot in Bimal da's (Bimal Roy) old house over on Mount Mary, Bandra.'

Next to Roy's old house in Mount Mary, there was an outhouse, which was in a dilapidated condition. That outhouse was transformed into a police station for the length of the shoot. The police station in the film is a dimly lit, gloomy place full of cops with glum look on their faces.

The rest of the crew had a chip on their shoulder as far as Partho Sen-Gupta was concerned; after all, he was from the big bad world of commercial Bollywood. But in fact, it was Boney Kapoor, producer of *Mr. India*, who helped them with many of the props used in *Raakh*. Sen-Gupta went to Kapoor saying they were making this almost homemade, no-budget film. He rather generously opened the godown for him to take as many props as he would like. The guns used by Mogambo's soldiers and their uniforms were used to dress the cops in *Raakh*. The uniforms were dyed in black and stuck decals on them for them to look the way they did eventually.

Raakh is a classic example of 'jugaad' filmmaking that even today's indie film-makers swear by. Aditya's and Bimal

Roy's homes were used, friends chipped in. Sanjana Kapoor, who was going out with Aditya at the time, was on a trip to London, and picked up a black toy gun that looked real. That was the lethal weapon that Aamir uses in the film for killing all those people! Also, this was a post-apocalyptic, post-nuclear society — so the minimalism actually helped.

There was another aspect to the styling — stencilled lettering in various places in the film. In the opening scene, with Aamir's monologue, words like 'Crime', 'Homicides', 'Rape' float around the screen, in red stencilled lettering. Then you see the same illuminated lettering in the police station.

About that, Partho Sen-Gupta says, 'Bombay of that time had a lot of industrial warnings and railway warnings that used a lot of that kind of lettering. So the idea was to give the impression that the supra-state had taken over, you know. I think that way it worked quite well, because it gave the idea of a post-industrial state and an imaginary Bombay.'

Pankaj Kapur

Throughout the film, a lot of voice-overs and monologues have been used, which strongly reinforces conventions of film noir. Aditya Bhattacharya remembers that it was Pankaj Kapur who suggested the voice-over.

> He was the most senior amongst us and he was from NSD, so he got pretty involved with the creation of the film. I think I remember that while shooting one of the scenes, he was the one who suggested the voice-over and we went into the edit with that in mind. Also, the bookend thing, Aamir serving prison at twenty-one — *'ekiss saal ki umr mein meri zindagi raakh ban chuki thhi'* — the film begins and ends in the same place, that was not

in the script. It was added later on. You tend to work with people who are far more talented and have more life experiences and so, I tend to see the script only as a rough guide, and with the case of *Raakh*, it was definitely true, it changed as it went on.

But how Pankaj Kapur came upon the role of Inspector PK in *Raakh* was serendipitous.

He tells me, sitting in his office one afternoon:

I was looking for work of a certain kind...of a different kind than the regular stuff that was happening in the mainstream at that time. We were doing a certain kind of plays in Bombay at that time and I think Aditya happened to see one such play—*Woyzeck*, which sort of fascinated him and he photographed it...apparently at the same time, he was writing this script and that's how he approached me and said that there's a part in this film. I was open to any kind of ideas and interesting work that was happening... and I think if I remember rightly, he and I also happened to work together in a film called *Mandi*.

Kapur loved the experience of working on *Raakh*. It was like a home production for everyone working on the film—a bunch of people who got together to make a particular kind of film, and everyone was contributing in their own way. He in fact went out of his way and contributed in his own ways. His role as the cop was a fascinating presence in the film—there's an extended sequence where his loneliness is reinforced by him going on a rampage, breaking everything in his bleak little room.

What was more important for me, was that there was

somebody who, being part of the system, had problems with it but felt really helpless at the hands of the system....who was a kind of a conscientious cop who wanted to do things, but was unable to do because of the system in which he was trapped. And here, when he got an opportunity to help out a youngster, he thought of going all out with it...which in a very idealistic kind of a way, one was empathizing with, thinking of the kind of society in which we live, the kind of things that happen around us. For there is somewhere a person within us who stands up and says, 'Can we address this, yaar!' So, I think that's the kind of character PK was in this film; his rage was not just because he was thrown out of his job, but because he was thrown out for the wrong reasons... and he knew he was being thrown out because he knew the system well. What he does, was the only way he could raise a voice, the only way he could help out this boy.

Pankaj Kapur met Santosh Sivan on the sets of *Raakh* and then they became friends later. He was very excited about the way Sivan had lit the film. His cinematography actually was the soul of what the film was trying to achieve. Kapur got excited about the lighting, the framing and it got the two of them talking, a beginning of a friendship. Pankaj Kapur later worked with him on his directorial debut *Mausam* (2011).

Kapur also had a lot of regard for the young, would-be star like Aamir Khan who had agreed to work in a project like this. *Raakh* won three National Awards: Pankaj Kapur as Supporting Actor, Aamir Khan won a Special Jury Award and Sreekar Prasad won for editing.

'At that time, I was very happy to see a youngster

committing himself to a role like this, giving whatever best he can, into the given project...which was very nice to see. I think where we see him today, one could see a kind of promise at that time...that sense of commitment, that sense of understanding and commitment to the work that you are doing and taking that work seriously.'

Many would think that Aamir Khan's role in *Raakh* was an indicator of things to come. All his intensity and his acting chops were in full display. Although he was churning out good performances in his romantic roles, this kind of intensity came to the fore much later, in films like *Sarfarosh* (1999), *Ghulam* (1998), *Rang De Basanti* (2006), *Lagaan* (2001) and so on. In *Raakh*, one gets a hint of this let-it-all-loose Aamir Khan.

But Khan himself wasn't too happy with the way the film finally shaped up.

He tells me,

> I felt that we did not manage to make it the way it was meant to be. We did not manage to make it reach its potential. I felt we fell short. Partly the reason was budget. We didn't have money. So the way that Aditya could often not be able to shoot the film the way he wanted to shoot it. Whenever he could not shoot it the way he wanted to, and fell short either in terms of production design or equipment and lighting, he would say, 'Achcha, let's imagine that this is in the future and the police department wears black uniform,' and *aisa karke woh kuch wierd space mein chala gaya...* (and this way he reached some weird space) if you know what I am trying to say. I felt that we did not need to go into fantasy zone or into future, and all that....I felt we didn't achieve its full potential. I told Babla also. I said, 'Yaar,

mazaa nahin aaya.' I don't think the film turned out the way at least I had imagined.

He goes on to explain how the rape scene was supposed to have been shot at a five-star hotel, but because of budget constraints it was moved to a roadside dhaba.

But Aditya Bhattacharya and Partho Sen-Gupta had a very passionate, ardent logic behind the futuristic and surreal space the film inhabits. They wanted to say something powerful, they wanted to move out of the zone of escapist commercial cinema, but also wanted to strike a balance so they could still play around with things. As Sen-Gupta explains,

> I think the big problem with Indian films today is that it's all about hyper-realism. We are living in this hyper-realistic world where everything is as it should be. We didn't care much about this back then, because it's Cinema, and maybe places represent what is going on in the protagonist's mind. So it may not be 'really' how it is but probably how he sees it, or feels the space. I think that's something that's non-existent in the Indian independent cinema of today. We are still living in this hyper-realistic 1970s of French Cinema. I don't call it 'realism' because realism is constructed, but this is hyper-realism. And I think in that sense, *Raakh* is different. It's a different idea of cinema.

Today, *Raakh* exists only on YouTube — it looks like a bad VHS rip-off but that's the only way to see the film now. Many would agree with Aamir Khan, that it may have been too surreal for its own good, while many others may see Aditya Bhattacharya's vision of a post-apocalyptic thriller. But what cannot be debated, is that *Raakh* is an important film, a film that launched many a career, and contained some captivating performances. A film that has to be seen by more people now, almost three decades later.

Clerk

Cardiac arrest

Release: 1989

Cast: Manoj Kumar, Rekha, Shashi Kapoor, Mohammad Ali, Zeba, Anita Raj, Rajiv Goswami, Sonu Walia, Prem Chopra, Rajendranath, Satish Shah

Directed by: Manoj Kumar

Plot Summary: Bharat (Manoj Kumar) is an honest 'Cillerk' in a government office. His father and brother (Ashok Kumar and Mohammad Ali respectively) are both ex-servicemen (i.e., belong to the armed forces). Bharat, steadfastly following the path of honesty and patriotism, takes the fall when his other brother Balram (Rajiv Goswami) robs a bank. But eventually, the family's (and the audience's) perpetual state of misery forces him to join hands with the evil Vijay Kapoor (Shashi Kapoor) — also his ex-girlfriend's (Rekha) current husband — and amasses a lot of wealth quickly. Discovery of his indiscretion leads to his father's death by heart failure, which he had successfully evaded before, with the help of a cassette and a tape recorder (read below). Bharat finally sees the error of his ways, and sets about to redeem himself.

[Statutory Declaration: This piece is a figment of the writer's imagination, and bears no resemblance to anyone living or dead, barring the filmy references, of course.]

Chandrani Mukherjee is the enfant terrible of modern film journalism. Her unconventional approach and outspoken manner raises eyebrows everywhere—pseudo-intellectual critics sneer at her, and yellow journalists and the paparazzi laugh at her. But the public simply adores her. Her writings on cinema are lapped up by film buffs and the aam junta alike.

I was understandably intimidated and nervous at the prospect of interviewing her. That too about Manoj Kumar's *Clerk*. Her work on the film and its significance is widely known. Her TED Talk, *Clerk: A Modern Masterpiece* in which she speaks about how the 1989 film broke new grounds in sociology, is one of the most-viewed videos in the history of YouTube.

You have claimed on many occasions that Clerk *was the best film of the 1980s. Are you serious?*
I sense sarcasm in your tone. But I don't blame you. On the surface, *Clerk* might look like a trashy film. But a dig deeper, and profound meanings will emerge. Take the scene where Ashok Kumar is revived with the INA song. Everyone makes fun of it, but nobody realizes this was an allegory for Renaissance.

What? Surely you must be joking, Ms Mukherjee!
I am not. See, in the film, Ashok Kumar has had a cardiac arrest, right? So he is sort of lying on the bed. And here's his son Bharat (Manoj Kumar) who plays this old patriotic song, after a deeply moving social commentary about the

Hippocratic Oath. The music stirs Ashok Kumar and his limbs come back to life and he's hale and hearty again! Here Dadamoni represents the Indian public, and Manoj Kumar represents...well, Manoj Kumar, who is raising us Indians from slumber. There has never been such resounding symbolism in Indian Cinema.

I think I am going to be sick. Can I use the washroom?
No, later. Cigarettes and smoking play a key role in *Clerk*. Bharat smokes all the time, so does Sneh, the ex-girlfriend.

In Indian films, physical intimacy has always been depicted either by flowers bumping their heads or two doves pecking away at each other. Satyajit Ray had a more subtle, nuanced way of showing the couple in [the] Apu Trilogy getting intimate. In *Clerk*, Manoj Kumar employs a phallic symbol — a cigarette.

Gulp!
After a confrontation scene with Sneh (Rekha), Bharat smokes a cigarette. He leisurely allows the smoke to waft into the air. His colleague Pooja (Anita Raj), who is crazily in love with him, gulps all the smoke emanated from Bharat's mouth, and blows it away! Now, isn't that the most fascinating on-screen kiss in the history of Indian cinema, ever?

That actually makes sense. Dare I disagree?
There's another variation of this in the film. When Bharat and Sneh were in college together and...were dating, Sneh used to pick up cigarette butts discarded by him and smoke them. This was her way to 'touch his lips'.

Years later when they meet in wildly different circumstances, Bharat fails trying to light a cigarette, so Sneh lights it for him. When Bharat starts smoking it, she makes a profound observation about how their lips had met again, through the smoke they shared after so many years. How quaint!

Indeed!
Do I sense sarcasm in your tone?

No, not at all! Come to think of it, Clerk had an illustrious cast. What do you think of that?
It was a stellar star cast: Ashok Kumar, Dina Pathak, Anita Raj, Rekha, Shashi Kapoor, Prem Chopra, Sonu Walia, Rajendra Kumar, and the young and energetic Rajiv Goswami! Nobody talks about the sizzling performance of Rajiv Goswami in the film. The pace with which his face takes on widely variant expressions, is incomparable. Ashok Kumar is writhing in pain, and Rajiv brings back ominous tidings from the doctor. He quotes: 'Main doctor hoon, mujhe FEES chahiye!' His sullen, contorted face as he emphasizes on the word 'fees' is a resounding commentary on the unreasonable claim that doctors should actually charge any remuneration from their patients. When Sonu Walia mentions Rekha's character in passing, we have that priceless expression again—he swings toward the camera and spits venom, '*Naam mat lo uss naagin ka*!' Rajiv pulls off one of the most unique, not to say daring, bank heists ever conceived by a Bollywood writer—he just walks into a bank in the dead of the night, breaks the safe and scrams with the money! A solitary cop spots him and gives chase. Rajiv bumps into Manoj Kumar, his reel-and-real-life brother, and runs, dropping his shawl on him who is then mistaken by the cop as the bank robber. Bharat, realizing his responsibility to prove a role model for all big brothers out there, takes the fall for Rajiv and goes to jail. Later, when Bharat's family comes visiting and the eldest brother Ram

dares him, '*Khao Bharat Maa ki kasam ki tum mujrim ho!*' (Swear on Bharat Maa that you are a criminal!) Rajiv could bear it no longer and admits to his crime. His spectacular outburst, '*Mujh paapi ke liye jhoothi kasam nahin khana bhaiya!*' (Don't swear for a sinful individual like me, bhaiya!) has few parallels in Hindi cinema.

Prem Chopra's Sadhuram reminds me of his turn as the ill-fated Sukhdev from *Shaheed* (1965), his alma mater with Manoj Kumar. Both are rare examples of Prem Chopra in a do-gooder avatar, one who sacrifices his life towards the end of the film. In *Clerk*, Sadhuram is introduced as the orderly/peon in Bharat's office, who is later revealed to be an intelligence officer who is investigating the evil goings-on in the office.

Clerk also had an 'international' cast...
Yes, Mohammad Ali and Zeba Ali starred as Bharat's elder brother and sister-in-law, respectively. Mohammad Ali was the Dilip Kumar of Pakistan. Appearing in more than 200 films across three decades, Ali was dubbed 'Shahenshah-e-Jazbaat' by the Pakistani media. Zeba was a leading heroine of Pakistani cinema in the sixties. Collectively referred to as 'Ali-Zeb', Mohammad Ali and Zeba featured together in many landmark films. They got married in 1966.

The couple was invited by Manoj Kumar to act in his film. The then Pakistani Prime Minister Zia-ul-Haq also insisted. Besides, Manoj was an old friend, so they agreed. In the film, Mohammad Ali plays Ram, the eldest brother who Bharat looks up to—an ex fighter-pilot who lost his legs and part of his right cheek to the Indo-China War. Halfway through the film, when Ram realizes how unfairly he had doubted his wife's fidelity—a clever nod to Ramayana, you see—by a twist of fate both his face and limb are restored. Zeba's role as the dutiful wife Rukmini is one of the many examples of stark feminism in *Clerk*.

Did you just say, ahem, Feminism?
Positively. The three principal female characters in the film embody the New Woman.

Zeba's Rukmini steps up to earn some dough for the family when she realizes her husband is not up to the task. Knowing fully well that Ram thinks she is having an affair, she carries on her path undeterred. She sells her blood in a hospital and buys booze for her hubby, for crying out loud!

Instead of foolishly tying herself to a man with no future, Rekha's Sneh doesn't mind getting into a loveless marriage of convenience with Mr Vijay Kapoor (Shashi Kapoor). When he is proven guilty, neither does she hesitate to help Bharat fight him.

Anita Raj's Pooja, on the verge of being raped by her estranged father, decides to kill him. Despite being madly in love with Bharat, she bluntly protests when he is breaking bad.

Sonu Walia is probably one of those rare dames in Bollywood history who actually coined a word and used it in innovative ways: 'Titch'! As she elucidates in one poignant scene with Balram: *'Titch ka matlab Titch! Balram, Titch ek aisa lavz hai, jise jahaan dil mein aaye, fit kar do.'* (*Titch* means *Titch*! Balram, *Titch* is a word that could be fitted anywhere, to anything.) Shall I go on?

Ohmigosh no! I get the point.
There are some priceless moments in *Clerk* that will forever be etched into the minds of film-lovers.

The one-liners. Satish Shah screams, 'Hindi mein bolo!' (Speak in Hindi!) whenever he hears the Queen's language being spoken. Prem Chopra either says or is told from time to time, '*Is mein bhi ek point hai!*' (You have a point there too!) And then there's Om Shivpuri's lecherous 'Beauty, beauty, beauty, sweety, sweety, sweety' as he eyes a female.

The theme of poverty is more potent in *Clerk* than most Indian films based on the subject. Satyajit Ray was often accused of 'exporting poverty' through his film *Pather Panchali*, but all one could see in his film was happy people. Living in squalor but cheerful. In many scenes, the characters displayed moments of pure joy, even amidst despair and disease. Not so with *Clerk*, there's absolutely no respite. Bharat and his family are poor with a vengeance. They are perpetually unhappy. The earnestness of this is evident in the song that Bharat breaks into, in Mr Kapoor's party: [she stands up on the coffee table and starts crooning]

Sooraj ugte maine na dekha
Chand chamakte maine na dekha
Maine na dekhi khushi kabhi bhi,
Aur khushiyon ne mujhe na dekha...
Sab gham hai mere, main gham ka hoon
Pal pal jiyoon aur pal pal maroon
Kyunke, main ek Clerk hoon!

Never have I seen the sun rise
Never have I seen the moon shine
I have not seen joy, ever
Nor has happiness ever seen me
All sorrow belongs to me, I belong to sorrow
I live every moment, every moment I die
Because...I am a Clerk!

As Mukherjee continued, I felt an excruciating pain to the

left of my chest. I gasped for breath and tried to gesture to her for help, but she was too busy singing. Her voice wafted in the air as the world around me started going pitch dark...

'...*kyunki main ek Clerk hoon...*'

Agneepath

Of coconuts, dapper suits and a poem

Release: 1990

Cast: Amitabh Bachchan, Mithun Chakraborty, Danny Denzongpa, Madhavi, Tinnu Anand, Rohini Hattangadi, Neelam

Directed by: Mukul Anand

Plot Summary: Vijay Chauhan (Amitabh Bachchan), a revered gangster harbours a lifelong dream of releasing his village from the clutches of the evil Kancha Cheena (Danny Denzongpa). He makes friends with the guileless '*nariyal-paani wallah*' Krishnan Iyer M.A. (Mithun Chakraborty). As Vijay climbs up the rungs of the underworld, his goal seems clearer, but his idealist mother hates him and Kancha seems to have discovered his true identity.

Ye mahaan drishya hai
Chal raha manushya hai
Asru-shwed rakth se

Latpath, latpath, latpath
Agneepath, agneepath, agneepath!

What a grand vision
Of Man walking
Bathed in tears
And sweat, and blood!
Walk the fiery path, walk on!

[Author begs forgiveness for this blasphemy of an attempt to translate this classic poem. By way of defence, all he can offer is, 'Just couldn't resist'.]

These immortal lines are part of a poem composed by renowned poet Harivansh Rai Bachchan. They not only inspired whole generations, but spawned two films, at least one of which became a pop culture phenomenon. By his own admission, most of Bachchan's work is autobiographical and talk about his struggles and tribulations. No translation, however verbose, can hope to carry the fierceness of his lyrics, because the poet did live each word.

To me, *Agneepath* is not just about the venerable Vijay Dinanath Chauhan (more on that later), but an assembly-line of queer but memorable characters. An array of faces — Kancha Cheena, Krishnan Iyer, Commissioner Gaitonde, Dinkar Rao, Natthu and even Terylene!

Priest Kings and Film Institute

When Tshering Phintso was born to the horse-rearing Denzongpa family in Gangtok, Sikkim was a monarchy ruled by Chogyal Tashi Namgyal. Chogyals were priest kings, whose powers were said to have divine ratification. Tashi Namgyal was crowned by the thirteenth Dalai Lama himself. Tshering was passionate about horses since an early age, but as he grew up, the boy seemed more and more resolute to join the Indian Armed Forces. He also participated in the Republic Day parade as a young cadet. But during the Indo-China War of 1960s, dead soldiers' bodies were being sent back to the village. Tshering's mother was deeply affected by this and forbade her son from joining the army. Young Tshering, with a heavy heart, set sail for Pune to join the FTII.

While at the institute, the students had to introduce themselves to their seniors during the orientation day. As he announced his name 'Tshering Phintso Denzongpa', the others couldn't seem to understand, and kept asking him to repeat it. In the following days, friends kept making fun of him, making noises as if calling his name when they saw him. It was then that one of his best friends at the institute, Jaya Bhaduri, intervened. She rechristened him 'Danny' so that it's easier for people to pronounce.

In the next decade or so, Danny Denzongpa established himself as an actor in the Hindi film industry, then dominated by north Indian males who looked a certain way. Even with today's liberal and multicultural atmosphere, there are almost no mainstream actors who hail from the Northeast. Considering what he achieved in 1970s Bollywood, one would marvel at Denzongpa's career. He is said to have practised Hindi diction by speaking to the sea for hours on end. Today, many A-listers in Bollywood do not have the masterful command over Hindi or Urdu that he possesses. His career took off with Gulzar's *Mere Apne* (1971) where he got to work with the pristine Meena Kumari, and with B.R. Chopra's *Dhund* (1983) which allowed him to showcase his acting chops.

His friendship with the Bachchan family is well known, but despite that, he chose to stay away from any Amitabh Bachchan starrer for almost two decades. He later revealed in a magazine interview that he was not interested in being in the same film with Big B unless the role was meaty enough, a conventional villain part just wouldn't cut it. With the kind of presence Bachchan commanded in the 1970s–1980s, he believed that he wouldn't be noticed if they were to share screen space. They came very close to doing so in a film called *Andhaa Kanoon* (1983) where Denzongpa played one of the main protagonists and Amitabh Bachchan had an extended cameo. But his character gets killed off halfway through the film. Both of them made friendly appearances in the Jagdeep-starrer *Soorma Bhopali* (1988) as well. Even the mighty Manmohan Desai, who offered him *Coolie* and *Mard*, was unable to make Danny budge from his resolve. But eventually, destiny had other plans.

When Mukul Anand came to him with the role that became Kancha Cheena, it seemed irresistible. Finally, here was a part that possibly could not go unnoticed. Denzongpa and Bachchan teamed up, for the first time in eighteen years. The role became so integral to the film that in 2012, when *Agneepath* was remade, Kancha Cheena had a far stronger part to play in the script than even the lead, Vijay Dinanath Chauhan. Sanjay Dutt played the role, and it ended up as one of the greatest villain roles in recent times. But I would think they messed up the concept just a little bit. I believe that Kancha Cheena is a somewhat racist allusion to the mongoloid looks of the character: Kancha (Nepali) + Cheena (Chinese). Danny Denzongpa was the one who suggested the name.

Vijay Chauhan, Jr.

Manjunath Nayekar, from Malleswaram, Karnataka, was barely ten years old and was already becoming a known face in Kannada filmdom. At the age of seven, he appeared in T.S. Nagabharana's *Banker Margayya* (1983), based on R.K. Narayan's Malgudi story *Financial Expert*. It was just the beginning of his association with the writer's work. Manjunath aka Master Manjunath was also a regular fixture in the works of the Nag brothers—Kannada superstars Shankar Nag and Anant Nag. They worked together in films like *Nodi Swamy Navirodu Hige* (1983), *Makkaliralavva Mane Thumba* (1984), and the *Hero* remake *Ranadheera* (1988). So, when Shankar Nag offered him the lead role in *Malgudi Days: Swami and Friends*, there was no question of turning it down. Nayekar didn't know a word of Hindi, and neither did a lot of the cast members. But he learnt the language and dubbed his own lines. As most readers in their thirties and older might remember, Swami became a sensation among television audiences across the nation. Manjunath Nayekar was known as 'Swami' from then on.

In two years, Master Manjunath was contacted by Mukul Anand to play a young Vijay Dinanath Chauhan in *Agneepath*. All he cared to know, was that he was going to be part of an Amitabh Bachchan starrer. He didn't take a moment to say yes. But during the shoot, a seemingly minute detail kept bugging him. When Mukul Anand asked what it was, he said, 'I have curly hair, but the grown Vijay (Amitabh Bachchan) doesn't!' Anand told him not to worry about it too much. All he wanted the boy to do was to 'breathe life into the role'. And that's what Master Manjunath did. His transformation from the simple village urchin to the street-smart, crooked and somewhat cruel Vijay was one of the finest performances of *Agneepath*. The moment where young Vijay sets fire to the petrol pump where his mother was molested and walks away, tingles your spine and reminds you of the greatest gangster movies of the world.

Master of Coconuts

Actor Mithun Chakraborty used to live in a rented accommodation in Sion Koliwada, during his days of struggle. He shared his room with a Malayali gentleman, who paid the princely sum of ₹150 to sleep on the sole cot in the room, while he had to make do with the floor for ₹75. One night, a rat bit Chakraborty's leg. All the young actor could afford to do at the time, was to wash it with water and dress it. His Malayali friend was at work, so he hopped on to the cot for a quick nap. As luck would have it, he reached home early from work, and was furious seeing his ₹75 roommate lounging on his precious and hard-earned cot! The first thing he did was kick him and gesticulate wildly. His unique mannerisms and his verbosity in Hindi eventually became the inspiration for Krishnan Iyer M.A. The gender mix-up in language was inspired from the film-maker, K. Bappaiah.

Krishnan Iyer is the good samaritan who saves Vijay Chauhan, who is riddled with bullets, and takes him to a hospital just in time for his lifesaving operation, executed by Madhavi. Vijay acknowledges the debt and makes him his sister Neelam's bodyguard. This is one of the two major pieces in the film that makes it comparable to Brian De Palma's *Scarface* (1983). Mithun's Krishnan Iyer is strongly reminiscent of Manny Ribera, Tony Montana's best pal, played by Steven Bauer.

Mithun Chakraborty's histrionics as Krishnan Iyer, M.A. ('Yum-Yay') was one of the reasons for *Agneepath*'s resurgence much later, after it turned a damper at the box office. In fact, legend has it (throughout this book, I keep going back to this phase) that there were street fights in Kolkata between armies of both fan clubs. Both Amitabh Bachchan and Mithun Chakraborty have a sizeable fan base in the city. In many ways, both the stars started their journey there. Chakraborty hails from Kolkata, while Bachchan worked there for many years before joining films. In an otherwise dark, gloomy film, Chakraborty's role was not only a breath of fresh air, but also worked as a bridge between the cynicism of Vijay Chauhan and the righteous but somewhat utopian world view of his mother Suhasini. Also, what's a Bollywood movie without a romantic pairing? Mithun Chakraborty and Neelam spice things up a notch or two. They also feature in the only romantic song in the movie, 'Kisko Tha Pataa'.

From Selling Lampshades to Peddling Dreams

As Mukul Sudheshwar Anand came out of school, he realized his insatiable urge to get into filmmaking. But his family was in no position to afford him taking any risks. They had fallen on bad times. But how was he to fend for the family? He started designing lampshades and selling them at Linking Road, Bandra for ₹25 a piece. As he secured his family financially, he slowly eased his way into filmmaking, by assisting director Ravi Tandon in films like *Zindagi* (1976), *Muqaddar* (1978), *Chor Ho Toh Aisa* (1978), etc. He also ghost-directed many Gujarati and Punjabi films in the mid-1980s. Anand's career as a film-maker began with Hollywood remakes, starting with *Cape Fear* (*Kanoon Kya Karega,* 1984) and *Dial M for Murder* (*Aitbaar,* 1985) and then moving on to original concepts, especially *Sultanat* (1986), a grand spectacle that starred father and son, Dharmendra and Sunny Deol, and launched Juhi Chawla, and Shashi Kapoor's son and 'Bombay Dyeing Man', Karan Kapoor. He also relaunched Vinod Khanna in *Insaaf* (1987) after his much publicized sojourn at Osho Ashram. And then came *Agneepath*. The one common strand that ran across all of Mukul Anand's work, is the grandeur and scale of his cinematic vision. There was a finesse and style that he brought into his work while sticking to the Bollywood mainstream recipe. And his Bachchan films — whether it's *Agneepath* (1990), *Hum* (1991) or *Khuda Gawah* (1992) — were the zenith of this style. It all started with *Agneepath*: blowing up the gas station, Vijay Chauhan's suit, the dark atmospheric tone, fighting in the mud, Bachchan on the deck of his yacht while he sees the bomb drop in slow motion, quirky villains, and so on. All these were the hallmarks of Mukul Anand's style.

Who could have thought of a villain that went by the name of Terylene (Sharat Saxena in a suit and a pencil moustache)? I mean, it's fabric, for crying out loud! Terylene, however, dies an untimely (and rather unflattering death) as Kancha Cheena's henchman kicks him off a chopper. Deepak Shirke's Anna Shetty is not so unlucky, as his undoing is a part of one of the most spectacular high-adrenaline sequences ever filmed in Hindi Cinema. Shetty, rather foolishly, kidnaps Vijay Dinanath Chauhan's sister, and Chauhan launches a citywide manhunt, only to track her down (flanked by a whining Krishnan Iyer) in Shetty's lair. What follows is a riveting session of mud-wrestling-meets-the-Bachchan-punch, which is more than *any* money's worth!

Vijay Dinanath Chauhan

'*Vijay. Dinanath. Chauhan. Poora naam. Baap ka naam, Dinanath Chauhan. Maa ka naam, Suhasini Chauhan. Gaon, Mandwa. Umar, chhattish saal nau mahina, aath din — yeh solwa ghanta chalu hai — hain!*' (The name's Vijay. Vijay, Dinanath, Chauhan. Father was called Dinanath Chauhan. Mother, Suhasini Chauhan. Village, Mandwa. Age: thirty-six years, nine months, eight days...and it's the sixteenth hour now.)

In the Hindi cinegoer's minds, these lines hold pride of

place right beside epic intro lines like '*Rishtey mein toh hum tumhare baap lagte hain, naam hai Shahenshah*', '*Mogambo khush hua*' (Mogambo is happy now) or even 'The Name is Bond. James Bond'. But the first time they heard it, the audience could not make head or tail of it. What inspired Amitabh Bachchan's mannerism in *Agneepath*, was that of Mumbai don Varadharajan Mudaliar, who also inspired Mani Ratnam's *Nayakan* (1987). But his raspy, hissing voice didn't reach out to anyone. Most people were missing out on his dialogues as they couldn't understand them, owing to the voice. Amitabh famously redubbed the lines and it seemed better. But the menace of piracy had already spread its tentacles and bootlegged VHS Cassettes with his original act were circulating everywhere. Anyhow, the new voice didn't seem to help the cause of the film and it sank. But strangely, the lines lived on. And so did Vijay Dinanath Chauhan.

Vijay Dinanath Chauhan was born on 7 May 1953, a whole ten years, two months and twenty-one days after Amitabh Bachchan, considering that *Agneepath* released on 16 February 1990. Vijay was living the 1950s' Indian dream of the serene countryside.

Enter Kancha Cheena, and all hell's doors burst open. Kancha and zamindar Dinkar Rao bring ruin to the village, in effect demolishing Vijay's little cocoon of tranquility. But even before Kancha gets there, the engineer pays a visit and there are talks of electricity coming to the village. Progress, of course, is followed by the devil close on its heels. After his father is lynched, Chauhan flees to the big bad world of Bombay. This is around 1965. Cue vintage cars and sixties' clothes. Director Mukul Anand has been pretty meticulous there. The era is never really spelled out, but taking Chauhan's super-precise declaration to Commissioner Gaitonde, and back-calculating from there, one knows we are in that period. And then there's Terylene, the uber cool Sharat Saxena with a pencil moustache and parted hair, wielding a sword-cane. Terylene, Usman, Anna Shetty and Hasmukh Bhai notice the spark in little Vijay when he lights up a whole gas station owned by Kancha. Most Hindi film fans know and revere Deepak Shirke, who plays Shetty, but few know that he debuted with *Agneepath*. Usman was played by Mahesh Bhatt's blue-eyed boy Avtar Gill. The third goon, Hasmukh was played by legendary Gujarati stage and screen actor Arvind Rathod. So, these guys take Vijay in, and this is the point where he really takes off.

An Evening in Coney Island, 1918

As always, nineteen-year-old Alphonse 'Al' Gabriel Capone was waiting on tables at a shady named Harvard Inn in Coney Island, Brooklyn. Al couldn't take his eyes off the girl at the table. Though she seemed out of his league, he thought he will take his chances, and whispered to her sweet nothings about her posterior. The girl was accompanied by her brother, a local toughie named Frank Gallucio. Frank lunged at Capone with his knife and slashed his face, leaving a deep wound across his left jaw. That's how Al Capone acquired the name he loathed, 'Scarface'.

Al Capone went on to become the greatest mobster America had ever known. Around 1929, Maurice Coons, a young writer in his late twenties, wrote a fictional account of Capone's rise through the ranks, called Scarface, under the pseudonym Armitage Trail. The book was to set in motion a sequence of stories and characters that would eventually lead to Vijay Dinanath Chauhan, at the turn of the century.

Scarface (the book) talks of a boy named Tony Guarino

who kills his way to the top of the underworld. But destiny catches up with him and he eventually gets shot by his brother Ben Guarino, a cop. Sounds familiar? *Deewar* was always considered a precursor to *Agneepath*, in some ways.

The book inspired the Paul Muni-starrer *Scarface* (1932), which was remade fifty years later with Al Pacino in the titular role. The latter is, allegedly, a source material for *Agneepath*. The connections between the book and the three movies is breathtaking. In the book, the mother is almost non-existent. In the 1932 film, she warns her daughter Cesca to stay away from Tony: 'Tony no love you like he make you believe. All the time he smile on top but what he thinks…He got a lot of tricks!' In the 1983 film, Tony Montana's immigrant mother is disgusted by her son's descent into crime and how it shows badly on the immigrant Cuban community. She throws him out of the house when he comes visiting, forbidding his sister Gina from having anything to do with him. In *Agneepath*, the ideological differences are very clear and are foreshadowed in an early scene where little Vijay bumps into his mother while running in the house. She says, '*Vijay! Hazaar baar tujhse kaha hai, zara dekh ke chala kar. Jaldbaazi mat kiya kar!*', in effect reprimanding him for moving 'too fast'. Eventually, when he takes to a path of crime, she is ruthless in her admonishment of his evil ways, '*Apne haath dho le Vijay!*' (Wash your hands clean, Vijay) and in a scene seemingly mirroring the one in Al Pacino's movie, Vijay storms out of the house.

In the book, the sister appears only in the concluding part when she tries to poison Tony for murdering her beau Mike Rinaldo, also Tony's henchman. In the first Scarface film, Cesca literally drives the climax of the movie. She aims a gun at her brother who is holed up in his room, surrounded by police—for killing her husband Guino Rinaldo, his man Friday.

She realizes how similar they are, and says, '...you're me. And I'm you. It's always been that way', and chooses to fight on her brother's side, only to succumb to a stray bullet, seconds later. In the 1983 remake, the almost incestuous nature of the relationship comes to the fore in the climax where Gina is tired of Tony hindering her romantic liaisons, egging him on to take her for himself if he saw no other man to be worthy of her. In *Agneepath* however, Neelam is the dutiful sister, only once protesting her mother's scolding of Vijay. She falls for Krishnan Iyer, her 'bodyguard' but gets just a mild slap on the wrist from her brother, who eventually accepts their relationship.

There's a special mention of 'gun girls' in the book, femme fatales who helped assassins get away with murder by hiding the weapon on their person. Tony romances and settles down with one of these gun girls, the fiery Jane Conley, who eventually becomes instrumental in his downfall and death. In the thirties' movie, she is toned down to being a gold digger named Poppy who has no qualms shifting her loyalties at the slightest opportunity. In the remake, Michelle Pfeiffer dishes out a critically acclaimed performance as the neurotic and edgy Elvira, but the character lets herself be exploited by one mobster after another. *Agneepath* completes the process by making Mary (Madhavi) an absolute doormat. The only instance where she shows any semblance of agency is when she refuses to give birth to a baby (who she didn't want to be a part of Vijay's criminal empire), a rebellion Vijay promptly crushes.

And then of course there's the telephones. In the old movie, Tony is accompanied by this bumbling but fatally loyal sidekick Angelo, who could never make peace with the telephone and its evil machinations. Half the time he couldn't get what people were saying, and always struggled with the word 'seckertary' while introducing himself. The telephone is a recurring motif in the eighties' movie too, with Tony Montana almost ripping the phone off with his bare hands when the sinister Alejandro Sosa threatens him on a call. Again, *Agneepath* completes the loop. Vijay's mentors, the four goons, sit in an office surrounded with phones, which keep ringing incessantly. They've been plotting his assassination when Chauhan walks in on them, taking them by surprise. The shock is writ large on their faces and he says, '*Ye saala idhar telephone ka ghanti bahut bajta hai...galat cheej banaya telephone. Udhar se aadmi sochta kuch hai, bolta kuch hai, karta kuch hai...jaise tum log*!' (The telephones here keep ringing all the bloody time. What an invention, this telephone...men think of something, say something else, and do something else...like you guys!) Later in the film, he comes back to that office, now empty (he by now has killed Usman and Hasmukh Bhai) but phones still ringing. He answers one of them, says, '*Main andha dhanda bhi andhere mein nahin karta. Baat karne ka hai toh saamne aane ka, saamne. Samjha*?' (I don't conduct the business of darkness in the dark. If you gotta talk, come and see me. Got it?) and he throws the telephone on the wall, as the camera moves in on him.

Tinnu Anand

Over lunch with Tinnu Anand in his make-up van, we discussed *Agneepath* and his role of Natthu, the passionate old drunk who sticks by Vijay and vouches for him till his unceremonious death at the hands of Kancha Cheena.

Mukul Anand, who also happened to be Tinnu Anand's cousin and had earlier seen him act in films like *Nayakan* (1987) and *Pushpak* (1987), wanted Tinnu Anand to play Natthu in his new film. But there was a problem. Tinnu Anand was still in his thirties, but had to play a character who starts out as a middle-aged man and is in his early seventies by the end of the film.

He explains, 'The role was of somebody much older to Amitabh Bachchan. Mukul always feared how I'd manage to look older than Amitabh. [Bachchan is eleven years older than Tinnu Anand.] He said, "When Vijay is a child, you play your age. But when he grows up into Amitabh, that is when I need a totally different look." I said, "Leave that to me. I'll give you an authentic look."'

But he had a request—Tinnu Anand wanted the portions with the child shot first, where he plays his age. Once those were shot, he set about 'designing' his look for the older Natthu. He nearly shaved his hair, chopping off the bulk of his thick mop of hair (still visible in early part of *Agneepath*), only retaining the hair around the sides of his head and back. After whitening the residual strands of hair, he stepped into the studio where Mukul Anand awaited in anticipation. He was standing right in front of him but Mukul Anand showed no signs of recognition, till the former called out to him in his distinctive voice. He was shocked. Tinnu Anand had transformed himself totally!

Mukul Anand's brief was for him to go absolutely berserk, spouting the most profane abuses as he threw stones and stomped about. Tinnu let himself go and cursed with abandon. After every shot, the crew burst out clapping. They had never seen a senior actor abuse on camera like that. Mukul Anand was sure that if the members of crew loved it, the crowds will love it too.

But it's rarely that simple. *Agneepath* tanked on release. In the face of young guns, Aamir Khan (*Awwal Number, Dil, Deewana Mujh Sa Nahin, Jawani Zindabad, Tum Mere Ho*),

Sanjay Dutt (*Jeene Do, Khatarnak, Thanedaar, Zahreelay, Teja*), Anil Kapoor (*Jamai Raja, Kishen Kanhaiya, Ghar Ho To Aisa*) and Bachchan's own behemoth *Aaj Ka Arjun, Agneepath* just couldn't hold its own. But surprisingly, the characters and the lines survived and grew over the years. Despite a dark and moody remake in 2012 which was a massive box office money-spinner, film fanatics still swear by the original, Sanjay Dutt's terrific Kancha notwithstanding.

Back in the 1990s, the Press (that's what 'the media' was called those days) had a strange love-hate relationship with Amitabh Bachchan. Here's a quote from the May 1990 issue of *Filmfare*, from an article that lays down what's wrong with the Bachchan persona and why most of his films were 'bombing with mechanical precision'. A close look at the quote will tell you something's wrong:

> Is *Agneepath* 'different', as Bachchan claims, from the films he has been making over the years? The change of voice, though an innovative move, didn't give an extra dimension to the character of Vijay Sawant [sic], the underworld don. He's no different from the innumerable guilt-ridden, vengeful, trigger-happy introverts Bachchan has been playing since the *Zanjeer-Deewar* days. Though he invests the character with a few interesting mannerisms, the inner physiognomy of Sawant [sic] is untouched... The silver lining is nowhere in sight. And you begin to wonder if there is life beyond *Agneepath*.

It amuses me immeasurably to think what this writer would have written, if they had the gift of clairvoyance, if they had known that even twenty years on, the Bachchan Cult will show no signs of eclipse.

Andaz Apna Apna

Mad misadventures

Release: 1994

Cast: Aamir Khan, Salman Khan, Karisma Kapoor, Raveena Tandon, Paresh Rawal, Shakti Kapoor, Shehzad Khan

Directed by: Rajkumar Santoshi

Plot Summary: Amar (Aamir Khan) and Prem (Salman Khan) are two slackers who set about to marry a rich heiress, Raveena Bajaj (Raveena Tandon. Or is it Karisma?). And then there's her assistant, Karisma (Karisma Kapoor). Or is it Raveena? The histrionics of Karisma's father Ram Gopal and his evil twin Shyamgopal Bajaj (Paresh Rawal), the antics of Crime Master Gogo (Shakti Kapoor), are the stuff that legends are made of.

✎

Quaint Little Town

It was sometime in late 1994. Winter was setting in, and things were getting decidedly chilly in our sleepy little town. Nestled in a quaint corner of Assam, Silchar had its own charms.

It had an interesting film-viewing culture—in a town spread over just a tad more than 15 square kilometres, there were at least three major cinema halls (that's what movie theatres were called those days)—Devdoot, Gopinath and Oriental. Side by side, a number of video stores had cropped up that mainly rented out VHS cassettes. These stores were no less than Neverland for us movie-soaked buffoons. Their walls gleamed with posters of current and upcoming films and rows of shelves throbbing with an endless array of VHS covers (sometimes even empty covers as while renting out a cassette, it was often given away in a cringe-inducing generic sleeve). The popular stores were Benzer Video and Anandalok. I would walk in to Benzer and ask 'Kaku' (uncle, the rental guy) for a new movie devoid of any 'bad scenes' as they had to be seen with the family. This was said with a straight face. That wintery morning, Kaku proffered *Andaz Apna Apna (AAA)*. It hadn't made it to the theatres of Silchar yet. The reign of the Khans had set in, and anything with Aamir, Shahrukh or Salman in it was pure gold.

As the tape was rewound and played, little did I know what was in store.

Mumbai, Circa 2014

Rajkumar Santoshi was proving incredibly difficult to track down. Or maybe it was my being a commoner that made it seem such an insurmountable a task. A benefactor, following me on Twitter, provided a contact number and agreed to be named as a reference. But the rather unsporting lady on the other side announced with mechanical certainty that the phone was switched off. After repeated attempts, the benefactor was consulted again and a new mobile number came forth. The call went through all right, but there seemed to be a new problem this time around. My mouth went dry and heart sank. This was Raj Santoshi after all, the man behind *Ghayal* (1990), *Damini* (1993), *Ghatak* (1996), *Khakee* (2004) and of course, *Andaz Apna Apna*. Somehow sanity was restored—a couple of calls and a text conversation later, a meeting was fixed for the following weekend.

Silchar, 1994

Back in the day, most movies were watched with family, but like any dutiful Bengali father, mine avoided Hindi films like the plague—Hrishikesh Mukherjee's *Gol Maal* (1979) and Ramesh Sippy's *Sholay* being glaring exceptions.

As *AAA* unfurled itself for the first time, with my mother and sister in attendance, one could gather that this was no ordinary film. The opening credits of the film was a giveaway: 'Aamir Khan' was spelled with three Hs and 'Salman Khan' with three Ls! The film opens with Aamir on a bicycle, reminiscent of his character from *Jo Jeeta Wohi Sikandar*, Sanju. He spots a woman trying to fix her car, she turns out to be Juhi Chawla. What Aamir Khan says next confirms my feeling that this is not going be just another Khan vehicle: 'Aila! Juhi Chawla!'

Face off, 2014

On a lazy afternoon in August of 2014, I found myself sitting in Rajkumar Santoshi's drawing room, waiting in line as the director was busy in conversation with someone. While ogling at the palatial room, a familiar face presented itself. It was Master Raju—Raju Srestha, the child artiste from *Kitab*, *Khushboo*, *Parichay* and countless other films. He was also awaiting an audience with the director.

In an hour or so, Santoshi called me in. After some initial

stammer and fumble, we set about discussing the genesis of *AAA*. Sometime in early 1990, producer Vinay Sinha approached Rajkumar Santoshi with the idea of making a film that later became *Andaz Apna Apna*. Santoshi had just made *Ghayal,* and was well on his way to make *Damini*. *Ghayal* was a huge success. Nobody had quite made an action film like that before. It gave Sunny Deol the image of the one-man killing machine, a time warp he has been stuck in ever since. A cross between *Die Hard* and *Zanjeer*, *Ghayal* was Santoshi's directorial debut. He had been assisting Govind Nihalani on films like *Ardh Satya* (1983), the seething anger of which probably culminated in *Ghayal*.

After *Ghayal*, Santoshi was on the lookout for a playful, light-hearted concept for his next film. It was at this juncture that Vinay Sinha came to him with the idea of making a film with Aamir and Salman Khan. Aamir, though he really debuted with *Holi* in 1984, was launched on a huge scale in *QSQT* in 1988. Salman had a similar fate—starting his career with *Biwi Ho To Aisi* (1988), he was 'launched' with *Maine Pyar Kiya* (1989). Both were big stars by this time, but had never worked together. Santoshi decided to achieve a casting coup by clubbing them together in his upcoming project. It was no mean task. Since they were popular among young girls, it was decided to have a story where both the guys were chasing one girl, and both were trying in their own styles. Hence, *AAA*. That's all there is to it.

Revelation, 1994

Totally engrossed in the journey of Amar and Prem, and with the tomfoolery of Ram Gopal and Shyamgopal Bajaj, there were tears in my eyes. I hadn't laughed that hard in ages. This was a different kind of comedy—it was neither David Dhawan, nor Kundan Shah. It was the goofy, irreverent humour that Kishore Kumar introduced in films like *Half Ticket*.

Aamir comes to Sevaram Lodge, urges the owner Harish Patel (as Sevaram, of course) for a room. Harish says there's no room but relents and offers a makeshift arrangement in the attic. Aamir agrees and begins, '*Aap purush nahin...*' (You are not a man.) — Harish instinctively looks down as if to check — and Aamir completes the sentence, '*Mahapurush hain, mahapurush!*' (You are a great man.) The play is over the word 'purush', of course, and the fact that it is also part of a word that means hero, allows for the double-meaning (or not being a man, i.e. male, at all) to be rendered effortlessly.

Harish's instructions below are some of the most iconic conversations in the annals of Hindi Cinema:

> '*Sote samay aawaz toh nahin karte ho na? Paas mein hi kabristan hai, wahan se* complaint *nahin aani chahiye!*' (I hope you don't make too much noise while you sleep. There's a graveyard close by, see that they don't find a reason to complain.)
>
> '*Raat ko ek se do ke beech mein nahane ka paani aata hai, nahaa lena!*' (The water supply comes on between 1 and 2 in the morning, make sure you bathe then.)
>
> '*Idhar jo pankha hai, ussey chhedna nahin, kabhi bhi gir sakti hai.*' (Don't mess with the fan. It may fall.)
>
> '*Sooraj dhalne ke baad batti nahin jalana yahaan.*' (Don't turn on the lights after nightfall.)

When Amar wondered about changing clothes in the dark: '*Kapde badalne ke liye batti ki kya zaroorat?...Kisi ko kuch dekhna-dikhana hai kya?*' (Why do you need light for changing? Want to show something to someone, do you?)

I had never seen anything like *AAA* ever before. I rewound the tape and saw it again. It seemed even funnier the second time around. I called some of my friends, they'd had a similar experience.

Through the years, I'm not sure how many times I must have seen the film. It was much later that one got to know how it had bombed at the box office, and then attained something they called 'Cult Following'. It's arguable whether this following was caused by the internet or VHS tapes. But frankly, I've never known anyone who didn't like *AAA*. Ever.

'Zorambo Khush Nahin Hua', 2014

So far, all I got from Mr Santoshi was that *AAA* started off like any other comedy caper. In a while, we come to Gogo: Crime Master extraordinaire, *khandani chor, Mogambo ka bhatija*. Santoshi revealed that the original script had one more of Mogambo's relatives, to be played by a leading Bollywood bad guy of the time. Gogo had a smaller part to play. Why? In order to wrap our head around this, we will have to turn to comic books.

Any diehard *Superman* fanboy will be familiar with Bizarro and his Bizarro World. For the uninitiated, Bizarro is like a living mirror image of Superman. He attempts to mimic Superman, but ends up doing the exact opposite.

Rajkumar Santoshi originally planned to create a Bizarro-like character for Mogambo, a Yin to his Yang. A bumbling twin, who speaks and behaves the exact opposite. '*Mogambo ka bhai Zorambo*' (Mogambo's brother, Zorambo), also played by Amrish Puri. Zorambo was a part of the original script of *AAA*. Perennially upset, his pet-phrase was '*Zorambo khush nahin hua*' (Zorambo is not happy). But the role didn't make its way to the final film.

Santoshi explains, 'Mogambo used to wear black, Zorambo wore white. Mogambo had white hair, Zorambo had black hair. *Mogambo khush hota thha, yeh khush nahin hota thha. Uska aisa dialogue aata thha, "Zorambo kabhi khush nahin hota hai. Mera bhai baat baat mein khush hota thha, chala gaya."* (Mogambo used to be happy, this guy wasn't. He had a dialogue, "Zorambo is never happy. My brother used to be happy at small things, he died.") Always serious, never smiles. Amar and Prem used to say, "*Kisi tarha khush karo* yaar *isko!*" (Make him happy somehow!) It was like that. We had spoken to Amrish Puri and everything. But then we thought length-wise it is not working. But Crime Master Gogo was always a part of the script. He had a small part. *Ye bhai thha, woh bhatija.*' (Zorambo was the brother, Gogo was the nephew!)

Film *Mein* Film

There were in-film references aplenty. In a scene, Mehmood wants to make a film with Salman's character Prem, he has this production house called 'Wah Wah Productions' — a direct reference to Mehmood's role in *Pyar Kiye Jaa* (1966).

Often overlooked and grossly underrated, *Pyar Kiye Jaa* contained priceless performances by Kishore Kumar, Mehmood and Om Prakash. Prakash's effortless 'foiling' of Mehmood's histrionics in the iconic scene in which Mehmood's character, a wannabe film-maker, narrates his script, is an acting masterclass in itself. Twenty-seven years later, Mehmood repeated the act in a bizarre film called *Khal-Naaikaa* (1993), where his narration, even more bizarrely, was directed towards a little girl.

In *Andaz Apna Apna*, he was Johnny, proprietor of Wah Wah Productions, whose only obsession seemed to be to con youngsters into believing they were starring in his upcoming film. But by this time, he had already completed a film. On one of the walls of his office, one could see the title, *Jungle Mein Oye Oye* peeking from behind the hapless Prem. Ironically, a film bearing that title actually exists, starring somebody called Kapil Dev, an actor who also went by the name Irfan.

When Amar cuts the ribbon to enter jail, we can hear 'Papa Kehte Hain' in the background, referencing Aamir Khan's *QSQT*. *Sholay* is mentioned many times. When Prem says he'd seen *Sholay* ten times, Amar says, '*Haan, iske baap ne likhi hai!*' (His father has written it!), a hat-tip to the fact that *Sholay* was actually written partly by Salman's father, Salim Khan, one half of the writer duo Salim-Javed. Continuing the *Sholay* nod, when Amar and Prem arrive to 'rescue' their would-be father-in-law, and Teja rather wisely questions the money they were carrying, Prem quips, '*Maalik, jitne thhey, sab laaya hoon!*' (Lord, this is all I had!)

Jagdeep's character was called Bankelal Bhopali. The reference was too stark for anyone not to get it. In just a few minutes on-screen time, Jagdeep delivered one of his most spot-on performances as a comedian.

All this, coupled with the fact that Shakti Samanta was thanked in the credits, one would think that the names of the two protagonists, Amar and Prem, was a reference to Samanta's seminal film *Amar Prem* (1972). Rajkumar Santoshi strongly denies any link with that film. He couldn't recollect Shakti Samanta being thanked, and believed the producer Vinay Sinha had something to do with it.

Towards the beginning of the film, Amar says to his father (played by Deven Verma), '*Aap to purush hi nahin hai…*' Deven immediately looks down. Amar completes, '*…mahapurushi hai, mahapurush!*' This line today is part of Bollywood folklore. When Amar checks in to Sevaram Lodge, he repeats the act with Sevaram (Harish Patel), who reacts the same way (as mentioned before). Rarely would one find such a subtle way of pointing at something that was 'for adults only' or even potentially vulgar. When asked about this, Mr Santoshi says they were subtly done, without making it look raunchy or vulgar—it was all the actors' doing.

The scene with Aamir Khan entering the prison and Salman Khan taunting him is immediately followed by the part where Aamir checks in to Sevaram Lodge, without any explanation on how he escaped. Santoshi says, '*Peeche aaya hoga, chhudake aaya hoga. Salman pehle aa gaya, aake soya hua hai, Aamir Khan peeche se aa gaya.* (Must have followed him, must have escaped somehow. Salman comes first and lies down, Aamir joins him later.) He must have somehow managed to break out.'

After the interview ended and I walked towards my car, I thought that I had had a perfectly normal discussion around a perfectly abnormal film. Nothing in the interview was even remotely as mad as the film. And that's when it really hit me. Cults become cults, they are not made. It's the 'becoming' that is interesting, not the making.

Aamir Khan and the Marathon *Andaz Apna Apna* interview
It was like standing in front of Fort Knox. A gargantuan wooden gate looked down on me, as I wondered whether to knock or shout '*Koi hai?*' A couple of tough-looking kids pointed me to a calling bell hiding in plain sight. A security guard answered and I stated my name, adding that I have an appointment. I was respectfully shown to a lift and asked to go straight up to the sixth floor. On the sixth floor, as soon as the doors parted, I heard his voice floating in from another room, a voice we have been hearing for the past twenty-seven

years. Just a few more steps and he came into view, sitting cross-legged, propped on a table and addressing a group of people lounging in his couch. 'Um-bo-rish, right?', he asked and shook my hand, asked me to wait in the other room. I was too dazed to correct him. After minutes that seemed like years, Aamir Khan appeared, apologized for the wait, and said, 'Let's start!'

Aamir Khan says, 'See, this mad humour that you see in *Andaz Apna Apna* is actually all Raj Santoshi. It all emanated from his brain. And I think I was the only person in the crew who found it funny. Maybe Paresh.'

Before this, Santoshi had explained the story and characters to Salman and Aamir Khan, about the two characters who are really gold diggers and are after this rich girl. She's so rich that they waste no time in falling in love with her. But when one of them gets the girl, he realizes she's not the rich heiress after all, she's her secretary! So, the player gets played.

Aamir Khan says:

> It's a fun, mad comedy... Situational comedy, dialogue comedy, slaptick—you'll see every flavour of comedy in different scenes, in the film. And I don't know how much the others enjoyed that kind of comedy. I was like, you know, we're on a roll on this film. That's what I felt.
>
> I was doing three films. I had *Andaz Apna Apna*, I had one other film—I forget what—and I had *Baazi*. By the time I reached 1993, I shot for only twenty to twenty-five days, or thirty days in the whole year. Because I had *Time Machine*. And then Shekhar went off to make *Bandit Queen*. I was not signing any new films. Because first I wanted to finish the ones I had already taken on. One of them was *Andaz Apna Apna*.

Aamir Khan asserts that the joy of making a single scene of *AAA* was immeasurable. He had a whale of a time shooting those scenes with Salman Khan. Sometimes both of them would be focused on making the shot worth its while, and the camaraderie would show. There were moments when they would crack up, laughing on each other's shoulders.

> We have hugged laughing. We have cried together, with tears in the laughter, enjoying a moment that we have done as actors, because some of the scenes were truly hilarious.
>
> So we used to start laughing in the middle of the shot. Couldn't help ourselves. And [Salman's] character was of a simple guy, he didn't speak much. He doesn't realize what I've said quickly and gone away. *Usko baad me lagta hai,* 'Yaar *ye kuch galat bolke gaya mujhko.*' (He thinks later, this guy said something wrong to me.) I think I said yes to the wrong thing. So there's a very charming quality to his character.

The film began shooting in 1990 and released only in 1994. It was four long years in the making.

Finally, after a lot of trials and tribulations, they reached the day when the climax of the film had to be shot. Originally, it was to be shot in Mukesh Mills with an entirely different Crime Master Gogo.

> Finally, *girte, parte, marte,* somehow we came to the climax. The climax was to be shot at Mukesh Mills. Originally, it was in Mukesh Mills. And Crime Master Gogo was Tinnu Anand. And he was very good, he was fantastic....

And then some cast members didn't turn up, they were busy with other projects, and with so many big stars together, there may have been ego issues as well. This caused a long logjam, but things were finally resolved and people came together again, this time with greater focus to complete the film. In all this hullabaloo, four years had passed. In the mean while, Salman's hair kept growing and shrinking intermittently throughout the film, and a film that began well before Shah Rukh Khan's debut, ended up having a *Darr* reference: Juhi hums the tune of *Jadoo teri nazar* while Aamir stammers '*Ja-ja-ja-ja…*'. Juhi is startled, says, '*Mujhe laga Shah Rukh Khan aa gaya!*' (I thought Shah Rukh Khan is here!) But wait, Tinnu Anand was Crime Master Gogo? Aamir Khan responds,

> Yes. In fact when it was reshot, by then Tinnu's dates were unavailable. We got everyone's dates but Tinnu's. And since Tinnu was otherwise not in the film, Raj said we'll take Shakti Kapoor. But the most interesting thing was Zorambo, which Raj wrote for Amrish Puri.

After Zorambo with Amrish Puri didn't work out, Rajkumar Santoshi gave it a twist, according to Aamir Khan.

> (Zorambo was) kinda like Mogambo in *Mr. India*, asks people to jump and they jump into boiling water and all. I forget exactly what the scene was now, but basically we meet him for the first time and he comes and stands in front of us, face to face. And when you cut to a wide shot you realize he's standing on a table. He's actually a dwarf. *Toh woh humare level ka hai, then you cut to a wide, woh table pe khada hai, aur Salman aur main saamne khade hai*. So, in Raj's mind, this guy's a dwarf. And people lift him up and so on…

Rajkumar Santoshi actually arranged a casting session for it. Once when shoot was going on, people realized there was an army of dwarves around. Raj was screen testing them, one by one. He picked one guy, and asked his assistant to block him for the role.

Aamir Khan said, 'Yaar Raj, if you don't mind, I have a suggestion.'

He said, 'What?'

Aamir said: 'Whichever dwarf you choose, make sure he's very short. I mean real short. This one you've picked is almost the same height as me and Salman. Both of us are short too, *pata chala dwarf aur humare height me zyada farak nahin hai. So please choose a dwarf jo actual dwarf ho.*' (There isn't much difference between our heights and the dwarfs'. So please choose a dwarf who actually is one.)

Rajkumar Santoshi had laughed like there was no tomorrow. Ultimately, the midget character had to go out and Crime Master Gogo came in.

Rajkumar Santoshi is not only a very good director, but happens to be a very good comedian as well, and that percolated down in his writing.

Aamir corroborates:

> See Raj was a very good writer. He's very funny in real life also. And he was like in a zone, when he was writing. He's a very good dialogue writer also. And what is amazing about Raj is that he's a fantastic actor. Fantastic.

Andaz Apna Apna Part 2

For a very long time, fans have been speculating and praying for a sequel to *AAA*. Just type '*Andaz Apna Apna* sequel' on Twitter and witness the magic. Santoshi realizes there is a lot of demand for a follow-up, and he has been working on a script too.

'I am writing a script on it now. In a very short time I will finish the script.' On wondering whether he will cast the same team, he says, 'Preferably it will have the same cast. Let's see the economics and everything. Whenever we meet, Aamir and Salman both express the desire for a sequel. But we are also concerned that it should be a worthy second part. As soon as I am satisfied with the script, immediately we will lock everything.' In an interview to the newspaper *DNA* in 2017, Santoshi said that a sequel is in the works, but he will not be repeating the cast of *AAA* in the sequel.[*]

At one point, there was a significant amount of media chatter about Imran Khan and Ranbir Kapoor featuring in an *AAA* remake or sequel. Aamir Khan clears the air:

> I had told Raj, 'Write a script in which Salman and my characters are now aged.' So, it is twenty-five years later. They were young men then, now they are middle-aged guys. And they have a son each. *To ek ka beta Imran hai, aur ek ka beta Ranbir hai. Who dono bhi itne hi kamine hain.* (So one son is Imran, and the other is Ranbir—both of them as shameless as us.) I had suggested that make a story around these four characters. So maybe that's how the news came out...

---

[*]'Salman Khan, Aamir Khan won't be a part of *Andaz Apna Apna* sequel, says director. Here's why', *Hindustan Times*, 26 July 2017, http://www.hindustantimes.com/bollywood/salman-khan-aamir-khan-wont-be-a-part-of-andaz-apna-apna-sequel-says-director-here-s-why/story-8UwjZardHqyXhKKrcbhkjN.html

The Lines

Besides *Sholay*, no other Hindi film can boast of so many memorable dialogues. In fact, the scale would tilt ever so slightly in favour of *AAA* if one were to consider the sheer number of such lines. *AAA* also earns brownie points considering it was a flop—the lines etched themselves in public memory little by little, over the years. But today, each one of them is a gem, quoted by anyone at the slightest provocation. While I have translated a line or two earlier to give the reader a flavour of the kind of humour inherent in the dialogues, I provide a list below of some other lines but not hazarded a translation here since in that process, the fun in the puns, will assuredly be lost.

- *Aila, Juhi Chawla!*
- *Do dost ek hi pyale mein chai peeyenge, isse dosti badhti hai.*
- *Saala main bhi pheku aur yeh bhi pheku!*
- *Chit main jeeta, pat tu haara*
- *Tumhara naam kya hai Raveena?*
- *Yeh Vasco da Gama ki gun hai. Kiske mama ki gun?*
- *Aaya hun, kuch toh leke jaunga. Khaandani chor hun main.*
- *Suno suno duniya ke logon, sabse bada hai Mister Gogo*
- *Dr Prem Khurana, iss dhande mein bahut purana*
- *Woh humein teeley pe mil gaya tha na, isliye humne uska naam Teelu rakh diya*
- *Teja main hoon, mark idhar hai!*
- *Unka ek sawaal, humare do-do jawaab. Sawaal ek, jawab do.*
- *Gogoji aapka ghaghra!*

- *Bread ka badshash aur omelette ka raja – Bajaj – humara Bajaj!*
- *Yeh Teja Teja kya hai, yeh Teja Teja!*
- *Pehle se toota-phoota hai, ek marunga bikhar jayega.*
- *Galti se mistake ho gaya.*

The Music
Each song that was a part of the film is a classic now. Every last one of them. In a televised talk show, Ranveer Singh and Arjun Kapoor break into an impromptu rendition of 'Do Matwale Chale Zindagi Banane'. No party can be complete without someone playing 'Ye Raat Aur Ye Doori'. 'Elo Ji Sanam Hum Aa Gaye' is equally popular among cinephiles and comes to the rescue on those rare Antakshari nights when you get stuck on an 'E'.

The music of *AAA* was composed by Tushar Bhatia. Tushar is a classically trained sitarist and vocalist, but he didn't compose for any film after that.

'Tushar is an immensely talented musician. Unfortunately, he could never really adjust with the ways of the film industry. *Iss industry mein kya hai…music company bhi dictate karta hai, producer bhi dictate karta hai, ke aisa hona chahiye, waise hona chahiye…* (In this industry, right from the music company to the producer—everyone wants to dictate how the music should be). He is a very pure kind of an artist,' says Aamir.

Santoshi wanted music with a vintage, old world feel. Both him and Tushar were big fans of O.P. Nayyar and there was a deliberate harking back to the fifties and Nayyar's music.

Rising from the Ashes
But there's no denying the fact that *AAA* was a flop when it

came out. Maybe it was too ahead of its times, maybe people didn't get that brand of humour.

'The film wasn't handled properly,' says Santoshi, 'I got busy with some other film. So did Aamir. The distributors were new, so they couldn't do justice to the film. It didn't get a proper release. *Awareness nahin tha logon mein.* (There was no awareness about the film.) And youngsters at the time also took some time to grasp the humour.' He adds that had it been promoted well, it could have been a greater success.

Aamir elaborates:

> I would say it's two things. One is that the film was not promoted at all. At that time we didn't have the big studios who would release nationwide. Each territory was broken down into distributors and you gave delivery to each one. And each one paid you something. Distributors *ko lagta tha* yaar *yeh film ki* delivery *humko milegi ke nahin milegi, pata laga humne* publicity *kar dii theatre me aur phir* delivery *hi nahin mili!*' (Distributors weren't sure whether they will get delivery of the film, they were worried they will start promoting the film and in the end there will be no delivery!)

Besides, Salman and Aamir Khan were not looked upon as the bankable stars they are today. They had just about broken into the scene, so to speak. That may have been another reason for the lack of faith shown by the distributors back then.

> Salman and I were stars, but we were not the stars of today. We had given successful films, we were loved, but we were not that huge... Today one wouldn't be worried about Salman or me, distributor won't be worried whether the film will release or not. But at that

time it was different, often they didn't book theatres, they didn't put up the poster. They got the delivery on Monday. It's only when the film arrived on Monday and they got the final print from the lab, they were convinced that the film is releasing. They said, 'Now put up the posters.' The film was releasing on Friday. They called up on Monday, 'Put up the posters.' What did four days of publicity matter anyway, in those days? Today four days is a lot...But back then it took time for news to reach you. There was no TV. You know, right now you have so many TV channels but then you only had Doordarshan. So whatever best they could do in four days, they did. So as a result, the film didn't have an opening.

Also, Aamir agrees that the youth then were, by and large, not used to this kind of humour. Then much later, the younger generation discovered it on video and were taken by it, as their tastes had changed.

When Aamir's daughter, sixteen years of age at the time, discovered *AAA,* she was floored by it.

'For the first time in her life she saw it two months ago. And she tells me, "Papa it's an amazing film!" She and her friends saw it, they all loved it. On 31 December, they were all watching *AAA*. So as the generations are coming in, they are all watching it and all enjoying the mad humour. So, it failed the test at that time, but it's passed the test of time.'

Epilogue
4 November 2014, Mumbai
It was the twentieth anniversary of *Andaz Apna Apna*'s release, and I had a written a short piece about it on *DesiMartini.com*.

I was sitting in office, and I distinctly heard one of my colleagues gasp and exclaim loudly, '*Arre yeh to mere uncle hain!*' (This man is my uncle!) It was Tejas—Tejas Master, one of my two second-in-commands. Tejas did not watch enough movies to care about anniversaries (even if it were of *AAA*). He was reading my article and that led him to another article on *AAA* and therein, believe it or not, he had spotted his uncle.

Like everything else, the cult of *AAA* also flourished and thrived online, with the advent of the Internet. Possibly during one of these overtly passionate discussions on the web, someone noticed that a guy in the backseat of the bus in which Amar and Prem first meet, bears an uncanny resemblance with statesman and author Shashi Tharoor. Before you know it, it spread like wildfire in the cyber space, and people started claiming that it was the man himself! So much so that Tharoor himself tweeted, 'Will the guy in the middle of this still from *Andaaz Apna Apna* please identify himself so people stop claiming it's me?'

Not to be disheartened by these minor setbacks, people kept tweeting to Mr Tharoor incessantly, expressing their surprise that he was an actor too. There was a manhunt (no kidding) launched by a major newspaper to identify who the guy was, but nothing came of it. This has remained an abiding mystery among film buffs and fans of *AAA*.

Now, our dear colleague Tejas Master was staring at a still of the Tharoor look-alike, claiming it was his uncle, Indravadan Tailor. What were the odds? I questioned his assertion but he was positive that the man sitting at the back of the bus and smiling, was his uncle.

Indravadan used to be a struggling actor, and happened to have appeared in a number of films in the eighties and nineties, including *Tezaab*, *AAA* and *Hathkadi*. Unfortunately, he passed away in the late nineties.

Tejas promptly obtained a couple of photos of his uncle and wrote to *DesiMartini*, who announced this epoch-making discovery on their website. It was time to celebrate, in more ways than one.

Jo Jeeta Wohi Sikandar

There and back again

Release: 1992

Cast: Aamir Khan, Ayesha Jhulka, Pooja Bedi, Deepak Tijori, Mamik, Kulbhushan Kharbanda, Kiran Zaveri, Deb Mukherjee

Directed by: Mansoor Khan

Plot Summary: In picturesque Dehradun, slacker Sanjay Lal (Aamir Khan) from Model School whiles away his days drooling at girls and hanging out with his good-for-nothing chums. They are constantly at loggerheads with boys from Rajput College, a school for children of the rich and famous. The annual cycle race is the only arena where Model school can be a contender, and all eyes are on Sanjay's righteous brother Ratan Lal (Mamik) who can bring back the school's lost glory. The boys' father Ramlal (Kulbhushan Kharbanda) pins all his hopes on Ratan and despises Sanjay, dismissing him as a lost cause. Things come to a head when right before the race, Ratan is roughed up by the Rajput boys and is critically injured.

Suppose you were a successful film-maker, a doyen of an illustrious film family. After having made two of the most well-received films in history, would you abandon the glitz and glamour and take refuge in the hills? Let's say people accuse you of plagiarizing from a Hollywood film, would you venture to see the said film and call it one of your favourite films ever?

Mansoor Khan has done all of the above and more. Son of producer-director Nasir Hussain, he stepped out of his father's shadow for his own moment in the sun—*Qayamat Se Qayamat Tak*—which launched the careers of a posse of youngsters, Aamir Khan among them. Mansoor Khan directed the film at the behest of his father, but he had another film lurking within him, one that he had written long before *QSQT*. Story of two brothers—a domineering head of the family who wants to see his younger brother, a loser, succeed in life. But said young brother is a slacker, whiling his time away. The story was how the kid would 'come of age'.

Mansoor Khan wrote *Jo Jeeta Wohi Sikandar* when he was a naive kid himself, trying to prove a point. He had studied engineering, realizing well in time that it was hardly his cup of tea; gadgets and cameras always fascinated him. Tinkering with video editing on a Sony recorder, he came upon the idea of making a film about redemption. He was aimless, just like the protagonist Sanjay Lal from *Jo Jeeta Wohi Sikandar*. That's when he started writing.

Ostensibly to warm himself up, he made a short film called *Umberto* with his friend Amol Gupte acting in it, and it was this shot that his father happened to see and asked him to helm *QSQT*. Mansoor Khan obeyed.

But he was not willing to just carry things out like a robot. The pre-credits scenes were exactly as his father had written them on paper. After that, Mansoor took over and added his bits, especially in the characterization of the leads, Raj (Aamir) and Rashmi (Juhi). Contrary to conventional wisdom, he resisted keeping a happy ending to the film. Nasir Hussain always believed that the audience cannot handle sorrow. It's needed in the script, but smatter too much of it, and they are sure to reject your film. But in his son's view, that's how the story was destined to end, culminating in the pair's death. *QSQT*'s success vindicated him.

Despite such adulation in his very first film, Mansoor Khan refused to revel in it and turned his attention to his pet project. The reason he had written the elder brother in *Jo Jeeta...* as a father figure instead of there being an actual father in the story, was because he was sick of the clichéd father-son routine in Hindi films. But *QSQT* had already explored newer aspects of the relationship, with Aamir Khan playing son and Dalip Tahil as the father whose relationship doesn't follow the usual filmic pattern. Enter Ramlal Sharma (Kulbhushan Kharbanda), father to Ratan Lal and Sanjay Lal Sharma.

Film-maker and producer Kamran Khan was known for his stunt films. From 1960s to early 1970s, Kamran directed and produced action films like *Panch-Rattan* (1965), *Khoon Ka Khoon* (1966), *Ilzam* (1970), *Aisa Bhi Hota Hai* (1971) and *Mera Shikar* (1973), mostly starring Dara Singh or his brother Randhawa. The films are a treat, and most of them can be found in YouTube in all their glory. But at a certain point, his films stopped doing well. He had to go through a divorce and his two children, Farah and Sajid, had to fend for themselves. From an early age, both Farah and Sajid were deeply passionate about dancing, especially Farah. The kids played dancing cameos in films like *Saamri* (1985) and *Aag Se Khelenge* (1989). Farah indulged the passion and used to look for excuses to break into a jig at parties, or participate in dance soirees and contests.

A Walk in the Clouds
Mansoor Khan told me later in a telephonic interview:

> Farah had approached me to choreograph *Jo Jeeta Wohi Sikandar*. But I had already spoken to Saroj Ji (Khan) — I told her that, and said she can work as my assistant. She joined me as an assistant director and when she read the script, she said, 'I have somebody in mind for the brother.' She brought Mamik to me — the moment he walked into my office, I knew that this was guy who will play the brother Ratan Lal. We did a screen test, but I was very convinced that he was the one.
>
> Aamir was already a star. *Dil* had happened and *QSQT* had happened. So you needed someone who was believable as the brother who was one-up on Aamir. Mamik had a strong physique and yet had this endearing quality about him.

Farah Khan brought in Mamik for the role, and he fit the slot perfectly. In time, as destiny would have it, she also became the choreographer for the film, when Saroj Khan took off without informing.

Mani Ratnam's *Geethanjali* (1989), his first Telugu film, was a great success both commercially as well as among critics. It was later dubbed in Tamil and Malayalam, and remade in Hindi three years later: *Yaad Rakhegi Duniya* (1992, mostly known for one song — *Tere liye saari umar jagun*). The Press especially went ga-ga over the female lead of the film, a British-Indian named Girija Shettar. She was offered the role of Anjali, Sanjay Lal's childhood sweetheart.

Nandita Morarji stepped in as Devika, the Veronica to Aamir Khan's Archie. It would have been her debut in Hindi films. She was to be known by her screen name, Nagma.

The next big challenge was to cast Shekhar Malhotra, the antagonist, the bully. Mansoor Khan wanted someone who had an athletic build, looked good and exuded a certain amount of arrogance. A lot of young actors were auditioned for the role, including Rajiv Bhatia. Akshay Kumar was also auditioned for the role of Shekhar Malhotra, but he was turned down. Eventually, they zeroed in on Milind Soman.

Aamir Khan says,

> Milind Soman was this star athlete, full of arrogance — you know, the character is supposed to be very arrogant, sure of himself, really good at what he does, the girls love him. Unbeatable, the Greek god. That's how this role was written.
>
> When we cast Milind and we saw the test, we realized his voice and intonation lets him down. But the part was virtually written for him, because Milind is naturally arrogant. When he looks at you, you think you are something the cat brought in.

Milind Soman suited the role to a T, apart from the voice. When he was watching the footage of Soman's test, Mansoor Khan set the volume off and asked Aamir to dub the lines. And the whole thing changed — his performance seemed to improve a few notches. The way forward then was to get somebody else to dub for him. The casting process seemingly completed, the crew of *Jo Jeeta Wohi Sikandar* was about to leave for Ooty, when something happened that made them go back to square one and look through those screen test videos again.

That something was *Baaghi* (1990). Nagma who was playing Devika, backed out as she had been offered *Baaghi* opposite Salman Khan, the film that was to become her debut. The trigger for her decision might have been the realization that Devika was not a pivotal character. But fans of *Jo Jeeta Wohi Sikandar* would beg to disagree (if that were really her reason): Devika was the catalyst in Sanjay's transformation, and was one of the principal characters, albeit with some negative shades.

Nevertheless, the team went back to view the audition tapes, and this time they picked Karishma Pahuja to replace Nagma. Pahuja was a model and actress who had appeared with Aamir Khan in an FTII Diploma film — *Subah Subah* — that he did for his friend Inderjit Singh Bansal. She was tested for the part earlier and had been the second choice after Nagma. She was cast for Devika and the shoot began at Coonoor and Ooty.

A sixty-day schedule was completed, shooting at Ooty, Coonoor and Western Catchments. Western Catchments, about 20 kilometres away from Ooty is shrouded in clouds all year long, and one gets daylight for about three hours — from around 7 a.m. to 10 a.m. The cycle race was shot at Western Catchments, while juggling with daylight. The four-hour drive from Ooty was horrendous, the road condition in certain places was very bad. They had to start at 3 to even hope to reach the Catchments by 7 a.m. And then the wait began for the sun to peek from behind the clouds. After a twenty-day torturous and gruelling shoot, the cycle race was finally completed.

About 80 per cent of the film had been shot in a two-month schedule, including most of the climax. The cast and crew returned to Mumbai and got back to their lives, without any clue that they had to do the whole thing all over again.

Déjà vu

Aamir Khan was shooting for another film, when he got a call from Mansoor Khan. Karishma Pahuja, who was playing Devika, didn't seem to be working out for the movie. Aamir Khan maintains that she did her best, but somehow it was not Devika. The way the role was conceived, the part that it was supposed to play in the canvas of the film, just didn't pan out with Pahuja as Devika.

Mansoor Khan told Aamir, 'I think we'll have to recast and reshoot the film.' Aamir was flabbergasted. Acting for him is going through a whole gamut of emotional experiences, living those moments, and tapping into one's personal emotional reservoir. Having done that for *Jo Jeeta...* once, it seemed impossible to even attempt to recreate it.

He explains, 'As an actor, as a creative person, it has already come out of you, it's gone from you. Now when you are told you have to do it again, you start trying to remember what you had done then. How can I take it out again? It's gone!'

But Mansoor Khan persisted, and finally Aamir had to say yes. Now the next battle was to recast, get everyone together again and go back and shoot the film all over again. Karishma Pahuja was let go, and Pooja Bedi stepped in.

It was the early 1990s. Internet access was still a decade away, but 'Superhit Muqabla' and MTV were causing some fundamental changes in the way entertainment was perceived. On-screen kisses on TV shows were more commonplace than they are now, sex was still taboo (I still remember the embarrassment and discomfort of hearing *Sexy sexy sexy* from *Khuddar* as a teenager, with grown-ups around), but more risqué advertisements and photoshoots were to be seen everywhere. Indian advertisement had seldom seen such sexual candour before or ever since. Vatsyayan's legacy was revealed to adolescents across the length and breadth of urban India not via Mira Nair's eponymous film, but through an ad campaign that popped up on good old Doordarshan one fine evening. A rather generously endowed woman was writhing in the shower while a good-looking lad tries to moor his boat, and later joins the lady in the shower. As we collected our jaws from the floor, another lady would whisper 'Kama Sutra' in the background. The week's papers told us that the man was Marc Robinson, and the woman was called Pooja Bedi.

Pooja Bedi had a much-hyped debut in *Vishkanya* (1991), a film about mythical women with the 'kiss of death' (much like the Batman villain Poison Ivy) that poisoned the film itself. The very next film was the one that defined her career—as Devika in *Jo Jeeta Wohi Sikandar*.

The first thing that they shot was the song 'Jawaan Ho Yaaron' and the dance competition. After the shoot, Girija Shettar, who was playing Anjali, said she was leaving. She was going back abroad and couldn't continue the shoot unless Mansoor Khan could manage to wrap up the shoot in a month. He felt helpless—the entire film had to be made all over again, so completing it within a month was out of the question. Therefore, Shettar had to go too. But she could still be seen in 'Jawaan Ho Yaaron' as the girl in red who dances with Aamir Khan. Ayesha Jhulka joined the cast as Anjali.

Nagarjuna, the Telugu superstar (still remembered by Hindi film audiences for *Shiva,* 1989) seemed to have an interesting connection with the character of Anjali from *Jo Jeeta*.... The first choice for the role was Girija Shettar, who debuted with him in *Geethanjali* (1989), and then it was Ayesha

Jhulka whose debut as a lead actress was opposite him in *Neti Siddhartha* (1990). Jhulka first faced the camera as a child artiste, playing Kader Khan's adopted daughter in *Kaise Kaise Log* (1983), and after being the heroine in *Neti Siddhartha*, she had just worked on her first bunch of Hindi films—*Kurbaan* (1991) and *Meet Mere Man Ke* (1991)—when someone told her that Nasir Hussain was looking for a lead actress for his next project. She met Hussain, who then introduced her to his son Mansoor. After a round of discussion, Hussain let her go, promising to get back to her in some time. By the time she reached home, she got a call from them, outlining the dates. She had already committed those dates to Roopesh Kumar, yesteryear villain and producer, for the film *Hai Meri Jaan* (1991) opposite Kumar Gaurav. But Roopesh Kumar gladly accommodated, and congratulated her on bagging this big film.

Upon the departure of Karishma and Girija, the only other cast member Aamir Khan had the most scenes with was Milind Soman. Now, Aamir and Mansoor seemed to have a rather difficult time with Soman. Since most of the principal cast had already been replaced, it was finally decided to replace him too. Eventually, a role that a future superstar had auditioned for and lost, and a supermodel didn't seem to be doing justice to, fell on the lap of Deepak Tijori.

Tijori frequented the same theatre circles that Aamir Khan was a part of, in the eighties—which also had names like Paresh Rawal and Ashutosh Gowariker frequenting the proceedings. After doing bit roles in films like *Tera Naam Mera Naam* (1988) and *Parbat Ke Us Paar* (1988), in *Kroadh* (1990) Tijori was one of the villain's henchmen who attempts to rape the heroine Sonam. He had almost given up on a career in films when actor Avtar Gill came to him and told him that Mahesh Bhatt wanted to cast him for *Aashiqui* (1990). And then *Jo Jeeta Wohi Sikandar* came along, two years later. *Aashiqui*, *Jo Jeeta Wohi Sikandar* and *Khiladi* (1992) remain the three defining films of his career.

And the whole film was on the floors, all over again. But Nasir Hussain put his hands up when it came to spending money for shooting on location again. Milind Soman wasn't a part of the project anymore, so the cycle races that had been shot with him had to be reshot in the Western Catchments, but the rest of it had to be shot in Film City. In fact, the mall area and the Cafe shown in the film were also sets made at Film City.

Mansoor Khan explains,

> In my mind, Kodaikanal was the place where I was locating the film, but it was shot all over. Most of what we shot at Kodai, was unusable because we had changed the cast. We didn't go back there because Kodai gets very foggy and it gets very difficult to shoot there. That is why most of the shoot was done in Coonoor, Ooty and the Western Catchment Area. And the stadium had to be in Bombay because there is no other place where you could get a Velodrome (the arena where track cycling is held).

There were a number of cameos in the film. Imran Khan's appearance as the young Sanjay was a well-known and much-discussed aspect of the film. Aamir Khan's brother Faisal also had a cameo in the film, as did Aamir and Mansoor's old friend Amol Gupte. Mansoor Khan says,

> Amol was one of the announcers during the race. [He] is a very close friend, I did my first video film with him. We used to spend a lot of time together, so he happened

to do that part. In fact, he lent his voice to the film too—early in the film when Aamir and his friends were stealing the papers, the watchman's voice was actually Amol's. As for Faisal, he was assisting me on that film. He had to do a lot of stunts—when we were taking a point-of-view shot of a character reacting to a cyclist, Faisal had to run behind the camera and pretend to be the cyclist. So, in the process of assisting, he ended up playing one of the boys.

Floating on Cloud Nine

The doe-eyed Devika falls for Sanjay's charms and plants a kiss on his cheek. Sanju can't wait to share this news with his best pal Anjali and kisses her goodnight, leading her to believe he is about to reciprocate her feelings. Both are on seventh heaven, deep in love for the first time. To depict this, Mansoor Khan wanted a new syntax—a conventional romantic number would fall short of depicting the dreamlike quality. Here's where the idea of a slow motion song with lip-sync crept in, and *Pehla Nasha* took birth.

A similar experiment featured in *Geethanjali*, Girija Shettar's aforementioned Telugu debut. The song 'Jallantha Tullantha', choreographed by Prabhu Deva's father Mugur Sundar aka Sundaram, had Girija dancing about in the rain in slow motion, while lip-syncing in tandem. Eighteen years before this, Mehmood's *Lakhon Mein Ek* (1971) contained a song composed by R.D. Burman titled 'Jogi O Jogi' that kept switching between slow motion and regular speed, while keeping the lip-sync intact.

Mansoor says,

Sanjay is floating on cloud nine when Devika tells him

that she likes him. He couldn't even imagine Devika saying that to him, he was just trying his luck. I always had this sensation of floating in my head. When I had my first sitting with Jatin and Lalit and they played that song, it was clear to me that I wanted to shoot the song in slow motion—but I wanted to shoot the whole song in slow motion, not only the music parts. The simple trick to do that is to run your camera at twice the speed and run your Nagra (audio recorder) at twice the speed, while the actors move at normal speed, but the lip-sync is twice as fast.

Aamir Khan elaborates further,

The song was shot in high-speed lip-sync. When the camera runs at 48 frames per second—which is twice the speed—but plays back at 24 frames, the action appears slow. When we shoot songs, we play the song in the background, and we have to sing along. If we play the song at normal speed but camera goes at double the speed, my lip movement will be out of sync. In order to get it in sync, we had to sing it fast too. It sounded funny, but we had to maintain a calm expression…it was all Mansoor's idea. As an actor you had to precisely match the fast pace and do it right, because when it plays back in slow motion, any mismatches would be visible.

The Last Word
Aamir Khan says:

Even today when I speak to Nitish Tiwari who directed *Dangal,* he says he saw *Jo Jeeta Wohi Sikandar* while at Engineering College, and it was *their* film, you know—

the inter-college competitions, the sports meets, inter-IIT drama competitions, the concept of the underdog—a lot of people connected with the film on many levels.

It wasn't as big a success as *QSQT*, though for me, it's a better film than *QSQT*: the way Sanjay's character is written, the relationship between the younger and elder brother, his relationship with the two girls...it's a story about growing up, coming of age. It's got some amazing moments.

At the 2016 Jio MAMI Film Festival, Mumbai, the cast of *Jo Jeeta...* got together after twenty-four years to reminisce about the film.

Gunda

Where leaders steal shrouds

Release: 1998

Cast: Mithun Chakraborty, Mukesh Rishi, Shakti Kapoor, Ishrat Ali, Rami Reddy, Harish Patel, Mohan Joshi, Deepak Shirke

Directed by: Kanti Shah

Plot Summary: Nothing much to say here. To paraphrase Wise Man Morpheus, 'Unfortunately, no one can be told what Gunda is. You have to see it for yourself.'

⁂

What is common to *Cape Fear, Mean Streets, Philadelphia, Natural Born Killers, Face/Off, Black Hawk Down, Gangs of New York, Darr, Rock On!!, Veer Zara, Baazigar* and *The Lunchbox*, except the fact that they are all great films? As of writing this book, they were all rated lower than Kanti Shah's *Gunda* on IMDb.com. Similarly, films like *Kill Bill: Vol. 2, King Kong, District 9, The Exorcist, The Wild Bunch, Nosferatu, Rope* and *Rosemary's Baby* have been rated at par with *Gunda*.

They name *Plan 9 From Outer Space* (1959) as the worst film of all time. Clearly, 'they' haven't heard of Kanti Shah and his cult classic *Gunda*. Ed Wood's no match for Kanti Shah.

Saying something about *Gunda* is like talking about *Sholay* or *Andaz Apna Apna*—everybody has seen it, dissected it and the dialogues are etched in their memory. The Internet is full of temples, altars and idols dedicated to the divinity that is *Gunda*. The most notable of them is by the legendary Great Bong/Arnab Ray, ace blogger and writer of thrillers like *The Mine* and *Yatrik*. Great Bong is one of those prominent netizens who are responsible for the online frenzy around the kitsch fest. His ode to *Gunda* on his blog *Random Thoughts of A Demented Mind*,* is one of the most read and celebrated writings on the film.

No one can be told what *Gunda* is. You have to see it to believe it. In 1970, Dev Anand's director-brother Chetan Anand made a film called *Heer Ranjha* which is somewhat unique in Bollywood history as it was one big poem: the dialogues rhymed with each other. More than two decades later, a film-maker called Kanti Shah made another film with a similar attribute: *Gunda*. But that is only a teeny-weeny aspect of the epic. The film is full of one-liners, wisecracks, in-jokes, film references, ambassadors, auto-rickshaws, leopards and hanging cots.

Gunda was released in 1998 and lost in the barrage of other Mithun Da films from the south. It was almost a parallel industry that Prabhujee had set up, headquartered in Ooty. And 1998 was a particularly prolific year for him: *Mafia Raaj, Hitler, Hatyara, Ganga Ki Kasam, Do Numbri, Devta,*

---

*See 'Gunda—The Legend', 20 June 2007, http://greatbong.net/2007/06/20/gunda-the-legend/

Military Raaj, Chandaal, Ustaadon Ke Ustaad, Mard, Yamraaj and *Himmatwala* were all released that year. All classics in their own right. Prabhujee's cult was at its peak.

Gunda got a new lease of life with the advent of the Internet and online forums. Word about this film spread like wildfire, and before you know it, students of IIT had started an online movement to grant this classic the recognition it deserves: to be the highest rated film on IMDb.com. For a very short time, the movement succeeded and *Gunda* was right at the top of the heap, above *The Godfather* and *Shawshank Redemption*. Yes, *The Godfather* was trounced by *Gunda*, not *Sholay* or *Mother India*. Not even *Deshdrohi*.

Kanti Shah, the Auteur

If the auteur theory is about having a unique stamp of ownership on one's own work, Kanti Shah is most certainly one. His films have certain attributes that are to be found in his films and his films only. And like many auteurs, his films' titles are prefixed by his name, *Kanti Shah Ke Angoor* (2005) being a prominent example.

The identifiable features of Shah's cinema have been outlined in the Golden Kela Awards 2012, the Razzies of India:[*]

His films contain masala at its purest. No pretensions, no baggage. What you see on the poster is what you get.

His dialogues—they are rife with meaning, poetry and rhythm. Sample the following:

— '*Dikhne mein bevda, bhaagne mein ghoda, aur maarne mein hathoda.*' (I look like a drunkard, run like a horse, and hit like a hammer.)

---

[*]'Kanti Shah At The 4th Annual Golden Kela Awards!', *Randomxmag*, 5 April 2012, https://www.youtube.com/watch?v=965L5_LLx_I

- *'Main tera woh bura haal karoonga, jo deemak lakdi ka aur chhipkali makdi ka karti hai.'* (I will do to you what termite does to wood and a lizard does to a fly.)
- *'Kauwe ne Cheel ka chumma liya aur Cheel ne Choohe ka baccha paida kiya.'* (A crow kissed a kite and the kite gave birth to a mouse.)

Pedestrian, you say? You have no idea!

Surreal action. Dharam Paaji holds a helicopter down with a rope, and literally stops a bullet by catching it in his fist, Prabhujee hammers a man into the ground.

Social Messages. *'Aapka yeh kanoon, aur bhagwaan, jab bhi kisi ko deta hai, to chhappad faadke deta hai, aur jab leta hai, to thappad maarke leta hai.'* (When your laws and your god feel generous, they give through the roof, and when they decide to take it away, they snatch it by slapping you on the face!)

'Bhagwaan lakeeron ke zariye jeevan ka sirf trailer dikhaate hain, poori film nahin. Yadi woh humein poori film dikha dein, toh hum toh phir khushi se mar jaayein, ya gham se mar jaayein.' (Through the lines [on your palm], god shows you only the trailer of your life, not the whole film. If we were to be shown the entire film, we will die of happiness, or die of sorrow.)

Kanti Shah is also the uncrowned king of in-jokes, hat-tips and film references. For instance: *'Ye chahe Duplicate ho ya China Gate, main shaadi abhi isi waqt isi se hi karoongi!'* (I don't care whether he is *Duplicate* or *China Gate*, he is the one I wish to marry!)

The Case of the Disappearing Moustache

Prabhujee's father is played by Arun Mathur, a Doordarshan legacy who was known for his rather intimidating looks, towering frame and the singular style of clasping his hands at the slightest opportunity. He is Havaldar (Constable) Ram

Singh, Shankar's (Prabhujee) doting father, and like all filmy havaldars, he sports a twirled, thick moustache. The first time it vanishes is after his daughter's untimely demise at the hands of the villain's 'namard' (impotent) brother. One would assume the shaving of facial hair is to signify mourning. But bewilderingly it appears again in the very next scene, where the father and son deliberate on whether revenge should be opted for or not. In a few minutes, Ram Singh faces off Inspector Kale and accuses him of colluding with the villains. This he does sans the moustache. The only conclusion one may draw is that the moustache played a cameo in the movie, choosing to disappear and reappear at will.

Gunda opens with the rendezvous between a politico — a *kafanchor* neta (a leader who steals shrouds) — and a gangster named Lambu Atta. The first string of dialogues set the tone for the rest of the film:

KCN: *Maine gundagardi mein bahut naam kamaya,*
Kabhi dushmanon ko phaada, kabhi kaata,
Dikhne mein to tu naata,
Par tohar naam hai Lambu Atta.

(I earned quite a repute as a goon — ripped my enemies apart, hacked them.
You look rather *naata* [short], but your name is Lambu Atta.)

LA: *Kaam ki baat bata, jis kaam ke liye tu Billi ka doodh peekar Dilli se aaya hai.*

(State your business, for which you come all the way from *Dilli* (Delhi), after drinking the milk of a *billi* [cat].)

The philosophical ramifications of a political leader who steals shrouds and drinks cat's milk will not be lost on the fans of

Federico Fellini's and Luis Buñuel's early work. For further insights into the deeper meanings hidden in the dialogues, please refer to aforementioned blog post by Great Bong on *Gunda*.

The introduction of the villains is one of the most celebrated scenes ever conceived. Each one of them break the fourth wall, turning to the camera and introducing themselves. Here's the lay-down:

Mukesh Rishi — *Naam hai mera Bulla, rakhta hun khulla.* (My name is Bulla, and I keep it *khulla* [open].)

Shakti Kapoor — *Mera naam hai Chuttiya,* acchi acchon ki khadi karta hoon main khatiya. Bulli kahaan hai teri ungli, Bulla bhai ab hoga hulla gulla. Police aur hukumat karegi hai Bulla, hai Chuttiya. Sab bolenge hai Chuttiya, hai Bulla. Arre dhoondo dhoondo kahaan hai Chuttiya, pakdo pakdo kahaan hai Bulla.* (My name is Chuttiya, and I have vanquished many. Tell me Bulli where's your *ungli* [finger], come Bulla — let's raise some *hulla gulla* [noise]. The cops and the government will say 'Hey Bulla, hey Chuttiya!' Others will say 'Hey Chuttiya, hey Bulla! Find him, where's Chuttiya…catch him, where's Bulla?)

Mohan Joshi — *Mera naam hai Pote, jo apne baap ke bhi nai hote!* (My name is Pote, and not even my father can trust me!)

Harish Patel — *Mera naam hai Ibu Hatela, maa meri chudail*

---

*The extra 't' in 'Chuttiya' has been added to distinguish it from the similar-sounding swear-word in Hindi. It refers to the lock of hair that many Indians wear on their scalp. Shakti Kapoor's character sports this in the film, and hence the name. However, knowing Kanti Shah and his oeuvre, it is not unlikely that the Chuttiya's name is actually an allusion to the cuss word after all!

kee beti, baap mera shaitan ka chela, khayega kela? (I'm Ibu Hatela, my mother was born to a witch, my father was the devil's *chela* [devil's disciple]. Do you like *kela* [bananas]?)

Lambu Atta kills Bulla's sister, and another iconic scene ensues. Bulla holds his dead sister in his arms and laments:

Munni meri bahen Munni, Munni
Toh tu mar gayi?
Lambu ne tujhe lamba kar diya?
Maachis ki teeli ko khamba kar diya?
Arey mere dil mein kya kya armaan thhe tere liye.
Maine to tere liye teen-sau chhokre dekhe the...who bhi ekdam chikne,
Jo tujhe bhaata, wohi tera pati banta
Magar tu to katela gurda, yaane murda ho gayi.

Munni, my sister!
So you are dead?
Lambu has killed you!
I had so many dreams for you
I chose boys for you, handsome boys
You'd have liked them
But there you are
Just a corpse now.

The bad guys congregate on either an aerodrome or a dockyard, and Shankar seems to be a porter in both the spots. Shankar faces off with one of Bulla's henchmen, Kaala Shetty (Rami Reddy), and quips:

Main hoon jurm se nafrat karne waala,
Sharifon ke liye jyoti, gundon ke liye jwaala.

I am a hater of crime,
a beacon for the noble, but raging hellfire for the criminals.

Not to be disarmed, Kaala Shetty retorts:

Tujhe banakar maut ke moonh ka nivala
Tere seene mein gaadh doonga main maut ka bhaala!

I will feed you to death,
I will pierce your chest with the spear of death.

Such epic exchanges of words pervade throughout the film, and the actors and the music complement it appropriately. Sample this classic:

Kyon ye baraf peeta hai
Whiskey mein daal ke
Aa zara si aag peele
Baahon mein daal ke

Why do you drink ice,
Soaked in whiskey.
Drink the fire in me
Take me in your arms.

The significance of the stanza above has baffled researchers for years. Some say it refers to Prabhujee's cool quotient, while some others opine this to be another genius concoction of a brilliant mind, where the heroine beseeches him to gulp his drink without ice or water. The debate rages on.

Shankar's sister is raped and killed by the bad guys. Again, it has been discussed at length how Prabhujee's on-screen sister is almost always susceptible to this kind of violent end. Prabhujee/Shankar of course, goes on a rampage, sentencing his foes to death: '*Aaj maine tum logo ke maut ki date fix kar di hai. Yaad rakhna – aaj ek tarikh hai, do, chaar, chhay, aath, dus...bus! Intezaar karna.*' (Today I have fixed the date of your death. Remember – today is the first, second, fourth, sixth, eighth, tenth...that's it! Keep waiting.)

He proceeds to methodically dispatch all the illustrious villains to their maker. And unlike your run-of-the-mill vendetta seeker, Shankar does it with a lot of flourish. While ending Ibu Hatela by decapitation, he declares, '*Aaj ke baad koi tujhe Ibu Hatela nahin, Ibu Katela kahega!*' (From this day onwards, you will not be known as Ibu Hatela, but as Ibu Katela!)

There's another electric exchange when Inspector Kale sneers at our hero when he is framed for a murder: '*Jaate thhe Japan, pahuch gaye Cheen – samajh gaye naa?*' (We were headed to Japan, but ended up in China – understood?)

Prabhujee, with a divine smirk, responds, '*Bheegi hui cigarette kabhi jalegi nahin/ Aur yeh tai hai, teri maut ki tarikh kabhi talegi nahin!*' (A wet cigarette never lights. And one thing is for sure, the date of your death will never change.)

When it's known that Inspector Kale will almost certainly be the next one to die, Bulla and Chuttiya sing a rap as a tribute to him: '*Inspector Kale, ab lagnewale/ Tere mooh par maut ke taale/ Kitna bada risk hai, tere maut ki date fix hai/ Chal let jaa, chal mar jaa/ Mar jaa, let ja/ Let jaa, mar jaa.*' (Inspector Kale, soon on your mouth will there be death's *taale* [shackles]/ what big a risk it is, that the date of your death is fixed, come on, lie down, come on die, die, lie down, lie down, die...)

Kale encounters Shankar with a veritable army of white Ambassador cars and policemen. Shankar deftly waltzes between the cars and finishes off each one of them, ending with Inspector Kale. Again, it has to be seen to be believed.

In another celebrated scene, pimp Lucky Chikna has

instituted the world's first hanging brothel, cots hanging on ropes. Bloggers and netizens have long tried to interpret this, some drawing parallels with sex being a heightened sensation of pleasure, and hence beds hanging high (Visions and Perceptions Blog).[*]

Just before the final showdown, Chuttiya breaks the fourth wall once again. Tells the audience how he was not to blame, Bulla was the one who kept giving him pills ('Vitamin Sex': ask a *Gunda* fan), thus instigating him to commit crimes of passion. As destiny (read Prabhujee) would have it, he was killed inside the lavatory, castrated by our man of the moment.

As the film drives toward an epic conclusion, Prabhujee fights a fleet of auto-rickshaws, armoured cars, planes and choppers.

Gunda defines Cult. Or Cult defines *Gunda*. Both may very well be true. Nobody knew when it came to the theatres, ran its course and vanished. But today, every film buff worth their smoking salt has seen, has analysed and ranted about *Gunda* many times over.

If you haven't witnessed this gem or worse, haven't even heard of it, come out from beneath that rock and watch it. *Gunda* is a masterpiece of epic proportions. *Kanti Shah ki jai ho*!

---

[*] See 'Gunda—A Shakespearean Tale of the Existential and Metaphysical', 16 January 2008, http://visionsandperceptions.blogspot.in/2008/01/gunda-shakespearean-tale-of-existential.html

RGV Ki Aag

Sholay, demolished

Release: 2007

Cast: Ajay Devgn, Prashant Raj, Mohanlal, Priyanka Kothari, Sushmita Sen, Sushant Singh, Rajpal Yadav, Gaurav Kapoor, Veerendra Saxena, Abhishek Bachchan, Urmila Matondkar, and Amitabh Bachchan

Directed by: Ram Gopal Varma

Plot Summary: This is what happens when Ram Gopal Varma reimagines *Sholay*. Inspector Narsimha (Mohanlal) recruits Heero (Ajay Devgn) and Raj (Prashant Raj) to bring down gangster Babban (Amitabh Bachchan) who is terrorizing the residents of Kaliganj, which apparently is a Mumbai suburb.

⸺

'I want to remake *Aag*. When I tried to remake *Sholay*, it became *Aag*. If I remake *Aag* it might become *Sholay*.' — Ram Gopal Varma, when asked which film he would like to remake.

It was too good to be true. Every film buff from Kurla to Kalimpong was intrigued. The creator of *Satya* was going to

recreate 'The Greatest Film Ever Made', and that was not all—
Amitabh Bachchan was going to play Gabbar Singh. When
the first look poster with Bachchan in his uber-cool Gabbar
avatar was released, orgasmic shivers ran through the length
and breadth of the country. But it was to last barely a few
months. When the film released, first there was mourning.
Fans shed a tear or two. And then the anger kicked in. How
dare he? How could he? And anger eventually gave way to
ridicule. *RGV Ki Aag*, the cult, was born.

Once Upon a Time, there was a Fanboy

Ram Gopal Varma claims to have an encyclopaedic knowledge
of two motion pictures—*The Godfather* (1972) and *Sholay*
(1975). He knows the smallest of characters, every line, every
scene, every subplot of these two films. And he ended up
reinterpreting both these films as *Sarkar* and *RGV Ki Aag*.
But it's inconceivable that they sprung from the same womb.

Even for a teenager in middle-class Indian household of
the 1970s, Varma watched a lot of films. He watched and
was affected by cinema from a plethora of genres. And one
of them was *Sholay*.

It is part of celluloid mythology that when *Sholay* was
conceived, Sanjeev Kumar was ready to give his right arm for
Gabbar Singh's part in the film. He had his own interpretation
of the character, and reportedly offered to make some radical
changes to his looks in order to portray the bandit. But
Haribhai was known for taking risks and choosing quirky
and unconventional roles (the nine roles in *Naya Din Nai
Raat* [1974], playing Shashi Kapoor's father when he was, in
reality, four months younger to him, and the mute in *Koshish*
[1972]). Even Amitabh Bachchan, whose career had just about
begun and would become an A-list star while *Sholay* was being

shot, found Gabbar Singh's part so salivating that he insisted that the role be given to him. This is interesting, considering that for the next decade and a half, Bachchan didn't shift an inch from his 'image', till old age granted him that flexibility. But the makers of the epic had it clear in their heads who will play what, and that was not to be toyed with—Sanjeev Kumar was Thakur Baldev Singh, Amitabh Bachchan was Jai. Thankfully, better sense prevailed and the role went to yesteryear character actor Jayant's son, Amjad Khan.

Call it irony or quirk of fate that some thirty years later, the role fell into Amitabh's lap, and boy did he scoop it up! He liked Ram Gopal Varma's take on the character, especially the new look that had been designed. Having worked in *Sarkar* together, he knew Varma's style and had faith in him as a director. But above all, he was finally getting to play Gabbar Singh!

In Varma's interpretation of the character, Gabbar was a much older guy, with a face full of battle scars. To reinforce the dread and chilliness, it was suggested that the eyes be of different colour. He was made to wear military uniform and boots. In all, the look of this new Gabbar was…interesting.

So, Amitabh Bachchan who played Jai in the original *Sholay*, played Gabbar in the remake. But was he the only actor from the original to feature in this film? Think again!

Reincarnation

Ram Gopal Varma writes about the genesis of what eventually became *Aag* in his blog. It was Sascha Sippy, G.P. Sippy's grandson and at the helm of Sholay Media and Entertainment Pvt. Limited who gave him a call one fine day and informed that his father, the nonagenarian Vijay Sippy wanted to meet him. Varma gladly agreed. What Sascha broke to him was a fascinating tale in itself. He was interested in making a sequel to *Sholay*, and the story was in place. Here it goes:

In the aftermath of the 'Mehbooba Mehbooba' song, Gabbar Singh and Helen's character (the dancer) indulge in some hanky-panky and out pops Gabbar Junior. Gabbar lands up in jail in the end of *Sholay*. So, it's been thirty years and Junior vows revenge for his father. Veeru and Basanti, who are city-dwellers now, keep coming back to Ramgarh to meet the old Radha (Jaya Bachchan). Junior picks them up and locks them away. This is when Veeru's two sons arrive at Ramgarh to rescue their parents and destroy Gabbar Junior.

And then came the clincher: Sippy wanted him to introduce, in the aforesaid story, a character suitable for Jackie Chan! *Rush Hour* (1998) had been a huge success and its multicultural cast might have been the inspiration behind this interesting thought.

Varma turned it down, but this whole episode got him thinking. What if *Sholay* could be reinterpreted for the modern generation? What if these characters were to exist today? A *Sholay* for the 2000s, so to speak. A noble thought, no doubt.

The *Sholay* title could not be obtained, and Varma thought *Ram Gopal Varma Ke Sholay* would fit the bill nicely. Now to get the players.

Role-call

It was a *Sholay* cast cooked in a meth lab.

> Abhishek Bachchan as Veeru
> Mohit Ahlawat as Jai
> Amitabh Bachchan as Gabbar Singh
> Mohanlal as Thakur Baldev Singh
> Katrina Kaif as Radha
> Suniel Shetty as Sambha

Mohit Ahlawat had been launched by Varma in a film called *James* (2005). Though the film tanked, Mohit was noticed for his brooding intensity, exactly the kind of demeanour that one would expect from a Jai wannabe.

Ram Gopal Varma had already introduced Mohanlal to the Hindi film audiences in *Company* (2002). Though his sheer acting genius saw him through that film, his Hindi diction was a barrier. Mohanlal is known to have seen *Sholay* twice and was all geared to play Thakur.

The most bewildering casting choices in the whole lot, arguably, were Katrina Kaif as Radha and Suniel Shetty as Sambha. Katrina was inconceivable as the docile Radha. But she was firmly on her way to stardom and Varma had worked with her in *Sarkar* (2005). And why Suniel Shetty would want to step in to the shoes of Mac Mohan, is equally mysterious. But after some rewrites, the character of Radha went through some changes and Sushmita Sen stepped in to replace Katrina, while Sushant Singh replaced Suniel Shetty.

The new Jai, Mohit Ahlawat, wasn't too impressed by the way the film was shaping up. One can only marvel at his amazing precognitive skills. Mohit wanted out, and he and Varma reportedly fell out over this, the latter banishing him from any of his future projects. The search for a new Jai had begun.

Prashant Raj Sachdev achieved somewhat of a celebrity status among couch potatoes when he participated in the first season of AXN's show *Amazing Race Asia*. It was a team of two, also featuring fellow supermodel Sahil Shroff. After the show was over, Sachdev was planning to fly down to Los Angeles to meet a friend who was into event management. He got a call from Ram Gopal Varma's office. A long conversation ensued, and Prashant was hired for the role.

The media was abuzz with news that Abhishek Bachchan

was finding it uncomfortable to be able to pull off the action scenes where he had to face off against his own father. But the reality may have been different—Abhishek had a too-good-to-pass offer from Mani Ratnam, a film that required him to age considerably from a man in his twenties to a sixty-year-old. The film was, of course, *Guru*, which came out the same year as *Aag*. So, Abhishek Bachchan walks out, and Chhote Nawab of Pataudi steps in. *The Times of India* reported, 'Veeru in Saif hands'.

Saif was all kicked about it, but in a matter of weeks, he had to quit too. Langda Tyagi beckoned, and the character required him to undergo a major makeover. Veeru's mantle was then taken over by his *Omkara* colleague Ajay Devgn. Varma had earlier recruited Devgn for *Company* (2002) and *Bhoot* (2003). But Devgn's screen persona wasn't exactly sunshine and rainbow, and the Veeru we all know so well was a charmer, so the role had to be rewritten.

Sholay is a brand. I mean, of course it is a brand unto itself, but I don't mean that way. *Sholay* has a trademark, and there's a company that protects it. Honest. Google it and you'll know. So, with *Ram Gopal Varma Ke Sholay*, there was plenty of legal hullabaloo, that culminated into the title changing to *Ram Gopal Varma Ki Aag*. But that's not all, copyright laws also required the character names to be changed. So,

Gabbar Singh became Babban Singh,
Veeru became Heero (Yup, that's how it's spelt)
Jai became Raj
Thakur Baldev Singh became Narsimha
Basanti became Ghungroo
Radha became Durga
Sambha became Tambe

...you get the gist. Even poor Dhanno was not only made into an inanimate auto rickshaw, but also rechristened to Laila.

More than four decades ago, two young men teamed up and carved their insignia across the heart of Bollywood. Salim Khan and Javed Akhtar joined forces as Salim-Javed and changed popular Hindi cinema forever and their most abiding legacy to Indian films, arguably, was *Sholay*. Their trials and tribulations in writing it, and playing an active role in its birth is common knowledge now.

But what massive irony is it that *Ram Gopal Varma Ki Aag* was also written by a successful pair of celebrity writers? Sajid Samji and Farhad Samji, commonly known as Sajid-Farhad, are known for their collaborations with Rohit Shetty. It is from their illustrious stable that *Golmaal Returns* (2008), *All The Best: Fun Begins* (2009), *Golmaal 3* (2010), *Double Dhamaal* (2011), *Housefull 2* (2012), *Chennai Express* (2013) and finally *Dilwale* (2015) have been conceived. But their very first film as writers was Varma's *Shiva* remake called, uncannily, *Shiva* (2006). The very next film they wrote dialogues for was *Aag*.

When Jai and Veeru, erm, Raj and Heero meet the new Soorma Bhopali alias Sambha Bhai, Heero threatens him thus, '*Kaan kholke sun darling, aaj ke baad ek saal tak roz tujhe tapli marenge, aur tu inch inch chhota hota jaayega.*' (Listen carefully — for the next one year, we will keep hitting you on the head, and you will keep getting shorter by an inch every time.) And then the following flashes across the screen: '*365 tapliyon ke baad*' (after 365 knocks on the head), upon which we see our heroes leave Central Jail.

Iconic dialogues from *Sholay* are 'modified'. Babban asks his men, '*Kitne?*' (How many?) instead of the legendary '*Kitne aadmi thay?*' (How many were there?) Ghungroo says, '*Tere ko befizool baat karne ki aadat hai?*' (Are you used to talking nonsense?) Thakur/Narsimha says, '*Loha garam hai...*' (The iron is hot...) and leaves the rest to our imagination. While Gabbar says, '*Tujhe yaad rakhunga,*' Babban says, '*Bhuloonga nahin.*' (I will remember you. I will not forget you.)

Amitabh Bachchan as Gabbar Singh/Babban is supposed to be the big draw of the film. Amitabh Bachchan as an out-and-out villain—it was a huge deal, a second coming of sorts. And evidently Varma thought so too. The open credits declare: '....and introducing: Amitabh Bachchan as Babban'

In *Aag*, when we meet the indomitable Babban, he starts coughing in amusement. Apparently, it was intentional. Varma wanted to replace Gabbar's signature laughter with something equally quirky and impactful. He made him cough.

Babban barks to his men, '*Chaar aadmi chaar goli. Koi nainsaafi nahin.*' (Four bullets for four people. That's only fair!) One would presume claps and whistles were expected at this juncture. But there was utter silence in the theatre. Because everyone was marvelling at the sheer genius unfolding on screen, simultaneously surprised by their own tolerance levels. As Babban himself said, directly contradicting Gabbar Singh, '*Babban ke kahar se tumhe khud Babban bhi nahin bacha sakta.*' (Even Babban himself couldn't save you from Babban's wrath.)

Babban's ramblings were full of contemporary politics as well. *Aag*'s script is generously smattered with Iraq, Al Qaeda, CIA and USA references. Gently stroking a smoking pot of what I assume is tea, he says, '*Saala thanda na karo toh zabaan jal jaata hai. Main woh galti nahin karega jo America Iraq ke saath kiya. Ilaaka unka hai. Bina taiyaari ke jaayega toh...pooh!*' (This damn thing burns your tongue if you don't cool it. Let's not repeat America's blunder at Iraq. It's their land. If we go unprepared, then...pooh!) he pouts his lips. When he kills

Rehmat (Gaurav Kapoor playing the Ahmed-equivalent from Sholay), he mumbles, '*Beqasoor marta hain...America ke haath se, Al Qaeda ke haath se, mere haath se...par hum sabka maqsad kuch aur hain. America ka Al-Qaeda, Al-qaeda ka America, aur mera...Heero aur Raj!*' (It's the innocent who die...whether by America's hands, or Al Qaeda, or by my hands...but our goals are different. America's is Al Qaeda, Al Qaeda's America... and for me it's Heero and Raj!)

The saddest part of *Aag* is not that it attempted to remake one of our greatest films or the fact that it failed spectacularly. It's immeasurably agonizing to see two of India's most celebrated actors reduced to mere puppets in a sideshow. But there are also some (for lack of a better term) could-have-been moments between Mohanlal and Amitabh Bachchan. There's a point where Babban breaks in on Diwali celebrations (udhar Holi, idhar Diwali. Got it?), walks up to Narsimha and quips, 'Hello, Narsu!' then fondles the latter's beard and says, '*Tu buddha ho gaya re...*'. (You're getting old, buddy!) Imagine Gabbar Singh doing that to Thakur. It was almost a Batman-Joker 'You complete me' moment! When Narsimha finds that Babban has killed all his kins and confronts him, Mohanlal's seething anger leaps out of the screen and claws at your face. It's visceral.

Ramu also takes creative liberties. In *Sholay*, Jai played the harmonica, but here Babban does. We already knew about Gabbar Singh's father Hari Singh, but in *Aag* we get to know that Babban has a kid brother as well, named Ambar Singh, played by Sachin. Yeah, the same Sachin who played Ahmed in *Sholay*. In a flashback, Babban sneaks in to his brother's house, with gifts for his nephew. Consumed with love for his brother, Babban was just not Gabbar. He was just a doting elder brother. But Ambar, his goody-two-shoes sibling, will have none of it, and tells him to get lost. Narsimha gets to know about this and gatecrashes the party, holding a gun to Ambar's head. Babban must surrender, or else. But here's where things get murky. Our Thakur/Narsimha turns out to be quite the jerk. Even when Babban gives up, Narsimha shoots Ambar Singh on the chest, killing him instantly. In *Sholay*, the massacre of Thakur's family was Gabbar's way of avenging his arrest and imprisonment. But in *Aag*, Babban's grouse was different—vendetta for his brother.

Release

It was just like when *Sholay* came out. Everybody was in a daze—they couldn't believe what was happening on screen—because they hadn't seen anything quite like it before. And then all hell broke loose. The reviews were particularly caustic. For once, audiences and film critics saw eye to eye. Rajeev Masand wrote:[*]

> Much-loved moments from *Sholay* are parodied by Varma and for that, you want to wring his neck. One of the most memorable scenes in *Sholay* in which Dharmendra as Veeru climbs up the watertank and threatens to jump down to his death is turned around in this film with Ajay Devgan playing Hero, pulling a pistol to his head threatening to shoot himself. How you wish he'd pulled the trigger and spared us all the agony.

Raja Sen said, on Rediff.com wrote:[**] 'It's kinda fitting that Gabbar is now called Babban. Because *Ram Gopal Varma Ki*

---

[*]'RGV Ki Aag is RGV ka daag', http://www.rajeevmasand.com/uncategorized/review-rgv-ki-aag-is-rgv-ka-daag/

[**]'Ram Gopal Varma ki.. Aargh!', http://www.rediff.com/movies/2007/aug/31aag.htm

Aag, ladies and gentlemen, as its title suggests, is a B-movie.... As Devgan pulls a pistol to his head to make suicide threats, we sorely wish he'd pull the trigger.'

The much-scorned scene was Ramu paying a tribute to the 'soo-cide' water tank scene from *Sholay*. (One of the things that have puzzled *Sholay* fanatics all over the world was how the water tank really worked in a village with no electricity — all those lamps in Thakur's haveli means there's no power, right?) As the tune of 'Jeena Yahaan, Marna Yahaan' plays in the background, Heero leans against a well and promises to shoot himself if 'Gangu Mummy' doesn't allow Ghungroo to marry him. Yes, 'Mausi' from *Sholay* had transformed into 'Gangu Mummy'. As Heero screams that it'll be cold blooded murder if he were to die, someone steps up and reminds him that it will be a suicide, not murder. It was murder all right.

When the film was launched, there was a humongous amount of hype around the fact that Amitabh Bachchan was playing Gabbar Singh. Fanboys were drooling. When it released, *Aag* was a debacle of monstrous proportions. Over the years, it has become a pet hate and film-lovers — RGV included — use it as a benchmark to slander bad films.

No Smoking

King, Kashyap and Kafka

Release: 2007

Cast: John Abraham, Ayesha Takia, Paresh Rawal, Ranvir Shorey

Directed by: Anurag Kashyap

Plot Summary: K (John Abraham) is haunted by demons of his own making. A compulsive smoker, he is referred to 'Prayogshaala' helmed by Baba Bangali, to cure him of his addiction. Baba and his minions make it clear that smoking will cost him dearly. K learns the hard way that Baba was not joking. Every puff poses grave to not only to him but everyone he holds dear.

⁊

This book owes its origin, at least in part, to Anurag Kashyap's 2007 film *No Smoking*. I was in my mid-twenties, suitably confused and angsty, slightly bored. In short, for a twenty-something, I was completely in character. I had been fascinated by an Abbas Tyrewala interview in a film magazine where he spoke about the process of writing *Maqbool*. So when I discovered his blog, I started lapping up his posts written with his inimitable flair. One of the posts that particularly jabbed me on the nose and had it bleeding was a piece titled 'Surely you're joking, Mr Kashyap'.

Social Media hadn't yet strained our nerves and snapped our necks, and the Internet was a more inclusive place. Without having to articulate in 140 characters, people could speak freely and elaborate their points. It was the era of online forums and blogs.

So, coming back to Abbas Tyrewala's post. It was a tribute to the resolve and free spirit of this man called Anurag Kashyap, whose name sounded familiar (*Satya*, *Black Friday*). Tyrewala waxes on about how Kashyap went all out to make an Indian film noir and the now legendary story of what he had to encounter at the Censor Board. Finally, an underdog film-maker, if there was one. Kashyap's story was admirable, inspiring and goosebump-inducing. I just had to look him up. I landed up on a blog-post written by him, on a website called PassionForCinema.com.

No Smoking Diaries
Kashyap blogged about his experiences conceiving, pitching, selling and making this pet project called *No Smoking*. He wrote with an abandon and candour rarely seen in film-wallahs. And never been seen ever since. Those who followed Kashyap's posts religiously and interacted with him on the comments section would vouch for it. PassionForCinema (PFC) was a platform for film buffs to not only write but interact with others like them, and speak with unbridled passion about cinema—whether it was about Benegal or Bachchan, *Parinda* or *Pather Panchali*—it didn't matter. And Anurag Kashyap was

the incredibly benevolent emperor of this domain. So much so, that people started calling it his blog, which it wasn't.

His trials and tribulations while making *No Smoking* was being laid down on PFC, in Anurag's typical stream-of-consciousness style. He pulled no punches, held nothing back at all. It read nothing like a promotional exercise, it did not have the finesse or artfulness so common in such endeavours. It was a clumsy, disjointed, straight-from-the-heart account of how the film came into being.

The genesis of *No Smoking* goes back to Anurag Kashyap's mentor Ram Gopal Varma, the deity of all things irreverent and rebellious in Hindi cinema of late nineties to the early 2000s, and his horror anthology *Darna Mana Hai*. One of the stories starred Saif Ali Khan, a chain-smoker in the film, landing up at a motel where the owner is the sworn enemy of smokers. It was one of the most compelling stories in the film. The section was titled *No Smoking*. Much before this, while shooting *Satya*, Varma had sounded off the story with Kashyap. Kashyap loved it, but it also inspired in him another story idea about smoking. When he shared the concept with Ram Gopal Varma, he burst out laughing and dismissed it as outrageous.

When Kashyap's *Paanch* didn't show any signs of finding release, he was desperately looking to make a film that would see the light of the day. He had been fiddling with the 'No Smoking' concept since long, and decided to bounce the idea off others to see if anyone is interested in backing such a film. He named it *Cigarette Smoking Is Injurious to Health* and met Boney Kapoor with the idea. What Kapoor said upon hearing the concept would summarize what most of the industry thought about *No Smoking* even after its release, 'Go back to the planet you came from!' Actor Kay Kay Menon, the lead actor in *Paanch,* actually loved the idea, but he believed it was incomplete.

Raja Chaudhary, the hero of Anurag's later film *Gulaal* and his assistant on *Black Friday*, was at that time writing a short film in which he wanted Anurag to act. The story was about a compulsive smoker who wakes up one morning to find he was out of cigarettes. But there is a curfew outside and there is no way he can get a smoke for himself. Anurag loved it and agreed to do the role on the condition that Raja allowed him to complete his own script, incorporating elements from Raja's story.

Even those producer friends and acquaintances Anurag narrated it to, loved the narration but believed the project needed a star to back it. On narrating the idea to Angad Paul, the producer of Guy Ritchie's *Lock, Stock and Two Smoking Barrels* (1998) and *Snatch* (2000), he too felt that an A-list star was required. He placed his bets on Shah Rukh Khan. But there was no way Anurag would have anyone but Kay Kay Menon do it. After all, Kay Kay sailed with him through *Paanch* and was one of the few people who liked the concept and was ready to act in it. At this time, Anurag was at his lowest ebb—*Black Friday* was stalled on the day of release, *Gulaal* couldn't get a backer. The downward spiral began and Kashyap started drinking heavily and was sinking into depression. That's when Kay Kay's wife, Nivedita Bhattacharya told him to do whatever it takes to make and release a film, even if it means going ahead without Kay Kay.

Anurag Kashyap gathered all the confidence and courage left in him and went to see Shah Rukh Khan. Shah Rukh and he had been to the same college—Hans Raj College, Delhi. Kashyap studied zoology while Shah Rukh was pursuing a Bachelor's degree in Economics, only five years apart.

Shah Rukh Khan graduated in 1988, Kashyap in 1993. There was another connection: the college hockey team. Khan was the captain of the team, while Kashyap the vice captain, during their respective stints. Khan was preparing for *Don* at the time, he received Anurag warmly and listened to his story. He seemed to like the idea but advised him to stay away from such experimentation till he reached a position to do so. Anurag left again, empty handed.

Another blow to him was the stalling of *Gulaal* after a large portion of the film was shot. He had no clue who to turn to. It was then that as if by divine intervention, two people stepped in, who would eventually make *No Smoking* possible. Deepa Mehta's *Water* (2005) — the third and last instalment in her 'Elements Trilogy' that includes *Fire* (1996) and *Earth* (also known as *1947: Earth,* 1998) — had been made and released in Canada, and John Abraham's performance was being spoken about. Anurag had worked on the screenplay of the film, and it occurred to him to make a last ditch attempt by speaking to Abraham about the story idea he was nurturing all this while. John absolutely loved it. Since Kashyap didn't have a producer for the project, Abraham reached out to UTV, but they thought it to be too weird. In a while, Vishal Bhardwaj called Kashyap and wanted to know if he was interested to do a film with him. Anurag Kashyap narrated the smoking concept — Vishal instantly took a liking to it, and invited him over to the sets of *Omkara* for a narration to his producer, Kumar Mangat. On hearing the narration, Kumar was on board, and suggested casting Saif Ali Khan, who played the smoker in *Darna Mana Hai* (2003) and was doing Langda Tyagi in *Omkara*. But Kashyap was insistent that if it had to be made, it will be made with John only, considering he was the first actor to believe in the project and stand by him.

Symbolism in *No Smoking*

Probably the two most indulgent, intensely personal films included in this book are *Kaagaz Ke Phool* and *No Smoking*. Before you grimace and scowl and express your disappointment at this assertion, I would say I am not comparing these films; they couldn't be more different thematically and content-wise. But they were both inseparably wrapped around the lives of their makers and reflected their state of mind, and had very little to do with audience expectations and market forces. When Kashyap was writing *No Smoking*, he was angered, frustrated and shocked at the absurdity and machinations of the world around him. The fate of his debut *Paanch* was sealed, and his conversation with the Censor Board members is part of cinema legend. He was told that since cinema meant healthy entertainment, *Paanch* could not be allowed to be seen. Based on the Joshi-Abhayankar Murder Case, *Paanch* happens to be one of the most exciting films made on the nature of crime and criminals. It was the story of a bunch of youngsters who were part of a rock band whose rebellious nature and ambitions often put them at odds with the society. Led by the quirky, sociopathic Luke Morrison, one reckless night culminates in murder, and they are on the run. Greed, lust, jealousy and blind rage drive a wedge between them and they find themselves fighting each other as well. The film is yet to be released, but courtesy the Internet, everyone who cared to look for it, has seen the film, and those who have, not only swear by the film, but also its music. Some believe it to be the best rock album to have come out of Bollywood, ever.

Paanch never released, *Black Friday* was taken off theatres on the day of its official release, *Gulaal* began shooting but got stuck. To make matters worse, the Press refused to get off Anurag's back. He was labelled a jinxed director, and nobody was ready to work with him. It was almost as if the world had conspired not to let him say what he wanted to say. And it is this straitjacketing and stifling of individual voices that form the crux of *No Smoking*.

The film was made and promoted as an anti-smoking film. The censors cleared it, the Health Ministry lauded it, and even John Abraham kept reinforcing the 'social message' during promotions. By his own admission, Kashyap fooled the Censor Board into believing it was supposed to discourage people from smoking. After so many setbacks, he wanted the film to be released, and in the shape and form that he intended. And he pulled it off, and nobody realized till they couldn't do much about it.

All of it boils down to this: Smoking is about personal liberty (it does amount to self-harm but you are doing it to yourself with full knowledge of the risks), and the 'system' that will stop at nothing to get the hero K to quit. The 'system' consists of a godman, Baba Bangali Sealdahwale and his minions, K's wife Anjali, others like him who have been 'turned'—his friend Abbas Tyrewalla and his doctor. Kashyap's introduction to world literature was through Franz Kafka's *The Trial,* and its protagonist Josef K. seeps into *No Smoking* as simply K. Just like Josef K. was ostracized for his unknown crime by the powers that be, K from *No Smoking* has the whole world conspiring to keep him from his cigarette, even if it means doling out increasingly dire punishments, and eventually, robbing him of his soul. K is for Kashyap, K is for Kafka, and K is also for King. Stephen King. *No Smoking* also owes its origin to Stephen King's short story *Quitters' Inc.,* about a shady entity that would go to any lengths to make you to quit smoking. If adapted faithfully, this would have been the ideal anti-smoking film, but in Kashyap's film, the story of the smoker and Prayogshala – Baba Bangali's outfit – is just a device, a shell which cocoons the real story. A story about attempting to silence independent voices by the powerful godmen, making use of the oppressed – (the dwarf, the burqa clad women and the teeka-toting fanatics). There are plenty of references to World War II and Fascism – for example, the opening and closing scene in Siberia, and Anjali watching *Schindler's List*. The fingers being cut also refer to the writer rendered unable to hold a pen, and hence unable to express himself.

We all know how *No Smoking* was released and almost universally panned by Indian critics and audiences alike – it was widely acclaimed in the West. But even in India, a relatively small group of film lovers were intrigued by the film. They started writing about it online, with their own interpretation of the story. And in the months and years that followed, that group only kept getting bigger and bigger. *No Smoking* is probably the only film that has lent itself to so many interpretations and analyses. Someone proposed that the whole film was one big dream sequence – K was just hallucinating; another believed that like the German legend of *Faust* who made a pact with the devil, K was supposed to sign off his soul by signing the huge contract Baba Bangali presents to him. This is what film journalist and human rights activist, Pavithra Selvam wrote in her review for AOL Bollywood[*]:

> Analysing K's hallucinations and psyche is the most interesting aspect of the movie. Most of his hallucinations

---

[*]The original article no longer exists but Selvam quoted it on Quora; see https://www.quora.com/What-is-your-interpretation-of-Anurag-Kashyaps-movie-No-Smoking. Her interpretation was commended by Kashyap and featured on the *No Smoking* DVD cover as well.

are used as metaphors which draw parallels to real world scenarios. For instance, the theme of the movie, smoking itself is used as a metaphor to show how clouded the human mind can get. John Abraham's narcissist behaviour in the film alludes to how self-centered our lives can get in the mad race we run everyday to reach the inscrutable. John Abraham's illusion of his wife Anjali turning to his desirable secretary, Annie refers to the desires that consume the human self. The film is a tribute to how we end up losing our souls and forget to keep in touch with ourselves by neglecting to do small humane acts that would make our lives worth living for. It also refers to the natural order of the world that good prevails where evil is quashed by the superior power.

No Smoking is a tad difficult to follow (the biggest understatement you will find in this entire book; I like to sensationalize), especially for the regular Bollywood moviegoer. But even by those standards, one would feel the outright dismissal of the film was a bit harsh. Even unfair.

The film was a conclusive failure at the box office. But few other Hindi films have been dissected, analysed, and discussed the way *No Smoking* has been. There are fan theories aplenty, spread across scores of blogs and online forums. Every film buff worth their salt has had their own take on what the film tried to say.

Deshdrohi

No identification with actual persons

Release: 2008

Cast: Kamaal Rashid Khan (KRK), Gracy Singh, Hrishitaa Bhatt, Kader Khan, Manoj Tiwari, Ranjeet, Zulfi Syed, Raza Murad, Nirmal Pandey, Aman Verma, Yashpal Sharma, Aryan Vaid

Directed by: Jagdish A. Sharma

Plot Summary: Raja (Kamaal R. Khan) comes to Mumbai in search of work, but gets embroiled in a web of corruption and dirty politics. Soon, he realizes he needs to take things in his own hands, while making it a point to sashay with Sonia (Gracy Singh) and Neha (Hrishitaa Bhatt).

⁓

When a film begins with a note saying it bears no 'identification with actual persons' and ends with one that says 'THE BEGINING', you know there's something special about it. As the film unspools its layers before you, it's impossible not to be swayed by the grandeur of it all. More than a film, *Deshdrohi* is an experience without precedence in the annals of Hindi cinema. It gave us not only an extremely gifted actor who turned into a star overnight, but also one of the most revered film critics and trade analysts this country has known: Kamaal Rashid Khan, aka KRK.

When the trailers came out, it was almost too good to be true. One film that huddled three heroines together, all of whom had worked with the Khans in their heydays: Gracy Singh (*Lagaan*), Hrishitaa Bhatt (*Asoka*), and Kim Sharma (*Mohabbatein*). And the <cough> <cough> towering presence of KRK, spouting prophetic lines like, '*Aaj tumhaare dar se Mumbai chhodoon, kal kissi aur ke dar se Dilli chhodoon, phir ek din kahoge ki Hindustan chhod do!*' (If I leave Mumbai for fear of you — tomorrow I'll leave Delhi scared of someone else... and then one day I will be forced to leave the country!) And with the possible exception of Ashok Kumar, nobody ever fights the way KRK does — no sir.

Running Away

KRK hit the ground running, quite literally. *Deshdrohi* begins with a shot of KRK running through the fields of Gorakhpur, and the screen reads 'Introducing: Kamaal R Khan (KRK)', decidedly heralding the arrival of a star. But were we really witnessing this genius for the first time? Was this indeed Kamaal's introduction? Kamaal Rashid Khan had appeared in a Bhojpuri film with his *Deshdrohi* co-stars Manoj Tiwari, Ranjeet and Raza Murad, called *Munna Pandey Berozgar* (2007). So, *Deshdrohi* was still technically his Hindi film debut then? Not really.

Something inexplicable happened to director Partho Ghosh, post the 1990s. Ever since his feature debut with *100 Days* (1991) right up to *Yugpurush* (1998), Ghosh had never made a film sans mainstream stars. His career was sprinkled with films like *Dalaal* (1993), *Teesra Kaun?* (1994), *Agni Sakshi* (1996), *Kaun Sachcha Kaun Jhootha* (1997) and *Ghulam-E-Mustafa* (1997). But after that, he seemed to have turned over a new leaf and churned out one trashy pearl after another: *Khote Sikkey* (1998), *Chetna: The Excitement* (2005), *Mr. Hot Mr. Kool* (2007) and *Meri Life Mein Uski Wife* (2009). Among these gems was a film called *Sitam* (2004), starring Tara Sharma. The credits declared: 'Introducing: Kamaal.' And there's more. Dialogues were credited to Mehmood Ali and a certain 'Rashid Kamaal', lyrics were attributed to 'Kamaal', and finally the producer was 'Kamal'. If this is not sheer unadulterated genius, what is?

And believe me, we have only scratched the surface of this giant institution called KRK. A little digging on the Internet will unearth a 2005 video interview[*] of the producer of *Sitam,* a strikingly different looking Kamaal Rashid Khan. In the interview, he shyly admits his inability to speak Hindi, and lays down the film's plot in flawless English: 'It is a lou-shtory, with the message that okay, you can't decide about a girl by her cloths what she's wiyaring—if she is wiyaring short cloths or she is smoking or she is drinking it's not mean that she is a bad girl. And if one girl is having full dress, she is wearing sari or something you can't say that okay she will be good girl. So, anyone can be good and bad, you can't decide but the dress only.' He goes on to explain that he has written the dialogues as well as the lyrics of the film, also adding, 'I am playing the billlen in the mobie, yes.' Well in the movie, we have a different, more reined-in version of KRK. He will remind you of Zayed Khan's long-locks look from *Main Hoon Na* (2004), only with more style and angst.

---

*See https://www.youtube.com/watch?v=pbZr-stfKPA&t=130s

And imagine writing dialogues and songs in a language you can't even speak! As I said, genius. But this genius blossomed and flowered in full bloom only three years later, once he had brushed up his Hindi.

Coming back to *Deshdrohi*, our hero Raja (KRK) starts running from Gorakhpur and lands up in Mumbai. Mumbai of course is this hotbed of crime where goons in t-shirt and jeans pounce on innocent shopkeepers soliciting money. One such shopkeeper who says he has no money was shown just a minute ago peddling drugs. The goons start beating him to pulp, and that's when our heroine makes her entry. Astride a motorcycle, Gracy Singh breaks into the scene and fights the said goons. Raja, who is watching from a distance, munching on chana and going 'O teri!' now and then, is besotted by her and quips, '*Chehre pe itni rawaangi aur bholapan, maar-peet mein number one!*' (Such an innocent face, yet a number one fighter!) After a round of spectacular jumping and flying and landing on people's shins, Gracy leaves. Of course, she didn't forget to leave her handkerchief behind. Raja picks it up and another priceless nugget leaves his lips: '*Lagta hai itihaas ke panno se nikal kar Maharani Laxmibai khud Mumbai aa gayi hai.*' (It is as if the great queen Laxmibai has come out of the pages of history and landed up in Mumbai.) And we are instantly transported to a desert, where KRK in a dapper white jacket and trousers serenades Gracy in a red sari. Udit Narayan sings for Khan, and his dancing is a sight for sore eyes. One can only marvel at this peerless display of talent.

Raja is having vada paav. It's bright and sunny. Vada paav vendor quarrels with Raja. It's evening. Vendor slaps Raja. Voila, it's daylight again! Such cinematic brilliance permeates throughout the film! Raja is in Mumbai in search of his friend Shekhar, played by Bhojpuri superstar Manoj Tiwari. He is told by a magnanimous gentleman (Kader Khan) that he should look for his friend in Jogeshwari, as everyone from U.P. and Bihar lives there. One flashback, two songs and a fight later, Raja reaches Jogeshwari and sure enough, bumps into Shekhar in a matter of seconds.

Raja gets beaten up so many times that if I didn't know better, I'd almost believe that he had a fetish for that sort of thing. He is thrashed by his father back at his village for no apparent reason, thrown from the bus for not having change and calling the conductor 'bhaiya' (I will come back to 'bhaiya' later), beaten by the goons in the market for not allowing them to freeload. And we are not even halfway through the film. Each time something like this happens, KRK lets out a cry of agony quite unparalleled in world cinema. I call it the 'moan-scream'. Like *The Matrix*, no one can be told what the moan-scream is. You have to hear it for yourself.

When the goons are stomping all over Raja, Sonia (Gracy Singh) is back with her bike and fights with them again, but is soon overpowered. They are about to kill her with a toy gun, and Raja can't be just an onlooker this time. He urges people to help her, '*Arre usse koi bachao! Dekho ek lachar aurat par zulm ho raha hai. Arre aap log aiye na! Arre bachaiye na ussko! E bhai! Woh usse maar denge...arre koi toh aaiye...*' (Someone please help her! Look, a helpless woman is being tortured. Please come forward and help her...brothers! They will kill her! Anybody...please come forward...) Here again the method actor in KRK comes to the fore. His helplessness brings to mind Dilip Kumar's visceral cries for help in *Mashaal* when his wife is dying in the middle of the road. Utter blasphemy, you say? You have no idea.

When he realizes people are not going to help, Raja decides to take matters in his own hands. It is then that his superpowers are revealed. He takes flight, and hurls the guy holding the toy gun. KRK grimaces at the camera, telling you that he's really, really angry. Another goon starts at him, and KRK gets on his knees, slides to him and punches him straight in the family jewels. He gets into a scuffle with the leader of the pack, and ends up killing him with the toy gun. Sonia hurriedly takes him to her pad, where he laments how his Daadu wanted him to be '*Kanoon ka rakhwala*' (protector of law) and there he was, a '*mujrim*' (criminal) instead. It's really cathartic to watch KRK weep. You are sad. So sad that you want to gouge your eyes out.

From this point on, a new character is introduced every two minutes. There's encounter specialist Rajesh 'Killing Machine' Sharma (Shiva Rindani), who has killed '*ab tak pachpan*' (55 till now), just one short of a certain Sadhu Agashe. There's Rajan Naik (Mukesh Tiwari), the politician brother of the goon Raja ended up killing, there's Baba Kadam aka 'Problem Shooter' (Yashpal Sharma), leader of National Public Party and the messiah of north Indian immigrants Sanjay Narayan Srivastav (Aman Varma), Inspector Rohit Raghav (Zulfi Sayed), and so on.

Regionalism is a central theme in *Deshdrohi*. One of the most productive uses of the hours at your disposal is to count the number of times the word 'Bhaiya' has been used in the film in a derogatory sense. I lost track after twenty-five. While running from the cops, Raja runs into people beating alleged immigrants. After beating them with a plank of wood, Raja says, '*Jitni nafrat tumhare liye hamaare dil mein hai, usse zyaada pyaar tumhare liye hamaare seene mein hain!*' (We have more love for you in our hearts than the hatred you have for us in your minds!) *Deshdrohi* was banned in Maharashtra, but you cannot keep a classic down for long.

Sonia introduces us to her mute brother—'*Aaj tak maine jo kuch bhi kiya hai, isike khatir kiya hai. Yahin mera sab kuch hai, mere jeene ka maqsad.*' (Whatever I have done in my life, I've done it for him. He means the world to me, the very purpose of my life.) In an epic twist, the unnamed brother is shot by the Killing Machine, and Sonia abandons his body and within minutes, breaks into a romantic song with Raja.

Rajan sends for his shooter Kaalia to dispatch Raja. Kaalia is—wonder of wonders—Raja's friend Shekhar. Raja is only too happy to see Shekhar, and is about to embrace him when Shekhar aka Kaalia points a gun at him and goes, '*Aaj tumhe mujhe nahin, maut ko gale lagaana hai. Mera naam Kaalia hai, aur Kaalia ka matlab maut.*' (It is not me but death that you will be embracing today. My name is Kaalia, and Kaalia means death!) Kaalia shoots. Raja again does the legendary moan-scream and drops to the ground with a lot of flourish. As Raja lies bleeding on the ground, Sonia asks people for help, and as expected, the heartless people of Mumbai refuse any assistance. Sonia obtains a vegetable cart and carries Raja to the hospital and gets the reluctant doctor to operate on him at gunpoint.

After many trials and tribulations, just as you wrap your mouth around the cold nozzle and are about to pull the trigger, you realize KRK has finally reached climax. Of the film. In a showdown with the netas (read Deshdrohis), he emerges from beneath the ground, armed with toy explosives so no one can shoot him. In a deeply poignant scene, he asks said netas to sing the Indian national anthem. The netas try and flounder. KRK kills them anyway. The crowd roots for our hero, but he stops them and delivers a moving speech about not taking law into your own hands and hands himself over to the police. 'THE BEGINING'.

Deshdrohi remains a marvel of moviemaking and acting. It's been a decade since its release, and KRK is now a force to reckon with. His fans will vouch for the fact that had he not taken a break from acting and switched to reviewing films, all the Khans and Roshans and Kapoors would have had to hang up their boots.

Word on the street is, there's a sequel on the way. Has been for quite some time. KRK offered Mr Bachchan to be a part of the project. We live in hope.

You can put that gun down now. And stop laughing.

Joginder, The Magnificent

It was the late 1990s. Doordarshan, after dominating drawing rooms for years together, was slowly receding into the background. Despite a few popular shows now and then, the 'Golden Age of DD' was a thing of the past. Cable TV had arrived, and with its plethora of channels, viewers were spoilt for choice.

Around this time, a young man in his early twenties was hosting a show that was silently (and unwittingly) sowing the seeds of a mini-revolution. This man, in his own way, would change the face of film appreciation in India, or at least the way B-movies were perceived. That man was Sajid Khan. Sajid of the many *Housefull*s and a *Himmatwalla*. Back in the day, he anchored a show called 'Kehne Mein Kya Harj Hai' on Sony TV. In an era where most 'mainstream' Bollywood movies were scoffed at, Sajid Khan's show managed to both poke fun at and celebrate popular cinema, all at the same time. To quote from the *India Today* issue dated 6 October 1997[*]: 'Khan says it's "*Mad* magazine on TV". The programme brings out the funnier details of films which viewers may have otherwise missed. Like how humorous hamming can

---

[*]'Laugh it off', http://indiatoday.intoday.in/story/sajid-khan-now-has-a-new-show-kehne-mein-kya-harj-hai-on-sony/1/274940.html

be or how Hollywood could have found inspiration in Hindi cinema.'

In the course of regaling us with hamming escapades of character actors, or even A-list stars, sometimes, Sajid Khan introduced us to ham-king, Joginder. In a way, this would prove to be Sajid's abiding legacy to film buffs. Today, Joginder is worshipped with unwavering devotion across countless online forums like Facebook and Twitter, and screenings of his work are staged from time to time. Hindi film buffs across the board swear by his name and his films.

Who is Joginder Shelly?

Joginder Shelly hailed from Punjab. Born in Khanewal in undivided Punjab, he moved to Bombay in the 1960s. Like countless youngsters, he was in the city of dreams harbouring hopes of a career in films.

IMDb.com lists his first film as *Hum Hindustani* (1960) starring Sunil Dutt, Joy Mukerjee and Helen. The film encapsulated the dreams of a newly resurgent India, in the form of the song *Chhodo kal ki baatein/ Kal ki baat puraani*. Joginder, for some reason, was credited as 'Yogendra'.

Next up, was the swashbuckler *Saat Samundar Paar* with Dara Singh, in 1965. In the following years, there were a host of walk-in parts and bit roles: *Heer Ranjha* (1970), *Purab Paschim* (1970), *Chandan* (1971), *Bachpan* (1970), *Wafaa* (1978) and *Hungama* (1971).

Joginder had no dearth of work. And yet satisfaction eluded him—the prolific film-maker in him was waiting to emerge. By the time of *Heer Ranjha*, he had moved from being Yogendra to Joginder. But he was not cut out to be happy playing only the neighbourhood goon or barmy cop. He was too talented for that.

The 'Age of Joginder' began in right earnest in the year 1972 with a film called *Bindiya Aur Bandook*.

The Dot and the Gun

Roger Corman, despite being a B-grade moviemaker himself, is known to have introduced some of the greatest names in Hollywood—Martin Scorsese, Ron Howard, Peter Bogdanovich, Jack Nicholson, Peter Fonda and James Cameron being some of them.

If one were to draw an Indian comparison, the name of Shibu Mitra will invariably come up. He single-handedly caused the launch of Govinda (*Ilzaam*, 1986) and Chunky Pandey (*Aag hi Aag*, 1987). He also helmed one of Neetu Singh's first films as heroine: *Shatranj Ke Mohre* (1974). Shibu Mitra also made India's only adaptation of Zorro, called—you guessed it right—*Zorro* (1975; but you probably could never guess that Navin Nischol played Zorro)!

When young Joginder was striving to find his foothold in the industry, Mitra had just graduated from the FTII and started assisting another celebrated FTII alumni who was directing films, Basu Chatterjee. Mitra assisted Chatterjee on his debut *Saara Akash* (1969) and then on *Piya Ka Ghar* (1972).

Meanwhile, Joginder decided to take things in his own hands. He had his own vision and style, and it was high time he saw his own films made. It's still unclear who approached whom, but Shibu Mitra and Joginder decided to make a film together. Joginder was to produce, and Mitra would direct the film. *Bindiya Aur Bandook* was conceived. This was the beginning of a long, rewarding partnership. On online platforms, it has been insinuated that Joginder ghost-directed most of their films, but there's no way to validate this.

A lot of new faces were enrolled for *Bindiya Aur Bandook*,

names that would make a mark later on: Kiran Kumar, Raza Murad, Asha Sachdev. Kiran Kumar and Raza Murad went on to chart an illustrious career in on-screen villainy, while Asha Sachdev was second only to Aruna Irani in the sheer prolificity of playing sisters and prostitute-with-a-heart-of-gold routine.

Bindiya Aur Bandook spoke of a village infested with bandits, and of how the villagers were finally freed from their oppression.

Three years later, Hindi cinema was taken by a storm that it is yet to recover from. A storm named *Sholay*. One cannot conceive of saying anything more about this phenomenon than what has already been said, many times over. But in its own unique way, *Sholay* played an interesting part in our story.

Sholay is believed to have drawn inspiration from John Sturges' *The Magnificent Seven*, which in turn was inspired by Akira Kurosawa's magnum opus *Shinichin No Samurai* (*Seven Samurai*). Parallels are also drawn with Raj Khosla's *Mera Gaon Mera Desh* (the basic plot of a daaku (dacoit)-oppressed village to be rescued by a conman, similarities with the villain, Jabbar Singh and the very Thakur-like armless mentor/recruiter). Between this journey from Kurosawa to Sturges to Ramesh Sippy and possibly Raj Khosla, somehow Joginder comes in. When *Sholay* released, Joginder claimed to have noticed some plot similarities with *Bindiya Aur Bandook*, and dragged the makers to court. Now, one might think it was a deliberate act of fame-mongering. But Joginder actually believed *Sholay* was a rip-off of his film. On yet another of Sajid Khan's shows called 'Ikke Pe Ikka', there was a full-blown interview with Joginder about this. While Sajid couldn't resist guffawing every time Joginder opened his mouth to say something, the latter vehemently defended his claim and elaborated on his reasons.

And the cult of *Bindiya Aur Bandook* doesn't end here. Back in his heydays, Joginder's fans (also his target audience) were among the teeming millions in the slums and villages of India. Today, it's the urbane cinema-junkies and bloggers spread throughout the world. One of them is Todd Stadtman, a blogger from San Francisco, who has written much-loved pieces on Joginder's *Ranga Khush* and *Pyasa Shaitan*. In one of his posts[*], Stadtman draws parallels between Amrish Puri's iconic quip 'Mogambo khush hua!' and Joginder's (almost) equally celebrated utterance 'Ranga khush!' from *Bindiya Aur Bandook*. In fact, this phrase became so famous in the hinterland that Joginder couldn't help making another classic with it as the title.

Ranga Khush!!

Bindiya Aur Bandook was a big success with its target audience. Joginder developed his own dedicated fan following, those who didn't miss a single movie that had his name on it. And over time, he also cultivated his own style: a weird staccato laughter and sing-song voice, quite unique in the annals of Hindi cinema.

Just like the other film, just like most of Joginder's films, *Ranga Khush* too was about a village and a gang of bandits. But this time, he himself was captain of the ship—he not only wrote and produced the film but also directed it.

And as always, Joginder had no dearth of stars: Aruna Irani, Nazneen, Bharat Bhushan, Dheeraj Kumar et al. He

---

[*]'Die, Danger, Die, Die, Kill,' 5 September 2009, http://diedangerdiediekill.blogspot.in/2009/09/ranga-khush-india-1975.html

plays Ranga, a dreaded dacoit who terrorizes the village in question. The villagers, in true-blue Bollywood style, beseech their Gods to redeem them. One of the villagers is Devi, a devout do-gooder who is kidnapped by Ranga from the temple. Devi, at first, is repulsed by the bandit but in a change of heart, takes it upon herself to change this man for the better. Does she achieve this by turning him in or brainwashing him to do so himself? No, Sir. She has a better idea—she marries him! On the nuptial bed, within a couple of minutes screen time, Ranga turns over a new leaf as if by magic. And this is where the film takes an extremely 'Joginderesque' twist.

A lady in black robes appears out of thin air and reprimands Ranga for his weakness. She warns him that his deceased mentor would come back to haunt him, unless he carries out his 'duties'. From time to time, this apparition would appear and egg him on to fulfil his destiny.

There's more campy treasure in *Ranga Khush* than one could hope to find in a single film—a crimson-red statue of Ranga's mentor, also called Ranga, three half-naked children in a cave (*paap ka beta, zulm ki aulaad* [son of sin, child of oppression]), Joginder's weird look (a furry overcoat with a menacing bushy moustache and a mop of unruly hair), suitably trashy dialogues (*'Ranga majboor. Ranga ko yeh nahin manzoor. Ranga ko kar do nanga. Maaro danda. Phir bhi nahin batayega Ranga!'* [Ranga is helpless. Ranga does not like this. Strip him and hit him with a rod. Yet Ranga won't speak a word.]), an arch nemesis called Ratna, a fight sequence between Hanuman and Ranga, and a coterie of uncouth daakus.

What stands out in *Ranga Khush*, despite the campiness, despite the cheesy dialogues, is Joginder Shelly's unrestrained performance as Ranga. And from this film on, he would be called the 'Ed Wood of India', a nod to his trashy and minimalistic filmmaking style. A reputation that will only be reinforced with future films. Joginder had finally arrived, but Sundance was yet to happen.

Lota in Sundance

Sundance, potty rap, lota dance—it's known by many names, but none of them can match the quirkiness of the phenomenon itself. It was a huge hit when Sajid Khan unleashed it to the word on his show 'Kehne Mein Kya Harj Hai'. Today, film buffs and cult film enthusiasts swear by its massive impact on pop culture.

It's from a film called *Teen Ikkey* (1980). Joginder played Rocky, a Bollywood caricature of a devout catholic. Of course, he liked to call himself 'Raaki'. Now 'Raaki' is telling his girlfriend how '*Saara khudai ek side hotaa, Joru ka bhaai ek side hotaa!*' (All divinity on one side, and wife's brother on the other side!) Somehow while making this deep philosophical observation in chaste Hindi, Joginder aka Raaki decides to blow wind, letting out a terrible stench. When his girlfriend protests with a grimace, Raaki explains how he needs to go take a dump. What happens next is unheard of in the history of world cinema. Raaki, armed with a lota, breaks into a jig while heading to the bushes. Believe it or faint, the man danced bhangra all the way to take a poop! The whole thing is executed like a musical 'item'. And then, another inexplicable bit of 'Joginderism' happens. A pig shows up, looks at Joginder and then runs away.

This whole piece has attained legendary proportions in cult filmdom. This is what Joginder Shelly is all about. Nobody could do it like he did. Nobody.

The film itself is about that Holy Grail of Bollywood—

national integration. Ram (Romesh Sharma), Rahim (Kiran Kumar) and aforesaid Raaki (Joginder) bay for each other's blood — only to be turned into fast friends in an instant, when a cripple shows them the error of their ways. Now the trio is inseparable. Together they face the 'enemies of the country' who, in this case at least, is Kanhaiyalal. Yes, the Kanhaiyalal from *Mother India* and *Ganga Jumnaa*.

There is a scene where, when a bunch of goons 'attack' his pet pigeon, Joginder says, '*Tumne mere kabootar ka juice nikala, ab main tumhara juice nikaloonga!*' (You guys juiced my pigeon, now I will juice you!) and proceeds to punish the blokes with a flair and flourish that only he's capable of.

We've seen how Joginder always managed to recruit stars for his projects. But there came one film, in the early eighties, where he roped in one of the greatest star-actors this country has ever produced.

Thirsty Devil

A car parked in the woods — a hefty, middle-aged man is making out with a voluptuous woman. Passions run high. Interestingly, in this rather steamy sequence, the song playing in the background is a Pankaj Udhas ghazal, *Tumko maloom hai main sharaabi nahin...* As the woman steps out of the car, she is attacked by a supernatural entity, ostensibly The Devil himself, played by Joginder. Soon afterwards, she's raped by 'cosmic rays' emanating from the woods. Then we meet Joginder as sort of a shaitan/flying devil who needs help of a mortal being to help him achieve his ends. In search of such an accomplice, Joginder comes upon a devout priest who's been trying to attain eternal youth. This priest is played by Kamal Haasan. Thus begins *Pyasa Shaitan* (1984).

In the late seventies, Kamal Haasan did a Malayalam

film called *Vayanadan Thampan,* wherein he played a young priest who was trying to stall the ageing process. Joginder cropped certain scenes featuring Haasan from that film, and clipped them on to *Pyasa Shaitan.* How he pulled it off is a big mystery, considering Kamal Haasan was already a star by then. But this time it was his turn to be sued. Kamal Haasan filed a lawsuit against him.

When one watches *Pyasa Shaitan* today, it has Joginder's trademark all over it. With this film, he had switched from the curry western/daaku genre to horror. In the credits, he had these big animated fangs peeking out of his and Kamal Haasan's mouth. Of course, the idea of being 'raped by the rays', the flying devil, the seven virgins, the sleaze, it was all Joginder's handiwork.

Joginder Shelly passed away in 2009, and in a remarkable display of irony that characterized most of his work, one of the last films that he ended up doing was called *Duplicate Sholay.*

⁂

Today, Joginder is an online phenomenon. There are forums and blogs devoted to his work. And now there are even some who, going beyond the 'so-bad-it's-good' label, actually think that his cinema might have had some credibility after all.

The Ramsay Brothers

Veerana, Purana Mandir and *Do Gaz Zameen Ke Neeche*

The horror empire of Indian Cinema began in a modest radio shop in Karachi. Fatehchand U. Ramsinghani was proprietor of the Radio and Electric Company, with a massive showroom at Karachi. Legend has it that his British customers couldn't utter his full name, so they went with the simpler but regal 'Mr Ramsay'. During the Partition of India, Fatehchand had to come to Bombay and set up shop at Lamington Road, one of the biggest markets of electronic goods in the subcontinent.

Meanwhile, around the advent of the 1960s, the Hindi film industry was churning. What was once the sole preserve of big studios, was gradually becoming more fragmented and democratic at the same time. Small time businessmen were getting into financing modest films that would make good money in the nook and cranny of India's towns. This gave rise to a parallel industry where B-movies were being made with amazing regularity, and they almost always made money. Case in point is the Dara Singh swashbucklers of that era. Fatehchand, embracing the sobriquet the British gave him, decided to sink his teeth into the film production game by making *Shaheed-E-Azad Bhagat Singh* (1954) and *Rustom Sohrab* in 1963, starring Prithviraj Kapoor and Suraiya. The latter film clicked and F.U. Ramsay seemed to have tasted blood. He plunged into the film trade with all he had, and roped in all his seven sons one by one—Kumar, Tulsi, Shyam, Keshu, Kiran, Gangu and Arjun: the 'Ramsay Brothers'.

For a while, it was all hunky-dory. *Rustom Sohrab* had made them some money and then the Sindhi film *Nakuli Shaan* (1971) also fared well. But what dealt an almost lethal blow was the failure of the one big film they made in 1970, *Ek Nanhi Munni Ladki Thi,* starring Prithviraj Kapoor and Shatrughan Sinha. But the ruins of this film were to form the foundations of Ramsay empire. Tulsi and Shyam Ramsay watched the film in the theatre with the audience, and realized that there was just one particular scene to which they reacted most passionately. Prithviraj Kapoor, in a mask and a grotesque full body costume, entered a museum to steal something. As soon as they set their eyes on him, the audience shrieked. The Ramsays realized that many people actually came in to watch that particular scene and left. It was then that the truth finally dawned on them.

The audience loved to be terrified. It was horror that gave them a high, more than anything else. Back from the theatres, the brothers had to now convince their father to start making horror films. F.U. Ramsay was disillusioned with the movie business and wanted to bid adieu to filmmaking for good. But the boys were successful in persuading him to try their hand at this genre. They were already fans of films like *Dracula, The Mummy* and *The Curse of Frankenstein* and had a sketchy idea of how to go about it. Instead of just producing or writing, they now wanted to make a film all by themselves by distributing the major functions of filmmaking amongst the brothers. They obtained the one book on filmmaking that was to become their Bible — Joseph V. Mascelli's *The Five Cs of Cinematography*. Reportedly, the brothers locked themselves in a houseboat in Srinagar and conducted a three-month long workshop among themselves, to learn the basics of moviemaking. Thus was born their first Cult Horror: *Do Gaz Zameen Ke Neeche* (1972).

Zombie, Six feet Under

Name one horror genre and the Ramsays have made a film on it: zombies, vampires, werewolves, reanimated corpses, snowmen, and even Freddy Krueger from *A Nightmare on Elm Street*. *Do Gaz Zameen Ke Neeche* was India's first zombie film. They cast Surendra Kumar, who debuted with their earlier film *Ek Nanhi Munni Ladki Thi,* and introduced two more actors: Shobhana and Imtiaz Khan. Imtiaz was Amjad Khan's younger sibling. He went on to appear in films like *Yaadon Ki Baaraat* (1973) and *Dharmatma* (1975) but it was the Ramsays who gave him a break.

The entire cast of the film was bundled into a bus and they drove to the Government Guest House in Mahabaleshwar, where they canned the entire film in all of forty days, at a modest budget of ₹3.5 lakhs. With this film, they devised a model that was to see them through the next few decades of making financially successful horror films. The departments were split among the brothers — Kumar wrote the script, Kiran was in charge of sound, Gangu manned the camera, Keshu assisted on cinematography while doubling up as the production guy, while Arjun handled post-production and editing. The two remaining brothers, Tulsi and Shyam Ramsay, were to direct the film. Their mother and wives cooked food for the cast and crew, while also handling make-up. It was the perfect family model of filmmaking, and they made it work successfully for many years to come. They termed this model 'Tiffin Box Production'. The scenes were mostly shot in the jungles and, of course, the graveyard nearby.

There's also an apocryphal story that the brothers dug up a body by accident. It was the mother of all ironies, considering the title of the movie they were shooting. They were rounded up by local toughies in no time, and they had to calm them down, and bury the body back again, leaving an earthen lamp on the grave as a mark of respect for the dead.

In the film, the hero Rajvansh (Surendra Kumar) was murdered by his greedy wife (Shobhana) and her lover Anand (Imtiaz Khan). Rajvansh was, obviously, stinking rich and his wife and her lover were, obviously again, after his property. But in a cruel twist of fate, they were to realize that the *tijori ki chaabi* (the key of the vault) was also buried with Rajvansh. So they had to dig up the grave and—horror of horrors—the body was gone! It was then up to Rajvansh's zombie to torment the illicit lovers and get his revenge. But was it really Rajvansh's ghost? Or a horrible con pulled by someone on the unsuspecting couple? You have to watch the film, if you haven't already.

The film was released with an A rating, as are most Ramsay movies, for the generous sprinkling of gore and sex throughout. The film, and the underdog in that week's race, turned out to be a sleeper hit. The Ramsays orchestrated a radio spot on Vividh Bharati which worked as a preview of the film, full of the signature screams and suitable noises. The voice artist Sheel Kumar was roped in to do the voice-over—he urged listeners to watch *Do Gaz Zameen Ke Neeche,* and to shut their doors and windows. This piqued people's curiosity even more, and the film ended up garnering more than ₹40 lakhs on the box office.

This was just the beginning. Ramsay Brothers kept churning out film after film from what seemed like a virtual conveyor belt of horror flicks: *Darwaza* (1978), *Aur Kaun?* (1979), *Saboot* (1980), *Andhera* (1975), *Guest House* (1980), *Dahshat* (1981), *Sannata* (1981), *Hotel* (1981), *Ghungroo Ki Awaaz* (1981), *Maut Ka Saya* (1982), *3D Saamri* (1985), *Tahkhana* (1986), *Purani Haveli* (1989), *Bandh Darwaza* (1990) and so on. With this amazing prolificity and almost always striking gold at the box office, the Ramsays became an institution and a brand unto themselves. Back in the eighties, the whole industry was monitoring their moves—they were hiring A-list composers like Bappi Lahiri, Rahul Dev Burman and Usha Khanna, and actors like Shatrughan Sinha, Rakesh Roshan, Deepak Parashar, Navin Nischol, Bindiya Goswami and even Rekha. *Ghungroo Ki Awaaz* is still considered among R.D. Burman fans as one of his most underrated albums. *Hotel* was noted for its music as well as its stellar cast. The brothers were also known for introducing and frequently collaborating with new faces: Imtiaz Khan, Puneet Issar, Archana Puran Singh, Hemant Birje and Mohnish Behl, among them.

The Curse of the Old Temple

The year 1984 saw the Ramsays come up with another landmark film in their oeuvre, *Purana Mandir*. The mythical monster and devil worshipper Saamri is sentenced to death by decapitation by the Raja of Bijapur. Saamri proceeds to curse the Raja's lineage that as long as his head remained severed, the women in Raja's family will keep dying at childbirth. The youngest member of the Raja's family, Suman (Arti Surendranath) is in love with Sanjay (Mohnish Behl). Fearing her impending death once she inevitably marries him and begets his child, thereby invoking the age-old curse, Suman's father tries to separate them. As they rebel against his unsporting manoeuvres, the Thakur (Pradeep Kumar) reveals the truth of the curse to them. The couple resolves to go down to Bijapur and confront good ol' Saamri and ask him not to spoil the fun. They are accompanied by Sanjay's good samaritan friend, Anand (Puneet Issar). How the trio and their minions encounter the evil Saamri and overpower him, forms the rest of the story.

The film had a slew of new faces, with whom the Ramsays would continue to collaborate with in their later films. One of them was Arti Gupta, now the renowned Mumbai socialite Arti Surendranath, who handled the Indian production of Angeline Jolie's *A Mighty Heart* (2007). Arti became a staple in Ramsays' films and was their designated 'scream queen'. Another long-term collaborator who broke into the scene with *Purana Mandir* was Anirudh Agarwal. The name might not ring a bell for most people, but one look at the face and you will know who I am talking about. A civil engineer from Roorkee, what set Anirudh apart was his huge frame, and a distinctive face, which brings to mind wrestler-entertainer The Great Khali. He played Saamri in the film, and continued to star as monsters, ghouls and occultists in countless Ramsay films after this. Mohnish Behl played the lead in the film, and it became his first major success as an actor. The song shot on him and Surendranath—'Woh Beete Din Yaad Hain', composed and sung by Ajit Singh, another frequent Ramsay collaborator, became a chartbuster and is still quite popular.

Till *Purana Mandir*, Puneet Issar was known for the legendary super-punch that almost killed the greatest star of the millennium. *Purana Mandir* was his first great hit after the *Coolie* incident, and brought him to the fore. The film went on to become one of the greatest hits of the year. Video piracy was just setting in, and on one of the first major raids by Mumbai Police in a video parlour, *Purana Mandir* was being screened.

The Wilderness and a Lustful Witch

By this time, the Ramsay Brothers had established a signature style with films that contained monsters, ghosts and ghouls, homemade special effects, pedestrian humour, and oodles of sex (after all, monsters have carnal desires too!). In *Bandh Darwaza* (1990), the villainous vampire Newla craves young women. The Thakur's childless wife offers herself to him to, ahem, impregnate her! And one film that packaged all of this with peerless precision, was *Veerana* (1988).

A seductress witch by the name of Nakita haunts a village, and her favourite evening pastime is to lure young men, indulge in fornication and then disembowel them with delight. In a bid to stop her murderous orgy, the son of the Thakur (the only thing in Ramsay movies to parallel the number of ghosts is the number of Thakurs, I tell you), Sameer (Vijayendra Ghatge), allows himself to be tricked by her into her bathtub. While rollicking in the bubble-bath, Sameer snatches her tilismi bat-necklace, forcing Nakita to reveal herself in all her glory, dripping skin and all. He hands her over to the villagers, who lynch the witch. Years later, she is back for revenge and possesses the Thakur's daughter, Jasmin. Jasmin perpetrates her own round of seductions, songs and bubble-baths, and eventually her uncle Sameer and her cousin's good boyfriend Hemant release her from the clutches of the evil witch.

Till now, the Censor Board seemed too busy to notice

the sexual overtones in Ramsay films. But after *Purana Mandir*, the brothers were in the big league, and hence under the scanner. The Central Board of Film Certification (CBFC) suggested a whopping forty-six cuts, including some dialogues (*'Main tumhare jism ke har raaz ko dekhna chahta hoon'* [I want to witness all the secrets of your body]), suggestive scenes (Nakita stripping as Sameer looks on, Nakita descending on her victims), gory scenes (witch cutting the hand of a victim, sucking blood, bloodstained teeth), and violence (villagers stoning the witch while she is tied, a man being kicked on the crotch). The CBFC went on a rampage with this one.

But what remains in *Veerana* is a whole lot of all the above things, in good measure. Many viewers (mostly silly teenagers with raging hormones) remember *Veerana* for Jasmin, the young heroine who became an overnight sensation after this. She had debuted in a nondescript film opposite Vinod Khanna called *Sarkari Mehman* (1979) (in the credits, an explosion happens, and a bunch of flowers pop up on screen, declaring 'Introducing: Jasmin'), and starred opposite Vijayendra in *Divorce* (1984). Both the films were directed and produced by a certain N.D. Kothari. Jasmin disappeared after *Veerana*, never to be heard of again. If online forums are anything to go by, she had to hang up her boots because of threats to her life from the underworld, and is now settled in the United States. *Veerana* also happened to be Hemant Birje's first major hit after his smashing debut with *Adventures of Tarzan*, for which he missed the National Award for Best Actor by a whisker.

The fame and popularity of Ramsay Brothers' cinema isn't restricted to their home country alone. Their work has featured in the 'Mondo Macabro', a British show on international cult cinema, and many Ramsay films like *Tehkhana* and *Mahakaal* feature in their DVD releases also.

'Bacha Le!'

Any discussion on the illustrious brothers cannot be complete without mentioning another film, *3D Saamri* (1985), India's first 3-D horror film which reportedly ran into exhibition issues when some audience members, in those glorious days of single screen theatres, took off with a sizeable number of 3-D glasses. But it has great significance for Cult connoisseurs and Hindi film buffs for quite another reason—a seminal song called 'Bacha Le!' sang and composed by Bappi Lahiri. The song, inspired from Michael Jackson's *Thriller* (1982), featured ace comedian Jagdeep (who happened to be a brilliant dancer) in a Jackson persona, right down to the red jacket, dancing in a graveyard along with reanimated teenage corpses. Two of those 'undead' kids are themselves celebrated film-makers today: Sajid and Farah Khan.

The Also-rans

Too many movies crowd your mind when you think of the term 'Cult Film'. Films of all kinds, shapes and forms—too many to fit within the confines of a book such as this. This chapter huddles some of them together, films that deserve sole chapters (or even books) of their own. Some day.

Lamhe (1991)
Yash Chopra's timeless romance about love between a girl and her mother's silent admirer sank at the box office on release despite the stellar cast of Anil Kapoor, Sridevi and Waheeda Rehman. Shiv-Hari's music was the only thing about it that survived the carnage.

Virendra Pratap Singh (a clean-shaven Anil Kapoor) is hopelessly in love with Pallavi (Sridevi), but she loves Siddharth (the very successful model of the nineties, Deepak Bhatnagar). Pallavi and Siddharth get married, leaving Virendra to wallow in his misery. But sometime later, the couple dies in an accident leaving behind a daughter, Pooja. Pooja (Sridevi again!) grows up to be a spitting image of her mother, and she falls head over heels in love with the greying Virendra.

While watching *Lamhe,* one would inevitably be reminded of *Lolita* and *Daddy Long Legs*. But it's an original screenplay, written by Honey Irani (Javed Akhtar's former wife and Farhan and Zoya Akhtar's mother), and a brilliant one at that! The first half is about a young Anil Kapoor falling for an older Sridevi, while the second half is about a nubile Sridevi obsessed with a greying Anil Kapoor. Stroke of genius.

The film was considered too 'bold' for an audience busy with *Saajan, Phool Aur Kaante* and *Dil Hai Ke Manta Nahin*. But over the years, it has gained acceptance and acclaim among lovers of Yash Chopra's incredible oeuvre.

Daud (1997)

What can you say about a film where the hero introduces himself as Umaparvati, and the heroine calls herself Dayashankar? Better still, Ram Gopal Varma's *Daud* has one of the most curiously named villains of all time: Pinky!

The film is a delightful romp about a happy-go-lucky Sanjay Dutt who is hired to retrieve a box apparently containing gold worth ₹1 Crore. On discovering the worth to be double the amount, Sanjay holds on to the box, which is also important to the government. Urmila Matondkar teams up with him as they are chased by the bandits as well as the cops. They introduce each other thus:

> Sanjay: *Naam kya hai tumhara?* (What is your name?)
>
> Urmila: *Dayashankar...Tumhara naam kya hai?*
> (Dayashankar… What's yours?)
>
> Sanjay: Umaparvati. Nice meeting you.

Two characters from *Daud* that will go down in history are Pinky (Paresh Rawal), the leader of the bandits, and Chacko (Neeraj Vora). Sanjay Dutt and Urmila Matondkar bump into Chacko in a village in the middle of nowhere. Chacko is the village landlord, and is the last in a long line of hunters. His grandfather never got married. His father did, but his mother passed away before he was born! Chacko's origin, thus, is shrouded in mystery.

Written by Sanjay Chhel, there are some priceless dialogue exchanges in the film. After breaking a goon's wrist, Sanjay Dutt tells him, '*Arre ghar pe jaake thoda Tiger Balm laga lena. Sab theek ho jayega. Uske baad apna haath garam paani mein daal ke uspe thoda namak daal dena.*' (Just go home and put some Tiger Balm on it. Everything will be fine. After that, put your hand in warm water and put some salt on it.) Heroes have always thrashed bad guys, but seldom before has a hero advised a bad guy on home remedies.

Pinky breaks into the house of a cop and has an epic conversation with said cop's wife and child. He threatens the cop to turn his son into a Joker-like super-villain who endorses dental products:

'*Kya tum chahte ho ke tumhare masoom bete ke hothon ko cheer kar main do inch bada kar doon, ta ke yeh zindagi bhar hansta rahe, aur muskura kar toothpaste ke Ad mein kaam kare: "Imaandar baap ka jaandar beta. Roz istemaal karta hai Colgate. Ding dong!"*' (Do you want me to cut up your son's mouth by two more inches so he keeps smiling all his life, and features in toothpase ads, saying: 'A brave son of an honest father. Uses Colgate daily. Ding Dong!')

In another priceless cinematic moment, government officials discuss *Sholay*. Urmila has taken off once again by fooling a cop with the story of Basanti, Veeru and Gabbar. This epic conversation follows:

> '*Woh ladki kuch* Sholay *ka zikr kar rahi thi.* (The girl mentioned some *Sholay*.)

'Sholay? *Kaun* Sholay?' (*Sholay* who?)
'*Aap* Sholay *ke baare mein nahin jaante?*' (Don't tell me you don't know *Sholay*!)
'*Ji nahin, main kabhi mila nahin unse.*' (No, I haven't had the good fortune of making his acquaintance.)
'Sholay *ek bahut hit film hai.*' (*Sholay* is a very successful film.)
'*Par* Sholay *ka taluk iss case se kya hai?*' (But how is *Sholay* connected to this case?)
'Sir, *yahi toh pata lagaana hai!*' (That's what needs to be investigated!)

Go and get the DVD right now. I'll wait for you here.

Shaan (1980)

It was the follow-up to *Sholay*. Ramesh Sippy's second big action spectacle, *Shaan* had everything going for it. *Shaan* drew heavily from James Bond movies and had a rather spectacular cast: Amitabh Bachchan, Shashi Kapoor, Shatrughan Sinha, Rakhee, Parveen Babi, Bindiya Goswami, Johnny Walker and Sunil Dutt. And just like its predecessor, *Shaan* also introduced a relatively fresh face as the villain: Kulbhushan Kharbanda as Shakaal.

But none of these factors worked in the film's favour, and it didn't do as well as expected. Over the years, its kitschy sets and dialogues gained it a major cult following.

Vijay and Ravi (Amitabh Bachchan and Shashi Kapoor respectively) are petty tricksters whose brother happens to be a cop (Sunil Dutt). But when elder brother is executed by criminal mastermind Shakaal, the two swear revenge, combining forces with Rakesh (Shatrughan Sinha) who also has a score to settle with Shakaal.

This was the third film written by Salim-Javed where Amitabh Bachchan and Shashi Kapoor played characters named Vijay and Ravi, the other two being *Deewar* (1975) and *Kaala Patthar* (1979). The villain was also called Shakaal in *Yaadon Ki Baaraat* (1973), where it was played by Ajit. The name was inspired from a team member in Nasir Hussain's office, his publicity in-charge, G.P. Shakhaal. *Yaadon Ki Baaraat* was a massive hit, and somehow the character found its way into the *Shaan* script. *Yaadon Ki Baaraat* was a much bigger hit and Ajit was iconic in that film, but even today, when the word 'Shakaal' is uttered, the bald-headed Kulbhushan Kharbanda comes to mind. As is expected in a Salim-Javed film, he had some great lines, especially concerning his pet crocodile: 'Ajeeb janwar hai, jitna bhi khaye bhookha hi rehta hai!' (Strange animal. Always hungry, no matter what.)

Or a rather explicit warning that leaves little to the imagination: 'Yeh zahreeli gas dheere dheere mehfil ko aur rangeen banati rahegi.' (This poisonous gas will infuse more colour into the gathering.)

Shakaal's style, the grandeur of his hideout and his looks are still remembered and he remains one of the most recognizable villains in Hindi cinema. The brothers too had some memorable wisecracks. In one of the scenes, Ravi comments on Vijay's perpetual scepticism: '*Tumhaare dil mein seena nahin hai, patthar hai patthar!*' (You don't have a chest in your heart, just a stone, a stone.) Vijay deadpans in his typical style: '*Abe dil mein seena nahin, seene mein dil hota hai!*' (The heart is in the chest, not the other way round!)

Om Dar Ba Dar (1988)

Not having seen it is okay, but if you haven't even heard of *Om Dar Ba Dar*, you most likely aren't a film buff. It is India's answer to Luis Bunuel's or Andy Warhol's surrealist films.

Directed by Kamal Swaroop, an eccentric and flamboyant genius, *Om Dar Ba Dar* was made in 1988 and went largely unnoticed. The film itself is best summarized in an awesome blog review over on *The Seventh Art*,[*] and I quote:

> Here's the plot of the film: Horoscope, dead frog, cloudy sky, the moon, radio program, caste reservation, bicycle, Mount Everest, women's liberation, communism, sleeveless blouse, Yuri Gagarin, miniature book, Nitrogen fixation, man on moon, terrorist tadpoles, computer, biology class, turtles, Hema Malini, typewriter, sleazy magazines, hibernation, text inside nose, googly, James Bond, severed tongue, fish rain, shoes in a temple, World War, assassin creed, Gandhi, illicit trade, the lake, goggles, hopping currency, helium breath, counterfeit coins, underwater treasure, diamonds inside frogs, fireworks, the zoo, explosives, town at night, dead man, visit of God, the Panchsheel Pact, foreign tourists, Promise toothpaste, holy men, Fish keychain, Ram Rajya, food chain disruption, anti-cooperation movement, birth control, bagpipes, gecko, Jawaharlal Nehru, Aviation centers, Potassium Cyanide.

And I guarantee you, this is as lucid as it can get. The VHS of the film landed up in a closed gathering of renowned artists at Kasauli. With them watching, rewatching and copying the VHS, the film acquired a life of its own and spread far and wide, particularly among the intellectuals. It was selected for the Experimenta Film Festival, founded by film-maker Shai Heredia, and a DVD copy started floating around. Suddenly,

---

[*]See http://theseventhart.info/2009/07/11/flashback-63/

a print of the film became a coveted thing to own. Some had seen it, some hadn't, but everyone talked about it. Finally, after more than two decades, the film saw a limited theatrical release on 17 January 2014.

Urf Professor (2001)

One of the most delectable dark comedies never released, *Urf Professor* broke every rule in the book. It was directed by Pankaj Advani, the eccentric genius behind *Sankat City* (2009). Had it been released, *Urf Professor* would have been Sharman Joshi's first major role. Manoj Pahwa plays Professor, an adorable hired assassin (yes, these two words can be together. It's a dark comedy, remember?) who is obsessed with buying lottery tickets. Hilarity ensues when his car with the lottery ticket that just won him ₹2 Crore inside it, gets stolen. Irreverent, goofy and utterly crazy, *Urf Professor* is a delightful ride. Word of caution: if extreme profanity and sexual themes offend you, please avoid this film like the plague. Now, I don't know if that was a warning or an advertisment.

Waisa Bhi Hota Hai Part II (2003)

There are some films where the premise is so crazy, it has 'cult' written all over it. In *Waisa Bhi Hota Hai Part II*, the insanity begins with the title. From then on, it only gets loonier. A copywriter, wedded to a cop, saves a mobster, befriends him, and ends up wiping out two warring gangs. If that doesn't sound crazy enough, check out this conversation:

> '*Achha woh jo black & white tasveer lagi hai, tere boss ki hai kya?*' (Is that black & white picture of your boss?)
> '*Nahin, Gregory Peck ki hai.*' (No, that's Gregory Peck.)

'*Gregory...Bandra ka hai kya?*' (Gregory...from Bandra?)
'*Nahin, usske thoda aage hai – L.A.*' (Nope, a little beyond that...L.A.)
'L.A.?'
'*East mein.*' (It's to the east.)
'*Naale ke paas?*' (Near the drain?)
'*Haan...*' (Yes.)

Epilogue

As my friend Diptakirti indicates in his seminal book, *Kitnay Aadmi Thay*, the point of such books is to spark debates and discussions. There will always be those who disagree, point out glaring errors and exclusions, and talk about how the premise was all wrong. But that's the fun of conceiving a film/trivia book.

This tome doesn't claim to be an accurate or exhaustive list of cult films. It's a very personal compilation of films that, as far as my own experience/judgement go, do constitute as cult. Some titles that find mention here may particularly raise eyebrows. For instance, *RGV Ki Aag*. Cultmongers would understand why I include it. In the past decade, I have come across scores of people who refer back to *Aag* as if it were a benchmark for bad films, most noteworthy among them, RGV himself.

Similar questions may be raised about *Jo Jeeta Wohi Sikandar*. The film was somewhat commercially successful, but not on the scale one would expect a nineties' Aamir Khan vehicle to fare. It's a personal favourite, and has tremendous repeat value. We don't really talk about it often enough, but *Jo Jeeta...* has affected us filmy keedas in myriad ways: the brothers, the cycle race, Kulbhushan Kharbanda, 'Pehla Nasha', Pooja Bedi in her red dress, the brilliant music, the cameos and of course, the merry-go-round tale of its making.

Regardless, disagreements and debates are kind of what one hopes to instigate through this book. And hence, the films not included in here justify the book by virtue of their absence. Karma.

Made in the USA
Monee, IL
03 May 2026

49438696R00154